BY THE AUTO EDITORS OF CONSUMER GUIDE®

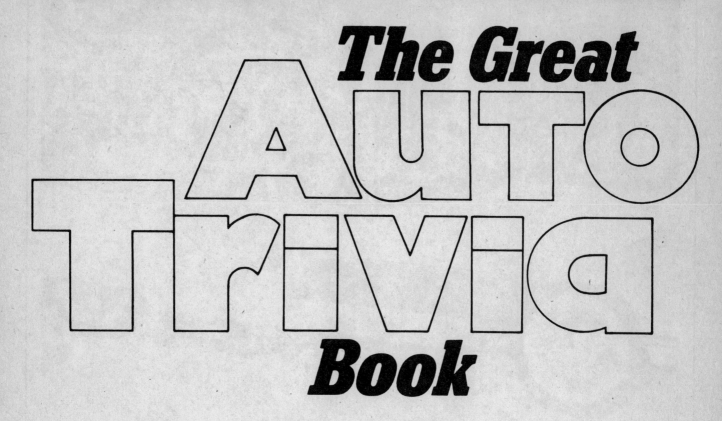

The Great AUTO Trivia Book

MITCH FRUMKIN

BEEKMAN HOUSE
New York

Louis Weber, President
Publications International, Ltd.
3841 West Oakton Street
Skokie, Illinois 60076

Manufactured in the United States of America
10 9 8 7 6 5 4 3 2 1

Library of Congress Catalog Card Number: 84–61078

ISBN: 0-517-45252-9

This edition published by:
Beekman House
Distributed by Crown Publishers, Inc.
One Park Avenue
New York, New York 10016

Book Design: Janet Fuglsang
Cover Design: Frank Peiler

Acknowledgements

Special thanks to the following for their aid in locating many of the photographs used in this trivia book:
Bernice L. Huffman—Motor Vehicle Manufacturers Assoc.
Karla Rosenbusch—Chrysler Historical Collection
Frank Mauthe—Chicago Automobile Trade Assoc.
Joe Blackstock, Chuck Sidor —Foster & Kleiser
Bill Buffa—Ford Motor Co.
Ron McQueeney—Indy Motorway Museum
Howard Mandlebaum— Phototeque
Bruce Reynolds—San Diego Aero-Space Museum
Phill Hall
Stan Hegberg

Also thanks to these clubs for their club page contributions:
Larry G. Mitchell—Classic AMX Club International
Jim Bollman—Crosley Automobile Club
J. P. Corbin— Auburn/Cord/Duesenberg Club
Bernard J. Weis—Pierce Arrow Society
Rick Kamen—Kaiser-Frazer Owners Club
Russ Brandenberg—Corvair Club

INTRODUCTION

Auto enthusiasts, start your engines, shift those gears and peel into this book created with your enjoyment in mind.

Here you'll find thousands of questions and answers, photo quizzes, picture puzzles, word games, and other diversions covering the wild and fascinating world of the automobile from the 1930s to the 1980s.

We've tried to make *The Great Auto Trivia Book* comprehensive as well as challenging, informative as well as intriguing. That's why the brain teasers assembled here test your knowledge on everything from styling and engineering developments to advertising slogans, model names, car company founders, racing facts, show vehicles, important dates and places, and dozens more.

Naturally, we've geared the book to all ages and knowledge levels, so even if you don't think you're an "expert," you're sure to know the right answers to many of these questions, maybe learn a little in the process, and—most of all—have fun.

Whatever your interest, *The Great Auto Trivia Book* is definitely going to keep you pleased and puzzled for many hours.

Fin Fever

The styling of rear fender fins took on all kinds of shapes during their final years in the late fifties and early sixties. Can you identify the year and make of car for each design?

1. _____

2. _____

3. _____

4. _____

5. _____

6. _____

Get a Horse

2. What hyphenated car name does this winged horse represent?

_____

1. A. What three car models used this stylized horse decal in 1976?

_____
_____
_____

B. What special name was given to the cars that wore this design?

_____

3. On what make of car does this world famous prancing horse belong?

_____

4. What make and model car displayed this noble looking animal?

_____

5. The rarest of cars wore this elegant horse emblem. Name it.

_____

Double Your Pleasure

This illustration, shows a rather unique set-up for transmission shift levers.

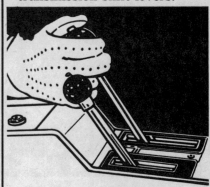

1. Which car maker offered this configuration back in 1963?

_____

2. What was the full advertised name for this optional equipment?

_____

3. How many forward speeds did this arrangement profess to give the driver?

_____

Slick Symbols #1

Can you name the oil company that this graphic symbol represented?

_____

Answers are on page 351

Identify the Imperials

Most of the Imperial front-end designs shown below are from the 1970's, but there are a couple of foolers. Give the correct year for each model.

1. _____

2. _____

3. _____

4. _____

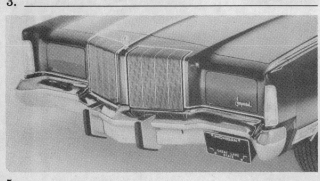

5. _____

6. _____

7. _____

8. _____

Answers are on page 351

Mercury Mug Shots #2

The eight Mercury front ends from the 1940-50's are poppin' through this page, so with wings on your feet, fly through this quiz with god-like speed, identifying the correct years.

1. _____

2. _____

3. _____

4. _____

5. _____

6. _____

7. _____

8. _____

Answers are on page 351

The Taxis that Hurried

While you're weaving in and out of traffic, can you identify the correct year and model of these four taxicabs?

1. _____

2. _____

3. _____

4. _____

Bird's~Eye View

Looking directly down on this yacht-like streamlined body design, can you answer these questions?

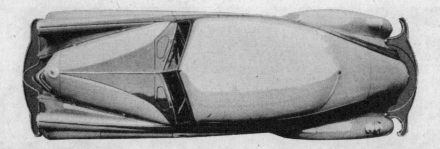

1. Car brand and model name: _____
2. First model year: _____
3. Number of cylinders: _____

4. Horsepower rating: _____
5. Wheelbase (inches): _____
6. Original price: _____

Outdoor Ads #1

1. Year _____ Make _____

2. Year _____ Make _____

3. Year _____ Make _____

Answers are on page 351

TURBINE TRUCK TEST

Chevrolet had been experimenting with turbine-powered trucks for 15 years when it introduced this driveable dream freighter. Think back over the years and try to answer these detail questions on the futuristic truck.

1. What did Chevrolet call this truck?

2. What year was this version unveiled?

3. How many horses powered the turbine engine?

4. Automatic or manual transmission?

5. How many gears?

6. What special steering system design did this truck incorporate?

Dealer's Choice (Imports)

Match the import manufacturer to their correct number of U.S. dealer franchises.

Number of Dealers	Import Manufacturer
1. 1101	A. Ferrari
2. 1081	B. Honda
3. 822	C. Jaguar
4. 416	D. Mercedes-Benz
5. 405	E. Nissan
6. 330	F. Peugeot
7. 316	G. Porsche
8. 189	H. Rolls Royce
9. 65	I. Toyota
10. 46	J. Volvo

Slick Symbols #2

Can you name the oil company that this graphic symbol represented?

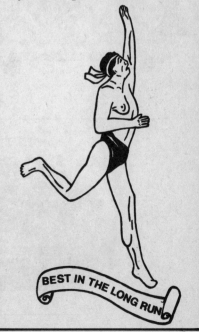

BEST IN THE LONG RUN

Answers are on page 351

Don't Tailgate

These eight car shots show the wild variety of rear ends that we've looked at over the years. Before you pull around and pass, identify the correct make and year for each design.

1. _____

2. _____

3. _____

4. _____

5. _____

6. _____

7. _____

8. _____

Answers are on page 351

LICENSE TO QUIZ

1. Which state back in the 1930's issued plates made of copper?

2. Which state issues special plates to members of the Seminole Indian tribe?

3. Which state had a baked potato with melting butter imprinted on its plate?

4. Which state for one year used the motto: "Lincoln Year"?

5. Which state once had the words "prison made" on its plates?

6. Which Canadian province has "100,000 Lakes" on its plates?

Woody Wagons #1

The natural beauty of wood added to station wagon designs over the past 50 years has given us some handsome and memorable vehicles.
What is the correct year and make for the six versions pictured below?
*Plus—List which ones used real wood, not simulated.

1. _____

2. _____

3. _____

4. _____

5. _____

6. _____

Answers are on page 351

Top These

Our continuing love affair with convertibles is easily understood when you view the six beauties below.
What is the correct model year and car brand name for each of these ragtops?

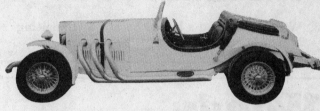

2. _____

1. _____

4. _____

3. _____

5. _____

6. _____

Answers are on page 351

Movie Car Trivia #1

Answer these car related movie trivia questions.

1. In the movie *Oh God* it rained inside what make and model car?

2. In *Rocky II* what size engine was in his black Trans-Am?

3. What was the year and make of the station wagon in the original *Halloween*?

4. What is the model year for the Pinto in the movie *Cujo*?

5. In what make and model car is Linda Blair (Regan) driven away at the end of the movie *The Exorcist*?

6. In the movie *The Deer Hunter*, in what year and make of car do Robert DeNiro and friends go deer hunting?

7. In *Rocky III*, Rocky poses for two car magazine ads. What kind of cars were they?

8. In the movie *Grand Theft Auto*, what kind of car does Ron Howard drive in a demolition derby race?

CORNER STATION

Parked in front of the local gas station sign are two oldies but goodies in need of some minor engine adjustments.
What is the year and make of these cars, and what three words appeared on the gas sign? What is the name of the winged horse?

Answers are on page 351

Firebird Fronts #1

Since day one, Pontiac Firebirds have always had a split grille and a pointed nose. Keeping this family resemblance may make it difficult for you to give the correct year for each front-end design.

3. _____

4. _____

1. _____

2. _____

5. _____

6. _____

Answers are on page 351

"Stock" Stumblers

Identify the correct year and make of these five gutsy-looking machines and the engine size they used.

Bonus: Can you name the race drivers most associated with each of these cars?

1. _____
   _____
   _____

2. _____
   _____
   _____

3. _____
   _____
   _____

4. _____
   _____
   _____

5. _____
   _____
   _____

Oriental Root Quickies

1. What was Nissan originally called when it started car and truck production?

2. What year did it start?

3. What year did it change its name to Nissan Motor Co., Ltd.?

4. What was Toyota's original company name when it began vehicle manufacturing?

5. What year did it start?

6. What year did it change to Toyota Motor Co.?

Answers are on pages 351-52

Past Shadows

Six silhouetted body designs are shown below. Can you identify them by model year and make of car?

1. _____

2. _____

3. _____

4. _____

5. _____

6. _____

Scrambled Suspension

The illustration below is a fine sketch of a coil-spring front suspension. The problem is that the component names have been scrambled. Can you decode the seven labels below and place them by the correct arrows?

1. _____
4. _____
5. _____
6. _____
7. _____
2. _____
3. _____

PART NAMES

LALB IOJTN
GENTSIRE CLEKKUN
MAFRE
PEPUR TONCLOR MAR
ICLO NIRGSP
WELOR TONCLOR MAR
KOCHS REBBOARS

18

Answers are on page 352

By the Seat of your Pants

PICTURE A

1. This man is demonstrating a new seating miracle. What is it?

2. What is the year and make of the car in the background that introduced this auto innovation?

PICTURE B

3. What auto corporation offered this swing-out seating idea?

4. What was the first model year these swivel seats were offered?

5. What was the last model year?

PICTURE C

6. How many adjustments did these seats have?

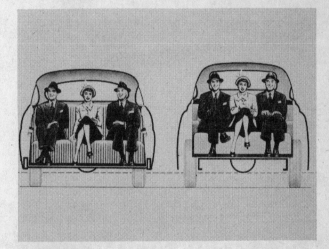

PICTURE D

7. What car company offered the seating arrangement shown on the left, which was lowered and positioned ahead of the rear wheels?

8. What model year was this design first offered?

Answers are on page 352

Passing Dreams #1

Seeing the rear 3/4 view of these "dreamy" cars, fill your head with what *might* have been. Identify the correct year, make and model for each of these creations.

1. _____

3. _____

5. _____

2. _____

4. _____

6. _____

Answers are on page 352

Short Cut

1. What year, make and model car is shown gliding down a flight of 8-inch stone steps in a dramatic demonstration of its new "full control" power steering?

2. What type and size engine was standard in this model?
   A. Flathead 6
      196.2 cu. in.
   B. L-head 6
      226.2 cu. in.
   C. Straight-8
      317.4 cu. in.

3. Was a McCulloch supercharged engine offered that model year?

4. What was the approximate factory price for this car?
   A. $2650
   B. $2950
   C. $3150

TV Car

Can you name the television show that featured these two road warriors?
What make of car did they always drive?

Muscle Car Unscramble

These mixed-up high-performance car names need to be rearranged so as to reveal their true identities.

1. RACOMA

2. GUEJD

3. EJIAVLN

4. GDEOD

5. CIAPTNO

6. SUTNGMA

7. ROTION

8. GORUAC

9. DAWTLIC

10. ZOAMN

11. FATSIRER

12. BSLYEH

Truckin' Spirits

Let's raise our glasses to the trucks that have delivered our favorite beverages over the many years.

Can you identify the tractor portion of these five beer trucks and one wine delivery shown below?

1. _____

2. _____

3. _____

4. _____

5. _____

6. _____

Answers are on page 352

Sink or Swim

Remember this split-personality automobile that would, with the flick of a lever, convert from land car to motorboat?

1. What was this vehicle's name?

2. Which country manufactured these unusual cars?
   A. Japan   B. Italy   C. West Germany

3. What was the first model year for the American market?

4. What type of engine design?
   A. Inline 4 cyl.   B. Flathead 6 cyl.   C. Inline 6 cyl.

5. What was the advertised mpg on land?
   A. 32 mpg   B. 24 mpg   C. 18 mpg

6. Fuel consumption in the water?
   A. 1½ gal. per hour B. 2½ gal. per hour C. 3½ gal. per hour

7. Approximate top speed on land?
   Approximate cruising speed on water?

8. What was the original advertised P.O.E. price?
   A. $2595   B. $3395   C. $3995

What's in a Name?

1. What contribution did this little girl give to the auto industry?

2. What was her first and last name?

3. What nationality was her first name?

4. What does her first name mean in its native tongue?

5. What nationality was her last name?

Auto Associations

Decipher these past and present automobile-related associations from their initials.

1. AAA _____
2. AABM _____
3. AEA _____
4. AERA _____
5. APMA _____

6. ASME _____
7. MEWA _____
8. MVMA _____
9. NADA _____
10. NAPA _____

Answers are on page 352

Cudas and Challengers

Slight design variations set the Dodge Challengers apart from the Plymouth Barracudas. The changes were subtle and may confuse you, but try to identify the years and makes from these front views.

1. _____

2. _____

3. _____

4. _____

5. _____

6. _____

Answers are on page 352

Identify the Imperials #2

The front-end look of the Imperials from the 1950's and 60's was always elegant and often opulent. Identify the years of the eight examples below.

1. _____

2. _____

3. _____

4. _____

5. _____

6. _____

7. _____

8. _____

Answers are on page 352

TV Screamer

1. For what TV show was this customized convertible designed?

2. What year GTO was customized?

3. What stage name was given to this car?

Deans of Design

Match the renowned American automobile designers with two of their more famous creations.

DESIGNER
1. Richard Teague
2. Elwood Engel
3. William L. Mitchell
4. Brooks Stevens
5. Raymond Loewy
6. Howard "Dutch" Darrin

YEAR AND CAR
A. 1966 Excalibur Series I
B. 1951 Kaiser
C. 1955 Packard
D. 1963 Avanti
E. 1963 Riviera
F. 1964 Barracuda
G. 1968 AMX
H. 1938 Cadillac Sixty-Special
I. 1962 Studebaker Gran Turismo Hawk
J. 1951 Henry J
K. 1961 Thunderbird
L. 1947 Studebaker

Answers are on page 352

Porsche Page

What was the first model year of production for each of these Porsche models?

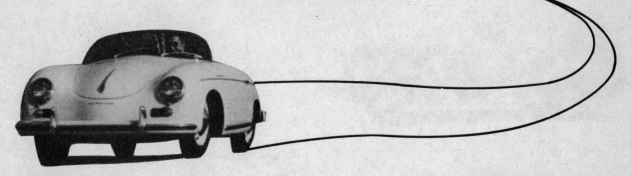

A. 356 Speedster _____
B. 911 _____
C. 911/912 Targa _____
D. 914 _____
E. 924 _____
F. 928 _____
G. 944 _____

Can you answer the following questions?

1. Which Porsche was intended as a Volkswagen sports car?

2. Which model claimed to be the first production safety convertible in the world?

3. What was the 911 originally called at its Frankfurt Auto Show debut?

4. What was the main difference between 911 and 912?

5. What does the "E" stand for in 911 E?

6. What model year did Porsche mark its Silver Anniversary?

7. What was this rear spoiler's nickname?

8. This spoiler also has a nickname. What is it?

POPULAR PANELS

Six very different panel designs are displayed below. Can you identify the year and make for each?

1. _____

2. _____

3. _____

4. _____

5. _____

6. _____

WILD PUT-ON

1. What truck line offered full-body dealer-applied decals like the "flame" design shown below? _____

2. What model year was this option first available? _____

3. What were the names of the four other decal designs? _____
_____
_____
_____

4. Approximately how long did it take a dealer to apply the decal? _____

"Hey, Taxi"

Quick, the meter's running. Identify the year and make of the four taxicabs shown below.

1. _____

2. _____

3. _____

4. _____

You Light Up My Life

Answer these illuminating questions and prove how "bright" you are!

PICTURE: A

1. What is the purpose for that little light designed into the grille, and what was it called? _____

2. What is the year, make and model of the car? _____

3. What was the first model year this option was offered? _____

PICTURE: B

1. True or false: this car was demonstrating a proposed six-headlight design.

2. What is the year, make and model of this bright idea car? _____

PICTURE: C

1. True or false: this lighting system is the first U.S. design to offer integrated, flush-mounted aerodynamic headlamps.

2. What is the year, make and model of this car? _____

PICTURE: D

1. What year, make and model taillight is this young lady showing off? _____

2. Was this taillight design standard equipment or a low-cost option? _____

Answers are on page 353

1930 Word Search #1

Find all the car brands that started and/or ceased production in the 1930's contained within this automobile shape. The words can be found horizontally, vertically or diagonally. They may read backwards or forwards.

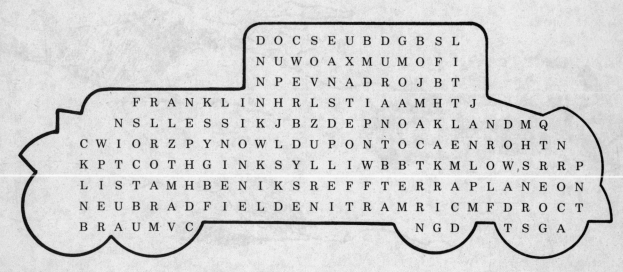

```
        D O C S E U B D G B S L
        N U W O A X M U M O F I
        N P E V N A D R O J B T
    F R A N K L I N H R L S T I A A M H T J
  N S L L E S S I K J B Z D E P N O A K L A N D M Q
C W I O R Z P Y N O W L D U P O N T O C A E N R O H T N
K P T C O T H G I N K S Y L L I W B B T K M L O W S R R P
L I S T A M H B E N I K S R E F F T E R R A P L A N E O N
N E U B R A D F I E L D E N I T R A M R I C M F D R O C T
B R A U M V C                       N G D   T S G A
```

ACORN	DURANT	LITTLEMAC	TERRAPLANE
AUSTIN	ERSKINE	MARTIN	THORNE
BRADFIELD	FRANKLIN	MOON	WILLYS-KNIGHT
CORD	JORDAN	OAKLAND	
DUPONT	KISSELL	REO	

Look but Don't Touch #1

Set up on a raised platform, so as not to have sticky hands all over its sleek body, is this limited production racing machine.

1. What was the full name of this car?
   _____

2. What do the numerals stand for?
   _____

3. What year did it first race? _____

4. What was the size in cubic inches of its original engine? _____

5. What was the second engine size raced in this car? _____

6. What was the largest engine block used? _____

Answers are on page 353

The Lower Forties #1

You're cruising down the back roads of mid-America and you come upon the proverbial farmer and his field of vintage cars. Before you talk turkey with Old Macdonald, you better identify the correct year and make of each automobile.

1. _____

2. _____

3. _____

4. _____

Spinners

You just opened a used hubcap shop, with 12 of your best spinner designs on display in the window. Somehow the name tags got mixed-up, so now you have to correctly identify the car make that wore these covers.

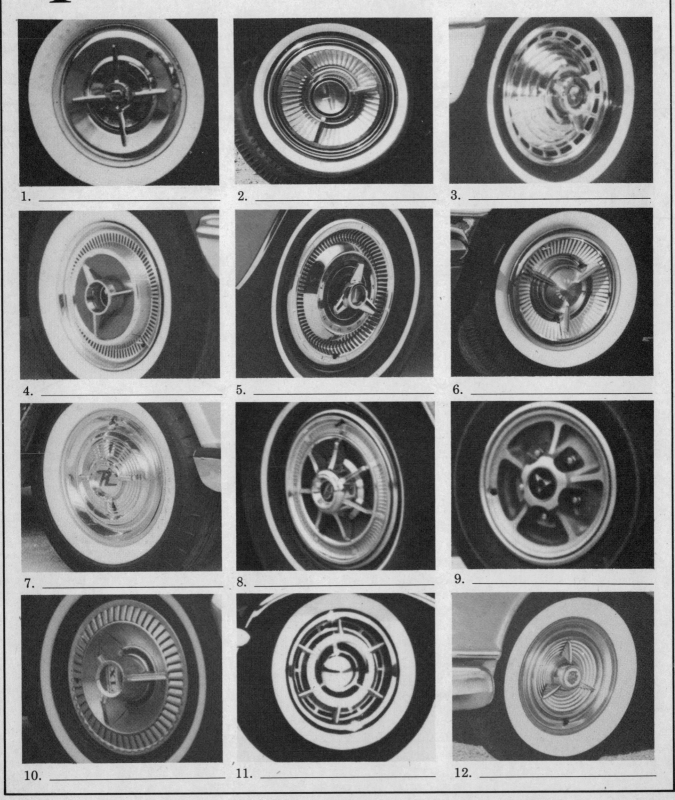

1. _____

2. _____

3. _____

4. _____

5. _____

6. _____

7. _____

8. _____

9. _____

10. _____

11. _____

12. _____

Answers are on page 353

INDY TWO TIMERS

Several drivers have won the Indy 500 two times. Three of those winners are shown below in their cars.
Can you identify these drivers and the double years they won?
In picture #1, name the mechanic.

1. _____

2. _____

3. _____

Joy Riding Jeeps

Can you identify when these Willys-Overland, later called Willys Motors, and Jeep Corporation models made their joyous mass production debuts.

1. Four-wheel drive Jeep_____
2. CJ model_____
3. Harlequin wagon_____
4. CJ-5_____
5. Wagoneer_____
6. Gladiator_____
7. Renegade_____
8. Cherokee Chief_____
9. Honcho_____
10. CJ-7_____

Blink Blink Blink

1. Which two car brands came with sequential rear turn signals that flashed in a three-step movement?

_____
_____

2. What was the first model year for each brand to offer this inventive system?

_____
_____

3. What was the final model year these turn signals were offered by both brands?

_____
_____

Smart Stick

This multi-purpose lever can be found on 1981 Toronados among other makes, and controls seven main functions. Name them.

1. _____
2. _____
3. _____
4. _____
5. _____
6. _____
7. _____

1940 Word Search

Find the car brands that started and/or ceased production in the 1940's. The brand names are in all directions—vertically, horizontally, diagonally, backwards, and around corners. Circle each name found.

```
  H V D        N A      R B    P L A Y B O Y    Q H S N A M E
 A M R C S     T M      N O    I T I S E X S    R E S I A K L
J I     T O    O E      E B    N I R U T I O    A I R H N E I
K D     R N    O R      I B      I L V          R C A N O L B
F R     E A    C I      R I      A A Z          O R       L O
S A B O N Z E  S C      E K      D S S          G O       E M
I D E L C A R  R A      M A      V A A          L S       R P
T E     R O    I N      A R      C L M        · Z L Y B O W U
R E     F C    A A U S T I N     O L B          I E C A B L H
U L     C A    D R E K C U T     M E Y          G Y A W R I A
K C     A R    T M O Z Y H P     F R O          P J N D L F O
```

AEROCAR	CROSLEY	KAISER
AIRSCOOT	DAVIS	KELLER
AIRWAY	DEL CAR	KURTIS
AMERICAN AUSTIN	FRAZER	LASALLE
AMERICAR	GRAHAM	PLAYBOY
BOBBI-KAR	HUPMOBILE	TUCKER

Answers are on pages 353-54

Auto Madness

In the opening scenes of the 1963 movie "It's a Mad Mad Mad Mad World," five famous comedians are driving various kinds of vehicles. Can you correctly match the actor to their set of wheels?

1. Milton Berle
2. Sid Caesar
3. Jimmy Durante
4. Mickey Rooney
5. Jonathan Winters

VW "Bug"
Ford truck
'62 Imperial convertible
'57 Ford
'62 Plymouth wagon

Bonus: Which car went over the cliff?

Show Stoppers

1. Freddie started his auto show career in 1970, and made appearances for almost 10 years. If you know the company he was the annual spokesman for, you'll know his full name.

3. This long-legged lady misunderstood when she was told to split the car 50/50. What company displayed this at the 1970 auto shows?

2. Auto salesmen will turn somersaults to sell you a car and, sometimes at auto shows, so will the cars. What year and make is this flippin' vehicle?

4. This charming two-wheeled, rear-engined gentleman was the auto show pitchman for what new 1960 compact car?

Answers are on page 354

Triplets

In 1958, Chevrolet brought out their first model featuring a six taillight design. This triple light theme continued on full-size Chevys for over two decades (except 1959).
Can you identify the correct model years for the eight designs shown below?

1. _____

2. _____

3. _____

4. _____

5. _____

6. _____

7. _____

8. _____

Answers are on page 354

The Faces of Oldsmobile

Oldsmobile's front-end look evolved slowly after World War II, but that's what makes it difficult for you to give the correct year of each design. Notice the subtle changes in the chrome upper grill "lip," the headlight/turn signal positioning, and the jet hood ornaments.

1. _____

2. _____

3. _____

4. _____

5. _____

6. _____

7. _____

8. _____

Answers are on page 354

GIMMICKS AND GADGETS #1

Mix pure genius with years of trial and error, and you have the formula for the wild innovations that have been created for our motoring pleasures.

What are the "marvels" illustrated in the six photos below? Give the correct year and make of car to all but #1 and #4.

1. _____

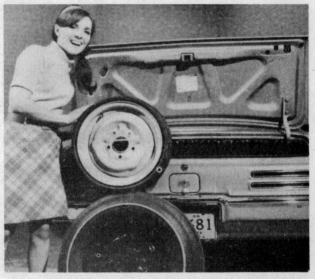

2. _____

3. _____

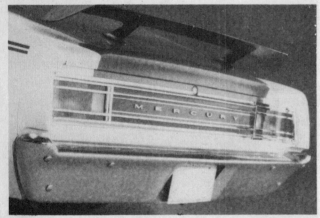

4. _____

5. _____

6. _____

Answers are on page 354

Radio Ha~Ha

1. Who was this wild and crazy radio comedian? _____

2. What oil company sponsored his show? _____

3. Identify the car dash with the unusual vertical radio. _____

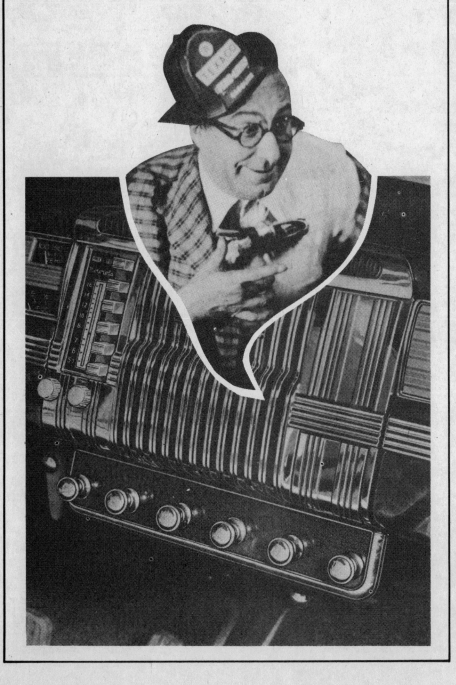

...and the News

1. What famous radio news correspondent/broadcaster is pictured above?
   _____

2. What independent automaker sponsored him in the early 1950's?
   _____

3. What other famous "hot flash" broadcaster did the above auto company sponsor?
   _____

4. What GM car division sponsored Henry J. Taylor News on radio?
   _____

Long Distance Information

What import car brand would you be calling from the numbers listed below? Decipher the numbers using your telephone dial.

236-8539 _____
248-7636 _____
337-7274 _____
738-4368 _____
767-7243 _____
874-8674 _____
786-2326 _____

Answers are on page 354

GAPERS BLOCK

We're traveling through a time warp, but seem to be stuck in a 1953 traffic jam. Well, as long as we're here, let's identify the year and make of cars that are gaping at us.

Answers are on page 354

Name Game #1

Six decades of car model names are listed below. You need to rearrange them so that they correctly match the year and make of the auto company that manufactured them.

CAR BRANDS

1. '58 Mercury
2. '35 Chrysler
3. '40 Cadillac
4. '70 Buick
5. '54 Henry J
6. '69 Plymouth
7. '59 Jeep
8. '36 Dodge
9. '54 Hudson
10. '41 Oldsmobile
11. '82 Imperial
12. '55 Packard

MODEL NAMES

A. Sixty-Special
B. GSX
C. GTX
D. Jet-Liner
E. Voyager
F. Frank Sinatra Edition
G. 78
H. Constellation
I. Airstream
J. Harlequin
K. Westchester
L. Corsair

What a Memory

What foreign car company in the 1960's used elephant mascots and the slogan "Mini-Brute"?
What American dealership sold these small imports?

Mechanically Minded #1

OK, you mechanics, decode these scrambled terms listed below, and then match them to their correct ignition system part.

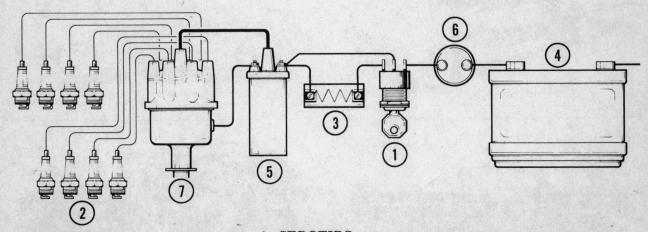

1. THWICS
2. KARPS GULPS
3. SEROTIRS
4. RAYBETT
5. TINNOGII LOCI
6. MATEMER
7. SUBITITORD

Top Dozen of '39

Out of the 21 different car brands back in 1939, these are the 12 best selling names.
Put them in the correct order to match their rank.

MIXED CAR MAKES	RANK	NEW-CAR REGISTRATIONS
Pontiac	1	598,834
Chrysler	2	481,496
Ford	3	348,807
Packard	4	218,995
Plymouth	5	176,585
Chevrolet	6	159,836
Studebaker	7	146,412
Hudson	8	84,660
Buick	9	65,884
Dodge	10	63,956
Mercury	11	62,855
Oldsmobile	12	62,005

Four~Fifty Wagons

Identify the year and make of these two- and four-door wagons from the mid-to-late 1950's.

1. _____

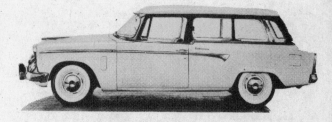

2. _____

3. _____

4. _____

Answers are on pages 354-55

Diesel Duzees

1. The car shown above boasts of being the first diesel powered passenger car. What year and make is it?_____

2. On the hood of this car is the name "Cummins," which is synonymous with American diesel engines. What was the first name of Mr. Cummins?_____

3. What is the name and title of the German inventor of diesel power?_____

4. What model year did Volkswagen offer its first diesel powered cars?_____

5. In what year did Mercedes-Benz build its 1,000,000th diesel powered automobiles?_____

6. What make of trucks during the 1940's and early 1950's traveled in "diesel caravans," educating the public about that engine's virtues? (See picture below.)_____

Answers are on page 355

DAY DREAMS #1

Dream cars make the blood pump faster, the mind hallucinate, and occasionally provide glimpses into our future. Identify the year, make and model name for each of the six visions shown below.

1. _____

2. _____

3. _____

4. _____

5. _____

6. _____

Movie Car Trivia #2

Answer these car-related movie trivia questions.

1. What year and make of car is the Blues Brothers "Blues Mobile"?

2. What size engine does Dan Akroyd tell us powers their Blues Mobile?

3. In the 1978 Superman movie, what is the year and make of car Lois Lane is nearly buried in?

4. Near the end of "Dirty Mary, Crazy Larry," what year and make of car does Peter Fonda crash into a train?

5. This same crash scene also appears in the opening of what hit TV program?

6. What year and make of car goes over the cliff in the "China Syndrome"?

Answers are on page 355

Fin Fantasies

Some wild looking rear fin designs are featured on these past dream/show cars.
Can you identify the year and full name for each?

1. _____

2. _____

3. _____

4. _____

5. _____

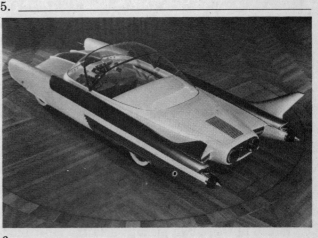

6. _____

Answers are on page 355

Personal Pickups

The Ford Ranchero and Chevrolet El Camino for 1959 are shown below. Answer the following questions to see how they compared.

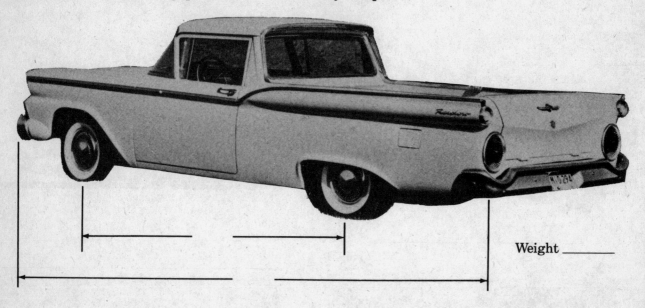

Weight _____

Weight _____

1. Which car had the longest bed capacity with the tailgate up? _____

2. Which bed capacity was the longest with the tailgate down? _____

3. Which make offered the largest V-8 option and how many cubes was it? _____

4. Which vehicle had more rated horsepower, and what was it? _____

5. What was the only color interior offered on the '59 El Camino? _____

6. Which of these two pickups sold the most models for 1959? _____

Answers are on page 355

Sneak Preview

Snow White is about to give you a sneak preview of the make of car that sponsored the early *Disneyland* TV shows.

What car manufacturer was the sponsor and also official car to the real Disneyland?

_____

COBRA QUICKIES

1. What Ford engine powered the first 75 production Shelby Cobras? _____

2. What size Ford performance engine did Shelby then change to?

   _____

3. What country built the Cobras' bodies and chassis?
   A. Italy   B. France   C. England

4. What material were Cobra bodies made of?
   A. Aluminum   B. Fiberglass   C. Steel

5. What year did Carroll Shelby switch from 289's to the monstrous 427 cu. in. engine? _____

6. What was the advertised top speed of the 271 h.p. 289 Cobra?
   A. 134 mph   B. 154 mph   C. 164 mph

7. What was the curb weight in pounds for a complete 289 Cobra?
   A. 2026   B. 2226   C. 2626

8. How many 427 cu. in. Cobras were built?
   A. 271   B. 356   C. 427

Top Ten 1942

The last year for auto manufacturing before World War II was officially 1942, though only a very limited run was possible that year. Correctly match car make with its production figure.

POSITION

1.____	45,472	A. Buick
2.____	43,307	B. Nash
3.____	25,113	C. Ford
4.____	16,601	D. Studebaker
5.____	15,404	E. Packard
6.____	12,230	F. Dodge
7.____	11,675	G. Chevrolet
8.____	9,285	H. Oldsmobile
9.____	6,085	I. Plymouth
10.____	5,428	J. Pontiac

PUSH/PULL POWER

only one wagon has "DRIVEPOWER"

PUSH   PUSH   PULL

In the illustration above, the half horse body represents conventional wagon rear wheel power. The drawing of the complete horse demonstrates front and rear—four-wheel drive. What was the only family wagon to offer "drivepower" back in the early 1960's?

_____

Answers are on page 355

School Daze #1

Many truck brands have powered school buses over the years. Can you identify the five manufacturers pictured below?

1. _____

2. _____

3. _____

4. _____

5. _____

Answers are on page 355

Faster than the Fastest

Back in the early 1930's a famous car driver would race his stock model automobile coast to coast against the most powerful trains, and beat them.

1. Who was this driver?
A. "Ab" Jenkins   B. Cannonball Baker   C. Sir Malcolm Campbell

2. What make of car did he use?
A. Studebaker   B. Mercury   C. Franklin

007

Answer the questions from these different James Bond movie scenes.

1. Movie Title _____
   Make of car _____

2. Movie Title _____
   Make of car _____

3. Movie Title _____
   Make of car _____

4. Movie Title _____
   Make of car _____

Name that State #1

Do you know which states used these slogans on their license plates back in 1955? The number combination on each plate represents an engine size offered by a car maker back in 1955. Identify the brand.

HEART OF DIXIE
❤1 8·265

1. _____

287
VACATIONLAND

3. _____

THE TREASURE STATE
8-341

2. _____

V8-259
.THE WHEAT STATE.

4. _____

Bite the ....

1. What movie does this crash scene appear in?

2. What is the year and make of the car shown in this movie still?

3. The male star raced against the above car. What year, make and model car did he race in?

4. Who was the male star?

Import Invasion

The names listed below are the 10 best selling import cars in America back in 1958. The problem is they're out of order. Can you rearrange them so the correct makes are in their right sales rank?

MAKE	SALES RANK
Hillman	1. _____
Simca	2. _____
Opel	3. _____
Renault	4. _____
MG	5. _____
Ford	6. _____
Triumph	7. _____
Volkswagen	8. _____
Vauxhall	9. _____
Fiat	10. _____

Answers are on page 355

The Dodge Dilemna

You could help solve our dilemma by just correctly identifying
the year and model name for each Dodge front-end design.

1. _____

2. _____

3. _____

4. _____

5. _____

6. _____

Answers are on page 355

Side Swipe

I've swiped just a portion of six different car side decorations.
Can you identify the year, make and model of car for each design?

1. _____

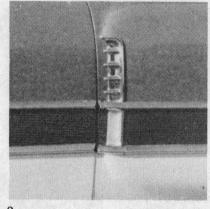

2. _____

3. _____

4. _____

5. _____

6. _____

Care-Free Cars

Which auto manufacturer, back in 1963, advertised their cars as
being from the "Care-Free State"?

```
1963



THE CARE-FREE STATE
```

REAR ENGINES

Besides the VW Bug, can you name two other German car makes and models that had a rear engine in the late 1950's?

1. _____

2. _____

Answers are on page 355

SPECIAL DELIVERY

Can you identify the tractor/cab portion of these six different delivery trucks?

1. _____

2. _____

3. _____

4. _____

5. _____

6. _____

Answers are on page 355

Revolutionary

"Ladies and gentlemen, this is our new revolutionary research and development sports car...", this was how the manufacturer introduced this beautiful gullwing dream.

1. Who was the auto manufacturer?
2. What was this model called?
3. What type of engine did it feature?
4. Where was the engine located?
5. What was the horsepower rating?

6. What was the manufacturer's claim for the top speed from this car?
7. How tall was this automobile?
8. What year was it introduced to the public?

KEY BOBBERS #1

Identify the correct car make by their key bob shown below.

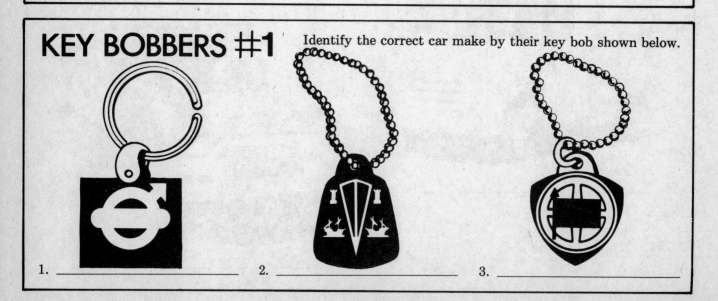

1. _____

2. _____

3. _____

Answers are on page 356

Kool~Aid

The illustration below is of a typical cooling system for a water-cooled automobile engine. Can you match the component parts to the correct arrows:

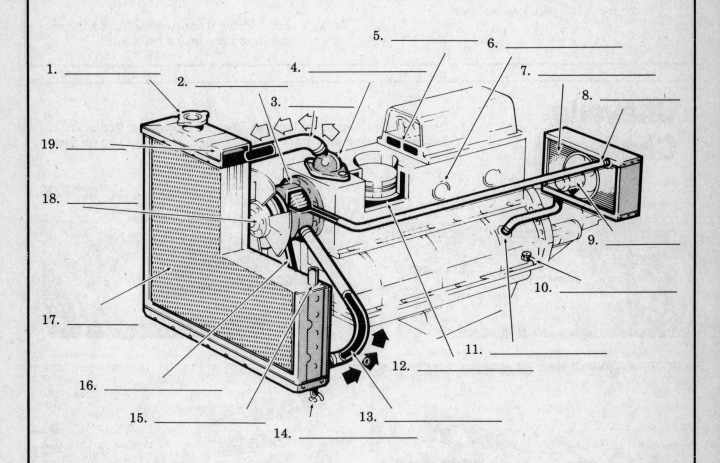

Automatic transmission coolant line
Cylinder head
Drive belt
Engine block drain
Fan
Freeze plug
Heater blower motor
Heater core
Heater hose
Heater hose return

Lower radiator hose
Radiator
Radiator cap
Radiator drain petcock
Radiator expansion tank
Thermostat housing
Upper radiator hose
Water jacket
Water pump

Answers are on page 356

LICENSE LAWS

1. What is the minimum driving age in Hawaii?

2. What states will issue either student, temporary, or restricted driver licenses to 14-year olds?

3. In what state do you have to be 21 or older to receive a full privilege license?

4. What's the minimum driving age in California if you don't complete drivers education?

5. In Louisiana you're prohibited from operating motor vehicles between 11 pm and 5 am if you are under what age?

6. You cannot drive a car in New York City at any time if you are under what age?

Chevelle Challenge

The 1964-69 Chevrolet Chevelles shown below are different in design, but some only have minor changes. Identify the six years with the correct picture.

1. _____

2. _____

3. _____

4. _____

5. _____

6. _____

Answers are on page 356

Toothy Buicks

The evolution of the Buick grille "teeth," are clearly displayed by these eight front designs. One by one, give the correct year.

1. _____

2. _____

3. _____

4. _____

5. _____

6. _____

7. _____

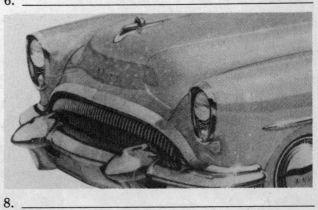

8. _____

Answers are on page 356

Up, Up, and Away

PICTURE B. This version was another company's approach to the flying automobile concept. Do you know its somewhat dubious name?

1. Cessna Skyauto
2. Waterman Aerobile
3. Anderson Aerocar

PICTURE A. Can you imagine the neighbors' faces back in 1939 when this car started flying around the block and landed in their back yard? Name the genius who created this twentieth century marvel.

1. Theodore P. Hall
2. Lawrence Phillips
3. Igor Sikorsky

PICTURE C. This flying car is the 1947 relative of picture "A"; Quite a change! Consolidated Vultee Aircraft built this model. Do you know what they called it?

1. Corsair Car
2. Corvair Car
3. Convair Car

Answers are on page 356

Indian Signs

For 1936, Pontiac designed these different hood ornaments to be symbols for the number of cylinders under the hood.
Which design was for the Eight and which was for the Six?

1. _____

2. _____

AUTO ART

Mel Wolff, a Chicago new-car dealer, created and sold these "OP" and floral decorated machines during the 1960's and christened them "auto art."
Identify the year, make and model of each design shown below.

1. _____

2. _____

3. _____

4. _____

Know Your Novas

How subtly the front ¾ view of Chevy's Nova (Chevy II) changed during the 1960's. Identify the correct model year for these six designs.

1. _____

2. _____

3. _____

4. _____

5. _____

6. _____

Answers are on page 356

Boss of the Bonneville

The picture below is of a world-famous speed king, who also was
the Mayor of Salt Lake City, and one of his many record-breaking
machines.

1. Who was this driver?
   A. John Cobb   B. "Ab" Jenkins   C. Cannonball Baker

2. What special-body automobile is he sitting in?
   A. Duesenberg   B. Marmon   C. Stutz

3. What world record did he set in this car, for a 24-hour run at
   the Bonneville Salt Flats?
   A. 99.47 MPH   B. 125.47 MPH   C. 135.47 MPH

4. This driver set even better times in another of these vehicles.
   What was this machine called?
   A. Super Salt   B. Bonneville Bomber   C. Mormon
      Special   Meteor

Merging Motors

First there was Nash, then Hudson, then they merged and formed
American Motors Corporation. This relationship brought out
many different automobiles with interesting names.
Give the correct debut model year for each listed below.

_____ 1. Nash LaFayette
_____ 2. Hudson Commodore (step-down)
_____ 3. Nash Ambassador Airflyte
_____ 4. Hudson Pacemaker (step-down)
_____ 5. Nash Rambler (compact)
_____ 6. Hudson Hornet

_____ 7. Nash-Healey
_____ 8. Rambler Rebel
_____ 9. Rambler Marlin
_____ 10. AMC Matador
_____ 11. AMC Hornet
_____ 12. AMC Pacer

Answers are on page 356

4 of a kind

Match the correct year to the four versions of the second-generation Buick Riviera.

1967   1968   1969   1970

1. _____

3. _____

2. _____

4. _____

Framed #1

This phantom view shows the framework for a car of the 1930's. The name of this frame is two letters of the alphabet, if you look carefully, you'll see them in the design. What are the letters and the year and make of the car?

Answers are on page 356

"TRANS"-PLANT

1. Where is the largest transmission factory under one roof located?

2. Which auto company owns and operates this plant?

3. How many transmission units can it manufacture in one day?

DASTARDLY DASHES

The instrument panels shown here all have distinguishing style characteristics that should help you identify the year and name of car they were designed for.

1. _____

2. _____

3. _____

4. _____

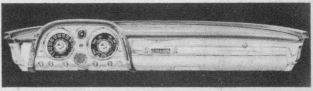

5. _____

6. _____

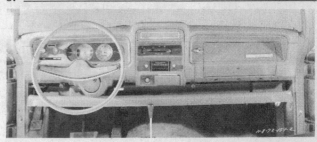

7. _____

8. _____

Answers are on page 356

Parking Garage of Time

What year and make of cars are parked on the three floors of this garage?

Answers are on page 356

"A Clean Sweep, but a Squeaky Finish"

1. What annual race gave this trophy as their Grand Prize to first place winners?

2. Who cosponsored this event?

3. What year did it officially start?

4. Which city and state held this race each year?

5. What was the name of the race track?

Dealers Choice (U.S.A.)

You have a lot of choices among domestic new car dealers, as the numbers below indicate. Your task is to match the auto manufacturer to their correct number of dealer outlets.

NUMBER OF DEALERS	U.S. MANUFACTURER
1. 5,155	A. Pontiac
2. 4,677	B. AMC/Renault
3. 3,175	C. Plymouth
4. 2,980	D. Oldsmobile
5. 2,945	E. Volkswagen of America
6. 2,831	F. Chevrolet
7. 2,796	G. Mercury
8. 2,744	H. Ford
9. 2,680	I. Dodge
10. 906	J. Buick

Duo-Door

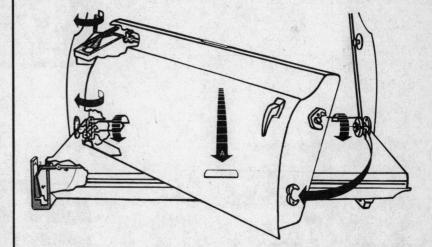

1. What two automobile brand names offered this ingenious two-way tailgate?

2. What model year was it first available on station wagons?

3. What was the advertised name for this design?

4. What was the last model year it was available?

Answers are on page 356

Open Sesame

Can you identify the year and make of these wide open vehicles by their rear entrances?

1. _____

2. _____

3. _____

4. _____

5. _____

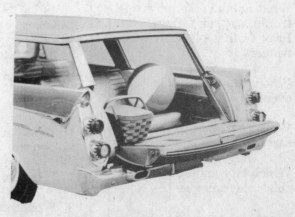

6. _____

Answers are on page 357

Fastest Thing on Wheels

Do you know the name of these three land speed record holder machines? Do you know who were the drivers for blur #1 and the 1931 vehicle in picture #3?

1. _____

2. _____

3. _____

Pleasin' Pickups

Six tasty pickup trucks are shown here. Can you identify their year and make?

1. _____

2. _____

3. _____

4. _____

5. _____

6. _____

Answers are on page 357

BIG IS BETTER

This car, in many ways, is considered one of the biggest ever produced in the world. Because of its price, only 10 were ever sold.

Can you name the manufacturer and model, and fill in the gargantuan dimensions, total weight, engine size and original cost?

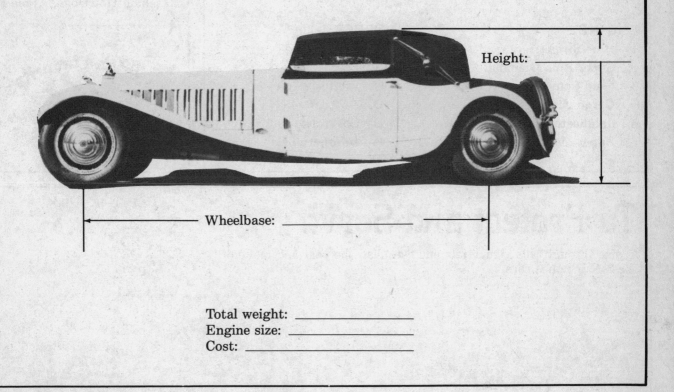

Height: _____

Wheelbase: _____

Total weight: _____
Engine size: _____
Cost: _____

TV Auto Trivia

1. What was the foreign make and model convertible that Columbo drove?

2. On the *Andy Griffith Show*, what make of police cars did Andy and Barney always drive?

3. *The Dukes of Hazzard* has made what year and make muscle car world famous?

4. What was the luxury car used by Mr. and Mrs. Douglas in *Green Acres?*

5. What year, make and model car does TV's Alice drive?

6. Ward Cleaver, Beaver's dad, drove what year and make car in *Leave It To Beaver*'s first season?

7. What make and model wagon did the dad drive in *My Three Sons?*

8. What year and make car starred in *Vegas?*

Answers are on page 357

Truckin' Engines

These six engine names are good examples of the imagination truck manufacturers used during the past decades. Match the engine name to the correct truck company.

ENGINE	TRUCK
1. Blue Streak	A. REO
2. Super Blue Diamond	B. Ford
3. Gold Comet	C. White
4. Cargo King V-8	D. Autocar
5. Jobmaster	E. Chevrolet
6. Super Mustang	F. International

Singing Slogans

Fill in the bottom line, to complete this famous car jingle.

Baseball, Hot Dogs, Apple Pie & _____ .

America's favorites

To Protect and Serve

Cruise through this visual quiz and establish the year and make of these four police cars.

1. _____

2. _____

3. _____

4. _____

Answers are on page 357

JUNKERS

A neighbor friend never trades his cars in, he just stacks them in his yard when they're worn out.
Can you name the cars he has owned and their model years?

Answers are on page 357

Visual Slogans

There have been renowned and obscure visual slogans which have symbolized various auto makes over the decades.
Name the cars that were advertised with these eight images illustrated below.

JET-SMOOTH RIDE

1. _____

2. _____

3. _____

win you over.

4. _____

No wonder the swing is to _____ !

5. _____

6. _____

lion-hearted

7. _____

ENGINE ←→ TRANSMISSION
PERFECT BALANCE

8. _____

Answers are on page 357

Club Page   Auburn~Cord~Duesenberg

The Auburn-Cord-Duesenberg Club submitted these questions in hope of stumping you. Do they, or can you answer them all with ease?

1. Why was the 1936 Cord designated as the model 810 by the factory?

2. What was the number of the first Model J Duesenberg?

3. Where were most of the Auburns and all of the Cords manufactured? What is the use of that factory today?

4. Who succeeded Gordon Buehrig as chief stylist for the Auburn-Cord-Duesenberg Company? What design change did he make on some of the 812 Cords?

5. What car was the first to use a gas flap door to conceal the gas cap?

6. Where were the factory showrooms for the Auburn-Cord-Duesenberg company located? What are they used for today?

7. How many hood louvers are there on the standard 810-812 Cord? How many on the custom Beverly sedan?

8. What American production car used the drivetrain design of the famous Miller race cars?

9. How many distinct body styles were there in the Auburn boattail speedsters?

10. What car was the first to use a horn ring on the steering wheel and a high beam light indicator on the dash?

Ride 'em Cowboy

1. What state uses this Bronco Buster logo?

2. What is the name of the real rodeo rider depicted on this license plate?
   A. Roy Rogers   B. Stub Farlow   C. Slim Pickens

3. Beside rodeo star, what other profession did he have?
   A. Movie star   B. Senator   C. Law officer

Emblem Quickie

What year, make, model and engine does this emblem represent?

_____

_____

Answers are on page 357

Boattail Rivs

Can you identify the years represented by these three different Buick Riviera fastback designs.

1. _____

2. _____

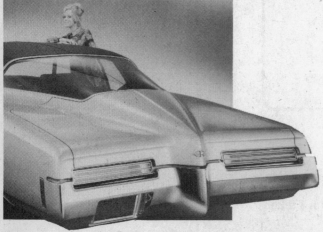

3. _____

SIXTIES SLOGANS

These 12 sayings listed below are excellent samples of some familiar and some obscure slogans from 1960's car advertisements. Who used these phrases?

1. Where the Action Is

2. The Roaring '65's

3. The Great Impostor

4. Ten Million Dollar Ride

5. _____ Tells It Like It Is

6. The World's 100,000-mile Durability Champion

7. Ride the Sports Car that Swims

8. . . .the Cars with the Bumblebee Stripes

9. Command Performance

10. Wide-Track Tigers

11. Unique in all the World

12. America's Most Carefully Built Car

Answers are on page 357

300's

The aggressive and powerful look of the Chrysler 300 front-end designs have shown considerable similarity over the years. Use caution in identifying the correct "letter" and year for each 300 pictured below.

1. _____

2. _____

3. _____

4. _____

5. _____

6. _____

7. _____

8. _____

Answers are on page 357

Glitter and Glamour

Each of these glamorous models was part of the stage presentations at the annual new car shows.
Can you identify the year and make of cars behind each hostess?

1. _____

2. _____

3. _____

4. _____

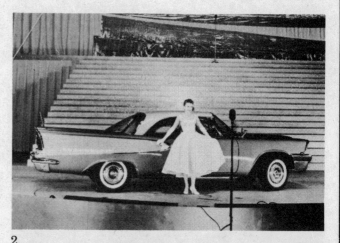

5. _____

6. _____

Answers are on page 357

Vette Quickie #1

Clever design details should give you clues in correctly identifying the years of these front views.

1. _____

2. _____

3. _____

4. _____

Queens for a Day #1

What show car are these two beauty queens riding in?

X Marks the Spot

One of the most desirable of all AMC cars would have to be the two-passenger AMX pictured below.
Answer the following questions about this muscle car.

1. What model year is pictured?

2. What engine block came standard?

3. What was the top optional engine block?

4. What was the maximum horsepower offered?

5. How high was the speedometer calibrated?

6. Was the hood scoop functional?

Answers are on page 357

First Class Delivery

Six different delivery trucks are shown below. Can you identify the maker of their tractor/cab section?

1. _____

2. _____

3. _____

4. _____

5. _____

6. _____

Answers are on page 358

ASSEMBLY LINES #1

Brand-new car bodies come down the long lost assembly lines of time in these six factory scenes. Identify the year and make of auto in each picture.

1. _____

4. _____

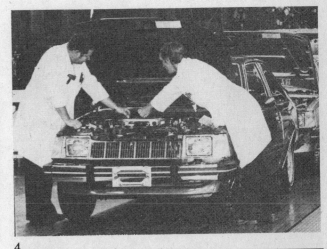

2. _____

5. _____

3. _____

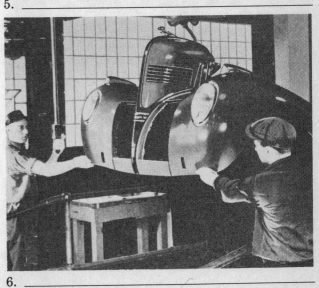

6. _____

Answers are on page 358

Daydreams #2

Auto companies have slowed down their output of show/dream cars lately, but the six experimental designs shown here are exciting examples of visions from various eras. Identify each by year, make and model.

1. _____

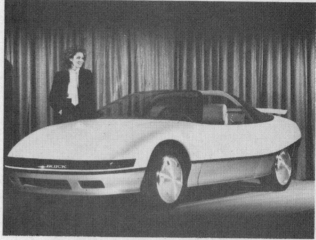

2. _____

3. _____

4. _____

5. _____

6. _____

Answers are on page 358

American Auto Graffiti

If you really think you "saw" the movie *American Graffiti*, then answer these auto related questions.

1. What is the year and make of car that Ron Howard loans to "Toad"?

2. Harrison Ford cruises around in what year and make of customized car?

3. The mysterious girl (Suzanne Sommers) taunts Richard Dreyfuss from what year and make of car?

4. What is the year and make of car that gets covered in shaving cream?

5. What year and make of police car does Richard Dreyfuss hook a chain up to?

6. What make of custom car did the Pharaoh gang members drive around in?

7. Cindy Williams had her parents' 1958 Edsel. What was the model name and exterior color combination?

Which Way Is Up?

What is the name of this famous hill climb, which has challenged auto manufacturers over the past 50 years?

_____

PANEL PROPHECY

The radical-looking panel delivery truck illustrated here is of a famous experimental vehicle of yesteryear.

How extensive is your knowledge on this dream machine? You'll find out after taking this quick quiz.

1. What was the full name for this show truck?
_____

2. What year did it premier? _____

3. What size V-8 engine was used in it? _____

4. What was the horsepower rating? _____

5. Where was the engine located? _____

6. What station wagon and pickup truck design of the 1960's did this dream influence?
_____

Fun-in-the-Sun

The beauty and variety of American convertible designs are very apparent in these six views, as is the promise of "fun-in-the-sun" driving. Identify the year as well as the make for each ragtop.

1. _____

2. _____

3. _____

4. _____

5. _____

6. _____

Answers are on page 358

Dash Detour

Take a little side trip and correctly give the year and make of the car that used these great dash designs.

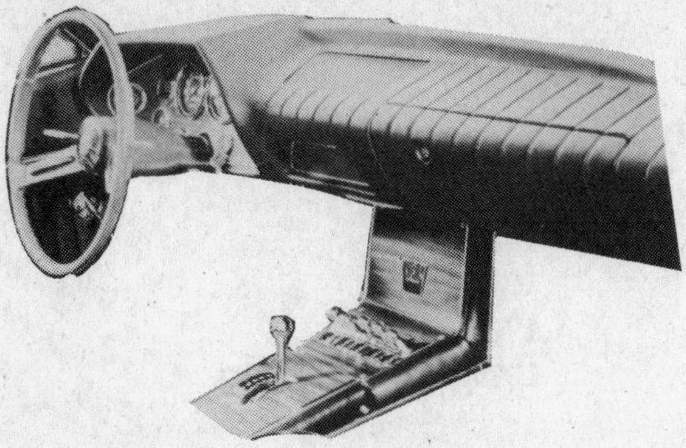

1. _____

2. _____

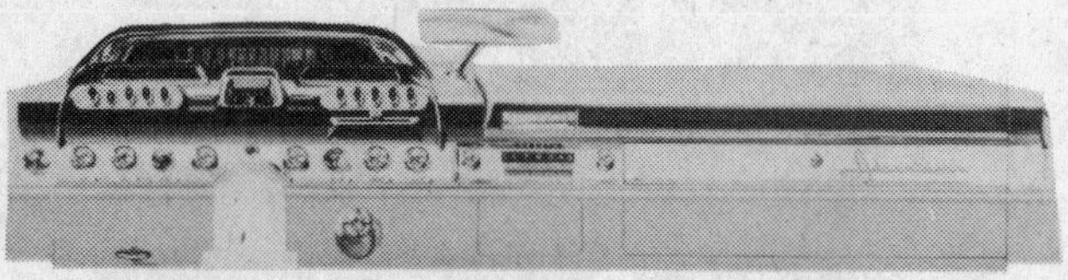

3. _____

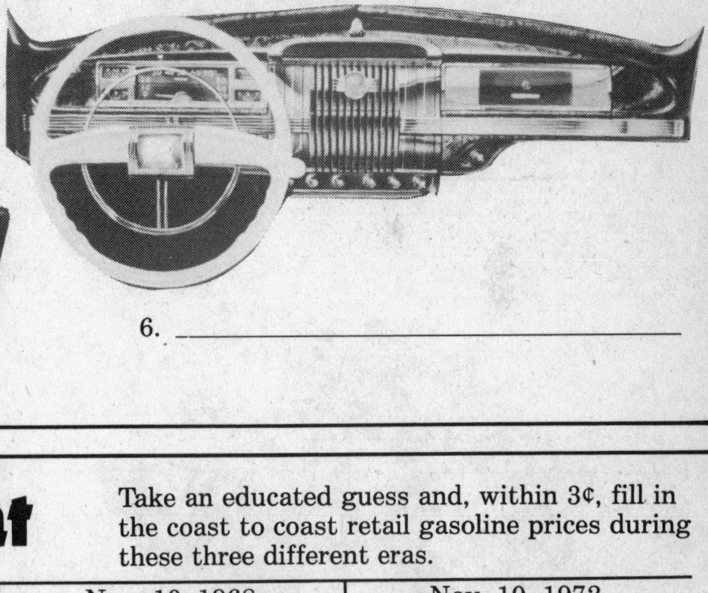

4. _____

5. _____

6. _____

The Price is Right

Take an educated guess and, within 3¢, fill in the coast to coast retail gasoline prices during these three different eras.

CITIES	Nov. 10, 1945 ETHYL	REGULAR	Nov. 10, 1968 PREMIUM	REGULAR	Nov. 10, 1972 PREMIUM	REGULAR
CHICAGO						
LOS ANGELES						
NEW YORK						

Answers are on page 358

Pontiac Power

Identify the correct cubic-inch displacement and
first model year for these four Pontiac engines,
using the answers listed below.

Cu. in.	Model year
301	1959
287	1970
389	1955
455	1977

1. _____

2. _____

3. _____

4. _____

Answers are on page 358

Muscle Car Word Search

How to play: The muscle car names are in all directions—vertically, horizontally, diagonally, and backwards. Circle each name found.

```
B I F I R A X M E F A I R L A N E F O B
A U T I R Y W T G A X E A C M M F A O A
R G J B R I T K N L B R M H U B X L V R
I V O S G E C P A E H O R N E T D C H A
V C Z K V J B A L B G X U P C S I O B M
C G N R C D F I C Y I T H D M V E N F B
H R O G O H A U R P M E B O Z D N L J L
E C F T M Y A G H D R O B S I A C G G E
C J L B E K N L J K X I U S R K A T Z R
H O R B T A L E L N L P D T D E M O N M
E Y H O T R F J O E E X F O H C R G P R
V T S S P D A U X R N T D T N A V E A E
E A U U C V Y N B T M G T A Y M D C B N
L M O P E P E I S G E O E I K A F H F N
L P G L T L R H M E B S T R V R M O V U
E A I T Z D E C H R Y S L E R O S D R R
F N E G O L R T R A N S A M E K I L H D
U O L J B S E M I A D U C A R R A B O A
R S O Y R U C R E M T R A U P Z J V N O
B A R R D G N Z S K Y L A R K T A B E R
```

AMX	Dodge	Mustang
Barracuda	Fairlane	Oldsmobile
Camaro	Falcon	Plymouth
Challenger	Firebird	Rambler
Chevelle	Ford	Rebel
Chrysler	GTO	Road Runner
Cobra	GTX	Shelby
Comet	Hornet	Skylark
Corvette	Javelin	Superbird
Demon	Mercury	Trans Am

Pickup Passion

Identify the year and make for these excellent pickups.

1. _____

2. _____

3. _____

4. _____

5. _____

6. _____

Answers are on page 358

DeSoto Discoveries

1. What model year did DeSoto put its crest on the headlight crossbar instead of the grill?
   A. 1930 B. 1931 C. 1933

2. DeSoto first offered its version of the Airflow in which model year?
   A. 1934 B. 1935 C. 1936

3. What was the last year that DeSoto used a crank-open windshield?
   A. 1935 B. 1937 C. 1939

4. Power steering came to DeSoto with which model introduction?
   A. 1949 B. 1951 C. 1953

5. The DeSoto nine-passenger Suburban body style was offered for which model years?
   A. 1946-48   B. 1949-50
   C. 1951-52

6. DeSoto first put the transmission shift lever on the steering column for which model year?
   A. 1939 B. 1942 C. 1949

7. Torsion bar front suspension was first used on which DeSoto?
   A. 1955 B. 1957 C. 1958

8. Which years did DeSoto have unitized body-frame structure?
   A. 1934-36   B. 1955-57
   C. 1960-61

9. DeSoto ceased six-cylinder engine production for which model year?
   A. 1949 B. 1955 C. 1960

10. What was the last model year DeSoto?
    A. 1961 B. 1962 C. 1963

Double Nickels

What month and year did the nationwide maximum speed limit of 55 mph become a permanent law?

By Sheer Drive

...and determination this transportation genius not only ran the Yellow Cab Motor Co., but pioneered a new concept for the use of cars and trucks. Who was this man and what field did he open up?

BILLBOARD #1

Year_____ Make_____ Models_____

Cut~Away Call~Outs

What year, make and model car is being
"X-rayed" in this line drawing?
Can you identify each and every one of the 29
components indicated by the numbered arrows?

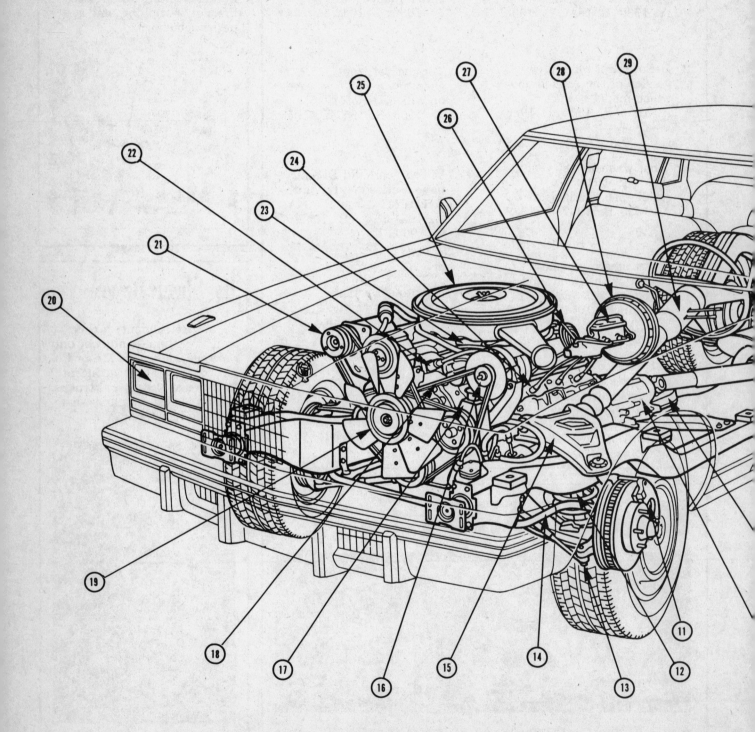

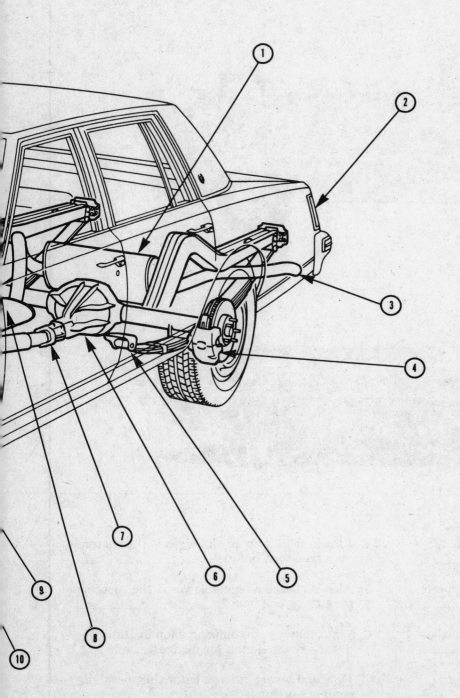

AIR FILTER HOUSING

FAN

FUEL LINE FILTER

MASTER CYLINDER

LEAF SPRING

SHOCK ABSORBER

POWER STEERING PUMP

ALTERNATOR

CATALYTIC CONVERTER

STEERING COLUMN

DISC BRAKE CALIPER

DIFFERENTIAL

DISTRIBUTOR

CARBURETOR

FRAME MEMBER

RESONATOR

UNIVERSAL JOINT

ALTERNATOR DRIVE BELT

TAILLIGHT

HEADLIGHT

AIR CONDITIONING COMPRESSOR

TAILPIPE

STABILIZER

SPARK PLUG

MUFFLER

TIE ROD END

DISC BRAKE

VACUUM OR POWER BRAKE UNIT

TRANSMISSION

Answers are on page 359

Before and After

Picture #1 is of the homely little Dodge pickup before it went in for a sex appeal beauty course and came out as shown in snapshot #2.

1. In picture #1, what is the model name for this production pickup? _____

2. What did Dodge call the custom version in picture #2? _____

3. What does the dream truck name translate to in Spanish? _____

4. Also in feet, how much longer is the custom over the stock body? _____

5. Also in feet, how much lower is the custom than the stock body? _____

6. What famous customizing shop in Detroit did the cosmetic job for Dodge? _____

7. How and where did you enter this low-slung compact dream?

_____

Answers are on page 359

Blinkin' Bobbies

In Birmingham, England, the local police experimented with a blue blinker light attached to the top of their helmets for night traffic duty. Do you know what year this novel idea was tried?_____

'55 Horses

The V-8 horsepower race was officially on in 1955, especially with Chevy, Plymouth, and others entering the field that year.
Match the car engines to their correct maximum 1955 horsepower rating.

MAKE / ENGINE (cu. in.)	MAXIMUM HORSEPOWER
1. Buick / 322	180
2. Cadillac / 331	208
3. Chevrolet / 265 (dual quads)	250
4. Imperial / 331	260
5. DeSoto / 291	225
6. Ford / 292 (automatic)	236
7. Hudson / 320	200
8. Lincoln / 341	177
9. Packard / 352	198
10. Plymouth / 260 (dual quads)	270

SILHOUETTES #1

It is much harder to recognize a car when all the characteristic details are gone and only a dark profile is shown. Identify the year, make and model for the five autos featured below.

2. _____

1. _____

4. _____

3. _____

5. _____

Two Sides to Everything

Above is "the other side" of actor Joe Higgins, who played the portly Southern sheriff in car commercials of the 1970's.

1. What make of muscle car ads did Joe appear in?

2. Of what city was he the sheriff?

3. What was his famous closing line in the TV ads?

Made By...

Can you name the company that built Fargo trucks?

MYSTERY CAR #1

The illustration below appeared in a car advertisement many years ago introducing a new import design.

1. What is the year and make of this car?

2. From what country was it imported?

3. What did the lowest price S440 model cost (f.o.b. east coast)?

4. Of what material was the engine made?
   A. Cast Iron   B. Magnesium   C. Aluminum

5. How many cylinders and what horsepower rating did it have?
   A. 2 cyl—30 H.P.   B. 4 cyl—35 H.P.   C. 6 cyl—45 H.P.

6. The ads claimed how many miles per gallon?
   A. 35   B. 45   C. 50

Daydreams #3

Dream and show cars give auto designers the rare opportunity to freely express their wildest imaginations and, in turn, their creations open our own minds to new directions.
Give the correct year, make and model name for each rolling sculpture shown here.

1. _____

2. _____

3. _____

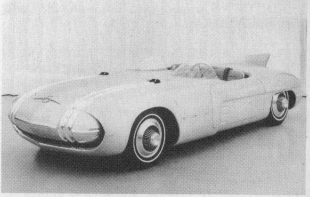

4. _____

5. _____

6. _____

Answers are on page 359

1960s and 1970s

1. What driver won both the NASCAR Grand National driving championship and most popular driver award in 1960?
   a. Joe Weatherly   b. Rex White   c. Lee Petty   d. Ned Jarrett

2. Marvin Panch won the 1961 Daytona 500 driving a:
   a. 1960 Pontiac   b. 1961 Chevrolet   c. 1961 Pontiac   d. 1961 Ford

3. Ford and Mercury both came out with new "fastback" hardtops mid-year in 1963. The design was aimed at racing, as was a new engine size. What was the size (in cubic inches)?
   a. 406   b. 409   c. 421   d. 427

4. Joe Weatherly won the 1963 NASCAR Grand National driving championship using two different makes. They were:
   a. Chevrolet and Ford   c. Dodge and Ford
   b. Pontiac and Mercury   d. Pontiac and Chevrolet

5. Richard Petty won his first Daytona 500 in 1964 driving a new Plymouth with what engine?
   a. 413 Wedge   b. 426 Wedge   c. 426 Hemi   d. 440 Wedge

6. In 1965 Ford drivers set a record with 48 wins out of 55 NASCAR Grand National events. Which make was second for the year?
   a. Plymouth   b. Mercury   c. Dodge   d. Chevrolet

7. A Mercury driver won the annual Pikes Peak Hill Climb's stock car competition in 1963 and again in 1964. He was:
   a. Bobby Unser   b. Ak Miller   c. A.J. Foyt   d. Parnelli Jones

8. The first Sports Car Club of America (SCCA) Trans-American Sedan Series was held in 1966. The winning domestic car was a:
   a. Ford Mustang   c. Plymouth Barracuda
   b. Dodge Dart   d. Chevrolet Camaro

9. Darel Dieringer was the surprise winner of the NASCAR Southern 500 on Labor Day in 1966 at the Darlington (S.C.) International Raceway. He drove a 1966 Mercury Comet owned by:
   a. Darel Dieringer   b. The Wood Brothers   c. Bud Moore   d. Junior Johnson

10. All of the following drivers have won USAC stock car races except:
    a. Bobby Allison   b. Richard Petty   c. Bobby Isaac   d. Dan Gurney

11. The 1968 Auto Racing Club of America (ARCA) stock car driving champion was:
    a. Ramo Stott   b. Benny Parsons   c. Iggy Katona   d. Les Snow

12. A.J. Foyt won the 1968 USAC stock car driving championship driving 1968 Ford Torinos for:
    a. Holman & Moody   b. Bill Stroppe   c. Banjo Matthews   d. Jack Bowsher

13. Ernie Derr won more International Motor Contest Association (IMCA) stock car championships than anyone. How many did he collect?
    a. 4   b. 6   c. 7   d. 12

14. The first NASCAR Grand National race won by a Dodge Daytona was at:
    a. Daytona   b. Talladega   c. Atlanta   d. Darlington

15. The first NASCAR Grand National race won by a Ford Talladega was at:
    a. Talladega   b. Atlanta   c. Daytona   d. Riverside

Answers are on page 359

Cannibalized Customs #1

My uncle Jack, Ace Auto Wrecker's chief mechanic, just doesn't like to throw things out. For years he's been saving car parts nobody else knows what to do with. Given his gift for making things fit, he could probably put an Isetta door on a Gullwing Mercedes . . . and make it work. In building his latest project car, he used parts from the fifties, sixties, and seventies. And it looks like he's built himself a real cruiser. He cannibalized 15 cars to make this beauty. How many can you spot?

Hello, Ma?

This photo taken in 1934 is of the film actress who later was the voice in the TV show *My Mother The Car.*
Who is this entertainer, and what make and model sedan is she standing next to?

Dealer Displays #1

These four window displays show the elaborate settings some new car dealers created back in the 1930's.
Can you identify the year and make of cars behind each window?

1. _____

2. _____

3. _____

4. _____

TV Auto Trivia #2

1. What is the year(s), make and model of the police car that comes out of the garage in the opening of *Hill Street Blues?*

2. In the very first opening scenes of the old *Mary Tyler Moore Show,* what year and make of car was Mary Richards driving?

3. What year and make of car did Baretta use?

4. Kojak used to smack his police blinker on the roof of what year, make and model automobile?

5. In the opening scenes of *One Day At A Time,* what year and make car do Ann Romano and daughters drive to Indianapolis?

6. What make and model car did Rockford drive?

7. What make of car did they customize to build the Green Hornet's car, called _____ ?

8. Do you remember *Car 54, Where Are You,* well what year and make of police car was #54?

Answers are on page 359

Downsized Duesy???

YEAR_____
MAKE_____ PLAYBOY

Easy Pickups #1

Match the pick up makes to the correct model names.

Makes	Models
1. Dodge	A. Caballero
2. REO	B. Arrow
3. GMC	C. Ranger
4. Ford	D. Sweptside
5. Plymouth	E. Scrambler
6. Jeep	F. Speed Wagon

Knock on Wood

Can you identify the year and make of cars that came decked-out in either real or simulated wood trim?

1. _____

2. _____

3. _____

4. _____

5. _____

6. _____

Answers are on page 359

Small Package

If you ever read an issue of *Popular Science* or *Mechanix Illustrated* during the 1950's and 1960's, you must have seen this car advertised in very tiny ads in the back of the magazines. Answer the following.

1. Name of car: _____

2. Front or rear engine: _____

3. Number of cylinders: _____

4. Cubic-inch displacement in 1957: _____

            and in 1967: _____

5. Air- or water-cooled engine: _____

6. Type of transmission in 1955: _____

            and in 1965: _____

7. Top speed: _____

8. Miles per gallon: _____

Proud Parent

Back in 1956, General Motors owned many subsidiaries that manufactured various car components. Seven of those GM companies are listed below, can you match them to the correct parts they manufactured back then?

COMPANY NAME	COMPONENT PART
1. AC	A. Horns
2. Delco	B. Cables
3. Harrison	C. Electronics
4. Klaxon	D. Carburetors
5. Packard	E. Steering
6. Rochester	F. Spark plugs
7. Saginaw	G. Radiators

Ice Capade

Can you name the rubber company that first explored the possibilities of a winter stud tire in 1959, with their BS3 design shown in this cutaway view?

_____

Answers are on pages 359-60

Detroit Hoods #1

The six mean-looking hoods are ganged up below to trip your muscle car memories. What year and make of cars from Detroit (and Kenosha) wore these power bulges?

1. _____

2. _____

4. _____

3. _____

5. _____

6. _____

Walter P's Legacy

In honor of Mr. Chrysler forming his car company decades ago, we challenge you to this bit of corporate trivia.

What was the first production year for each of these models:

1. Plymouth Fury _____
2. Dodge Coronet _____
3. Dodge Silver Challenger _____
4. DeSoto Adventurer _____
5. Chrysler Airflow _____
6. Chrysler New Yorker _____

Give the correct model year that these events occurred.

7. Dodge drops "Brothers" from its name. _____
8. First year for hemi-head V-8 _____
9. Introduction of push button transmission _____
10. DeSoto offers hidden "Airfoil" headlights _____
11. Debut of PowerFlite fully automatic transmission _____
12. Wagon tailgate window washer system _____

Let's Make a Deal

"Let me make myself perfectly clear, Mr. Petty, I will throw in a set of rubber floor mats if you buy this car today!"

1. What make and model car is being negotiated in the above photo?

2. What other number should be on the door next to the four?

3. When this picture was snapped back in 1971, NASCAR star Richard Petty had just won his _____ Grand National Championship.

Sixes from the Sixties

Can you match the make of car to the six-cylinder engine size offered in the 1962 models?

CAR MAKE	ENGINE DISPLACEMENT
1. Tempest	A. 144.3
2. Ford	B. 145.0
3. Rambler	C. 169.6
4. Corvair	D. 182.5
5. Buick Special	E. 194.5
6. Falcon/Comet	F. 195.6
7. Mercedes-Benz 300	G. 198.0
8. Chevrolet	H. 223.0
9. Valiant/Lancer	I. 225.0
10. Lark	J. 235.5

CONVOY UNSCRAMBLE

The truck names from different decades are listed below, each slightly mixed up. Rearrange the letters to discover their identities.

1. AOIDNMN _____

2. LERCEHOVT _____

3. KAMC _____

4. TUACRAO _____

5. PATARELERN _____

6. EWITH _____

7. KSOHSOH _____

8. TIBELPTER _____

9. DEERLAF _____

10. ROWHTENK _____

Answers are on page 360

Son of Cobra

The illustration below is a portion of a full-page magazine ad on Carroll Shelby's first GT 350. Can you answer the questions below on this wild and wooly muscle car?

SHELBY G.T.350 IS "SON OF COBRA"

ADULTS ONLY!

Shelby-American presents America's fastest, race-bred stock car!
You'll thrill to its performance, you'll hold your breath behind the wheel!!
Every minute is something new never seen before!!!

1. What was the first model year for this GT 350 design?

2. What size engine was standard?

3. How many horses were packed into this engine?

4. What carburetor was standard?

5. What was the advertised 0-60 mph time for the GT 350?
   A. 4.9 sec.   B. 5.7 sec.   C. 6.2 sec.

Answers are on page 360

Bullet Nose

The grille and bumper designs grouped below are from late-1940's and early-1950's Fords.
Can you give the correct model year for each of these bullet noses?

1. _____

2. _____

3. _____

4. _____

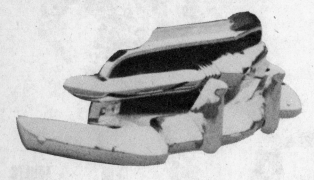

5. _____

6. _____

Door Fin

1. What year and make of car had this fin-like chrome panel mounted on the rear door of its first four-door hardtop?

2. What was this four-door hardtop model named?

3. The simulated air scoop on this production door was copied from which dream car?

4. What size engine was standard for this car?

5. This engine put out how many horsepower?

6. How many model years featured the door fin?

Window Sticker Price~1959

Can you put the correct port-of-entry price on the window sticker for each of these 1959 European imports?

PRICES

$1,353	$4,667
$2,175	$10,418
$2,330	$13,250

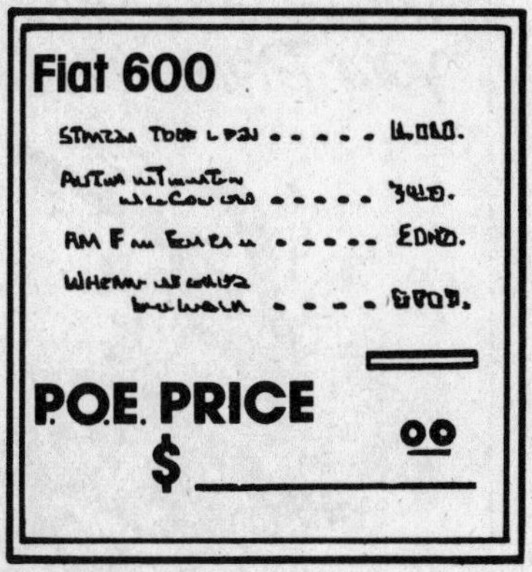
Fiat 600
P.O.E. PRICE
$
00

1. ______________________

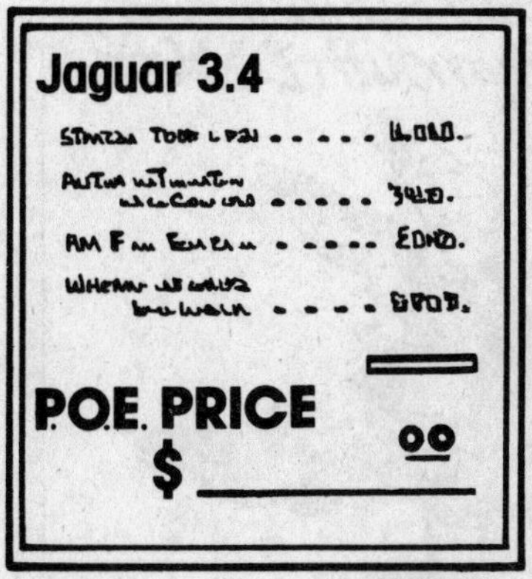
Jaguar 3.4
P.O.E. PRICE
$
00

2. ______________________

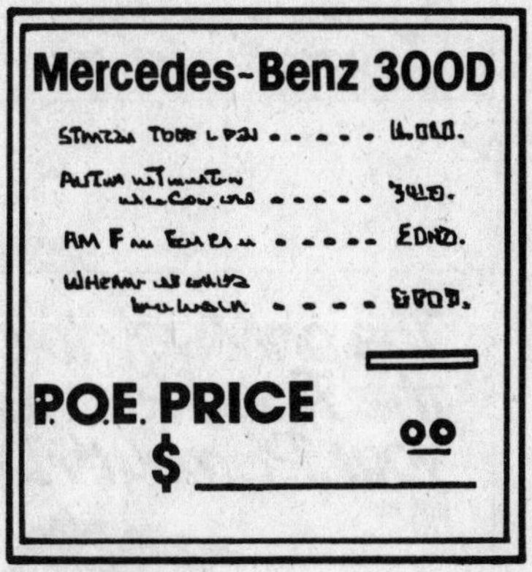
Mercedes-Benz 300D
P.O.E. PRICE
$
00

3. ______________________

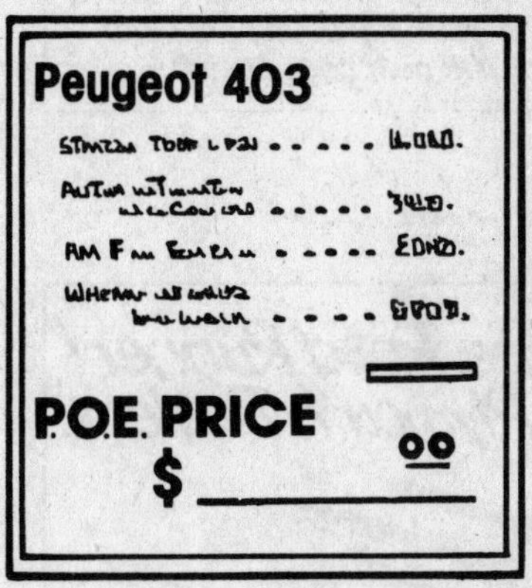
Peugeot 403
P.O.E. PRICE
$
00

4. ______________________

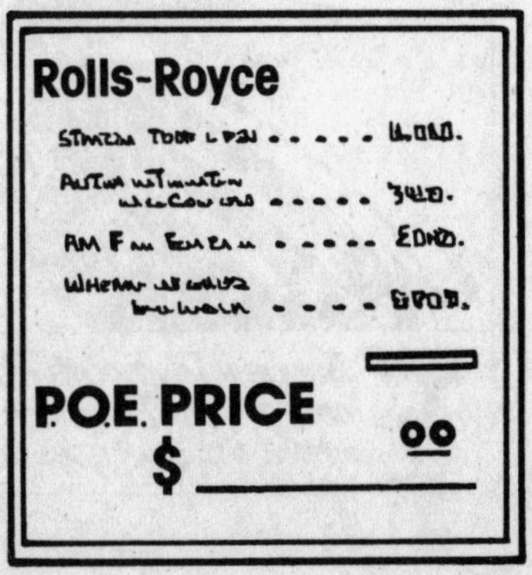
Rolls-Royce
P.O.E. PRICE
$
00

5. ______________________

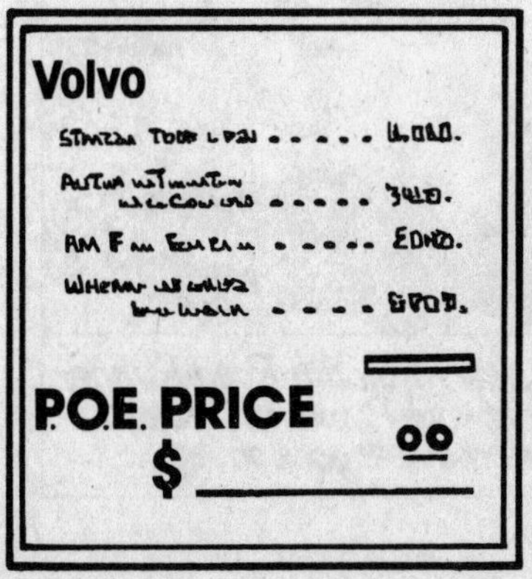
Volvo
P.O.E. PRICE
$
00

6. ______________________

Answers are on page 360

Beep Beep My...!

What is the full name of this determined but unlucky Road Runner hunter? _____

Answers are on page 360

Munchin' Motorist

Can you identify the year(s) and make of cars at your local drive-in restaurant?

5. _____

4. _____

3. _____

8. _____

7. _____

6. _____

TELETRAY SERVICE

1. _____

2. _____

THE BIG BOYS

Can you correctly match the truck manufacturer with the model name it introduced?

MANUFACTURER	MODEL NAME
1. Federal	A. Lone Ranger
2. White	B. Big Chief
3. International	C. Magnum
4. GMC	D. Brute
5. Fruehauf	E. Style Liner
6. Dodge	F. Bison
7. Kenworth	G. Sightliner
8. Chevrolet	H. Rogue
9. Diamond Reo	I. Bighorn
10. Studebaker	J. King of the Highway

TV Repair

This master auto mechanic and TV spokesman should be recognizable to all you public television viewers, so name him, the car-related show he hosts, and the year it premiered.

Answers are on page 360

Cars of Presidents

Lincoln automobiles have served as official White House limousines since the days of President Coolidge, and have earned the title of "Car of Presidents."
Fill in the missing information about these four official Lincolns.

1. Year _____
   Wheelbase _____
   Overall length _____
   Height _____
   Nickname _____

2. Year _____
   Wheelbase _____
   Overall length _____
   Height _____
   Nickname _____

3. Year _____
   Wheelbase _____
   Overall length _____
   Height _____

4. Year _____
   Wheelbase _____
   Overall length _____
   Height _____

Rubber Cord

1. What was the first model year for the 8/10 Cord roadster?

2. What special material was used for this limited volume replicar?

3. Which contemporary production automobile engine powered the 8/10?

4. Was this car front- or rear-wheel drive?

5. Who was most responsible for the 8/10?

6. What was the suggested factory price?

7. What was the last model year for the 8/10?

8. Approximately how many were manufactured?

Answers are on page 360

WELCOME ABOARD

These six cars are being loaded into the hulls of ships for passage
to distant shores.
Identify the year and make of each seafaring car.

1. _____

2. _____

3. _____

4. _____

5. _____

6. _____

Answers are on page 360

DETROIT HOODS #2

Look out, another gang of Detroit (and Kenosha) hoods are gathered below. Can you identify these hoods by their correct year and make of car?

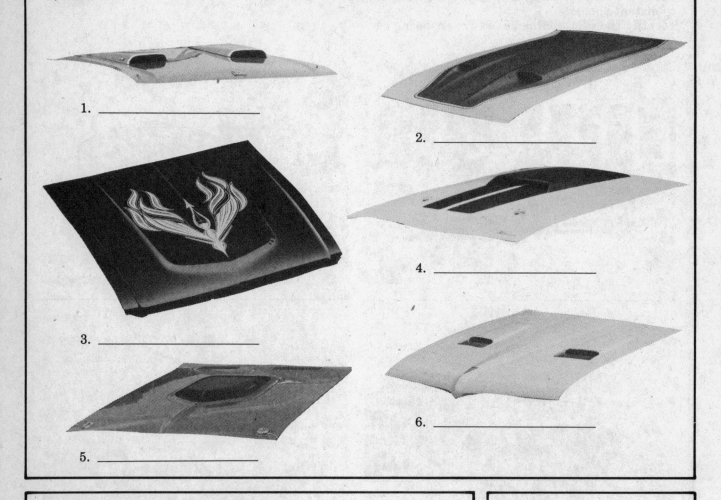

1. _____

2. _____

3. _____

4. _____

5. _____

6. _____

Traveling Trunks

What is the year and make of the two cars shown demonstrating the differences in their trunks' luggage capacities?

_____   _____

_____   _____

Life Like Logos #1

OK, all you parts freaks, can you identify the company that uses this logo?

_____

Answers are on pages 360-61

Stormin' Stockers

Answer the questions under each of these stormin' stockers.
Extra credit if you can name the correct drivers.

1.
Year & make _____
Engine size _____ cu. in
Driver _____

2.
Year & make _____
Engine size _____ cu. in
Driver _____

3.
Year & make _____
Engine size _____ cu. in
Driver _____

4.
Year & make _____
Engine size _____ cu. in
Driver _____

5.
Year & make _____
Engine size _____ cu. in
Driver _____

6.
Year & make _____
Engine size _____ cu. in
Driver _____

Answers are on page 361

Mustang Dimensions

Three different Mustang body designs are illustrated below. Can you fill in the correct dimensions and weight for each?

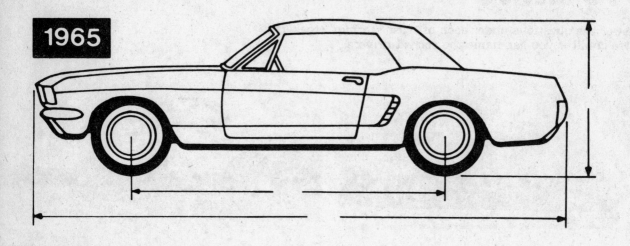

1965

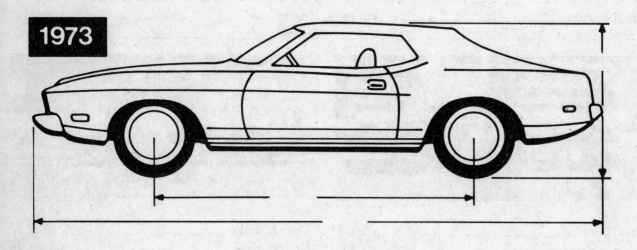

1973

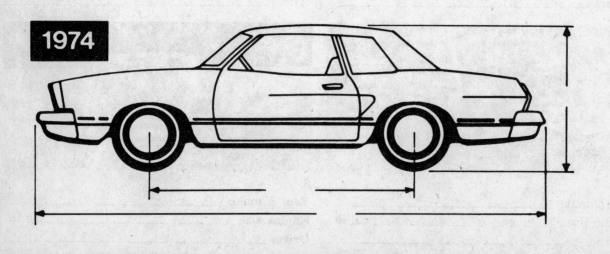

1974

Answers are on page 361

PUSH BUTTON TRANS.

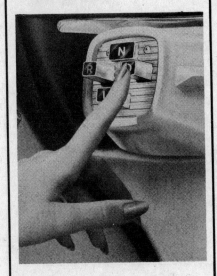

1. What did Edsel call their automatic transmission in 1958? _____

2. What was the last year that Chrysler Corp. offered its pushbutton transmission? _____

3. Packard first offered an electrically activated pushbutton transmission in which model year? _____

4. What did Mercury title their pushbutton transmission? _____

5. Which manufacturer offered pushbutton transmission the longest, and for how many consecutive years? _____

6. What did DeSoto call their pushbutton transmission when first introduced for 1956? _____

Faraway Places #1

There have been exotic and not so exotic geographic locations used as names by American and European car makers. Give the correct model name that fits the 13 definitions shown below.

1. Cadillac city in southwest Spain _____
2. A Mercury resort town in central Idaho _____
3. Maserati North American country _____
4. An AMC seaport in northeast Spain _____
5. An island in New York city that's a Fraser _____
6. A Chevy gambling resort town in Monaco _____
7. A Ford city in northwest Italy _____
8. A Chrysler village in eastern New York state _____
9. A Pontiac town north of Los Angeles _____
10. Willys island off North Carolina _____
11. A Dodge ski resort area _____
12. An Oldsmobile seaport in northern France _____

MEMORIES #1

Can you identify the brand of truck illustrated above, and which oil company name should be on the sign?

Answers are on page 361

WOODY WAGONS #2

Some of the six cars shown below have genuine wood body parts, while others are faking it. Give the correct year and make for each design. Bonus—Which ones are true woodies?

1. _____

2. _____

3. _____

4. _____

5. _____

6. _____

114

Answers are on page 361

CAR PETS

Identify these high-performance mascots and the car makes they represented.

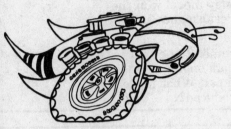

1. _____

2. _____

3. _____

4. _____

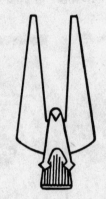

5. _____

6. _____

Horsin' Around

This comical drawing of a winking horse standing in a bathtub was a famous symbol during the 1930's.

1. Do you know what auto related service he represented?

2. What was the name of this happy horse?

3. What company did he represent?

Club Page-Crosley Quickie

Thanks to the Crosley Automobile Club, Inc., of Williamson, N.Y., you can tackle these five toughies.

1. Crosley claimed to be the first American production car with four wheel disc brakes. What month and year did this occur?
2. What does "Cobra" stand for in the Crosley engine?
3. In 1948, it was Crosley that produced the most station wagons. How many?
4. What Crosley model won the Index of Performance at Sebring in 1950?
5. Crosley claimed to be first with an overhead-cam engine in a low-cost production car. What model year was it introduced?

Winners #1

Six proud drivers pose in their winning Indy 500 race cars from the past. Can you identify these men and the years?

1. _____

2. _____

3. _____

4. _____

5. _____

6. _____

You Auto be in Pictures

This car was custom-built for a specific job. Do you know what it is?
What is the year, make and model of the car?

Birds of Prey #1

Below are quick sketches of four winged car emblems. Can you identify the make each represents?

1. _____

2. _____

3. _____

4. _____

Birds~Eye~View #1

While this car was not quite as small as this picture suggests, it was smaller than all intermediates and many compacts of its day. Can you answer these questions about this car?

1. Brand and model name _____

2. First model year for this body design _____

3. Largest engine option, original year _____

4. Overall body length (inches) _____

5. Original base price _____

6. Last year for this body design _____

GROOVY IDEA

This experimental "tire of tomorrow" may leave you in the dark unless you can explain what Goodyear had in mind with this design. Also identify the year and make of car.

_____

_____

_____

Star Wheels

Who are these stars and with what cars are they pictured?

1. Star _____
   Year and make of car _____

2. Star(s) _____
   Year and make of car _____

Answers are on page 361

Gimmicks and Gadgets #2

Give the explanation behind each of the auto innovations pictured below. Can you identify the car make that featured these special features?

1. _____

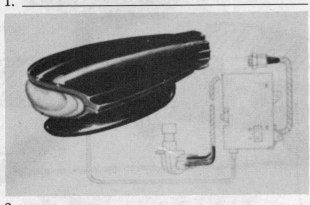

2. _____

3. _____

4. _____

5. _____

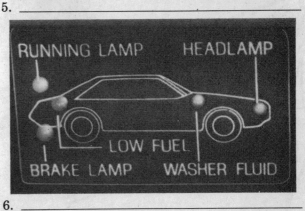

6. _____

Answers are on page 361

BACK OF THE BARN #1

In the open field behind the barn of an Arizona dude ranch you discover these antique automobiles.
Can you identify the year and make of these cars?

2. _____

1. _____

Answers are on page 361

Muscle Cubes

Match these 10 cars to their correct cubic inch high performance engine.

CAR	Cubic Inch
1. Buick Wildcat	A. 327
2. Chevy Impala SS	B. 400
3. Corvair Monza	C. 390
4. Chrysler 300	D. 425
5. Dodge Charger	E. 164
6. Ford Fairlane GT	F. 389
7. Mercury S-55	G. 427
8. Oldsmobile 442	H. 428
9. Pontiac GTO	I. 426
10. Rambler Marlin	J. 383

Soft Top Quickies #1

1. Which 1960 convertible had a glass rear window that raised and lowered electrically?

2. What was the single model year for the Mercury four-door convertible?

3. In 1971, Dodge offered a convertible in only one model line. Which one?

4. Two 1949 car makes simultaneously introduced the first high-compression V-8 convertibles. Name them.

DECAL DISGUISE #1

Chevrolet offered the above white Vega, Nova and Impala with a special trim package of red and blue stripes plus American eagle decals. What was this decor option called and what model year are the three cars?

1. _____

2. _____

3. _____

Answers are on page 362

Long, Luxurious Limos

Give the correct year and make of each of these six lengthy limousines.

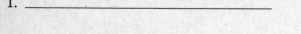

1. _____

2. _____

3. _____

4. _____

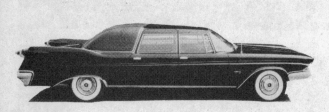

5. _____

6. _____

TV Auto Trivia #3

1. On the old *Perry Mason* show with Raymond Burr, what two cars did Paul Drake usually drive?

2. What kind of sports car originally was used in the opening scenes of *Get Smart?*

3. After a new sponsor took over the *Get Smart* show, what new sports car did Maxwell Smart drive?

4. What two cars star in *Simon and Simon?*

5. What brand of car did Samantha always drive in *Bewitched?*

6. What was the name of the cop show in which the heroes drove a Rolls Royce?

7. The Saint drove what make and model sports machine in the English-made detective show?

8. There was a very short-lived TV series called *B.A.D. Cats.* What make and model car did the heroes use?

Answers are on page 362

What is it? ________________

#1

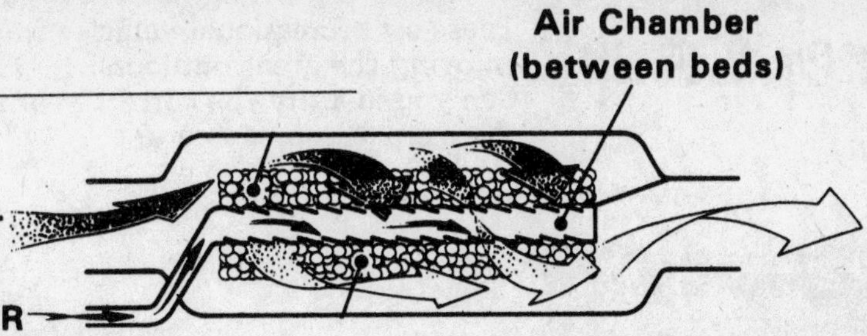
Air Chamber
(between beds)
ENGINE EXHAUST
INDUCTED AIR

WINNERS

#2

These smiling faces belong to six first-place Indy 500 racing drivers from past decades.
Can you identify them by name and the winning year; as a bonus try to name the mechanics in pictures #1 and #4.

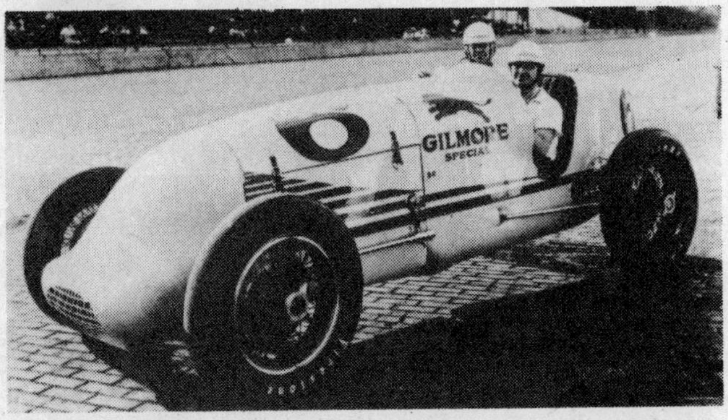
GILMORE
SPECIAL

1. ________________

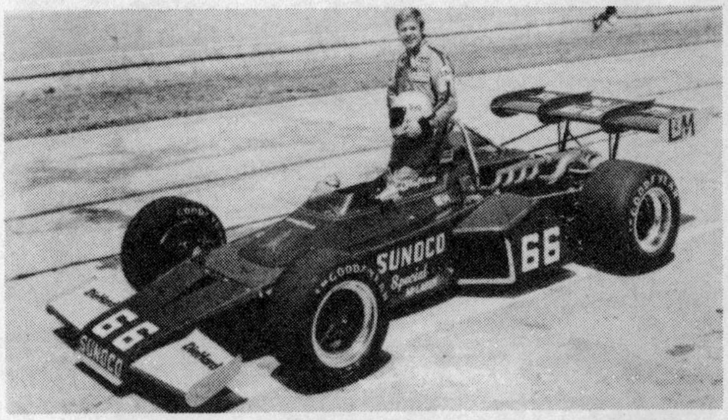
SUNOCO
Special
66

2. ________________

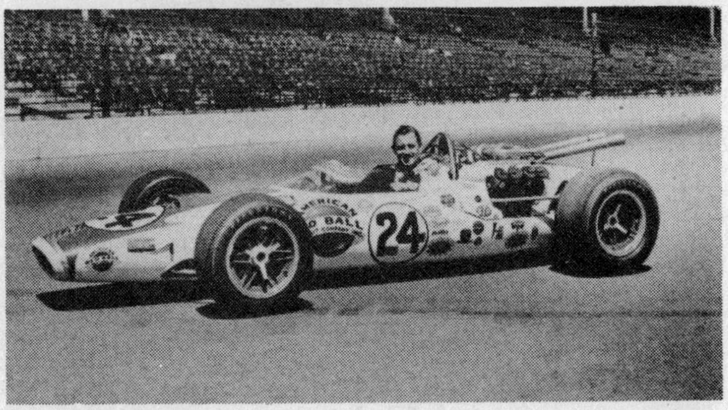
24

3. ________________

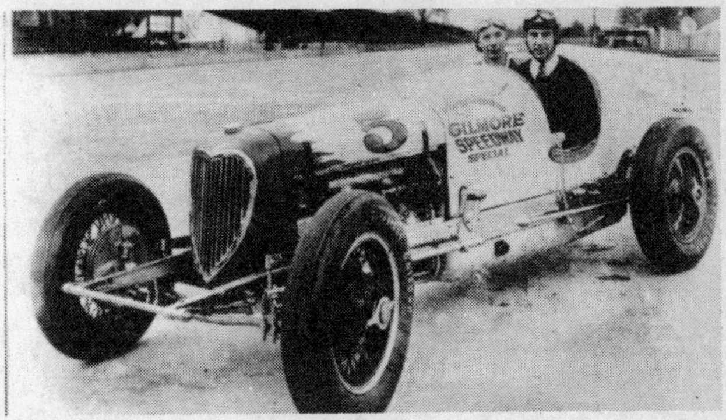
GILMORE
SPEEDWAY
SPECIAL

4. ________________

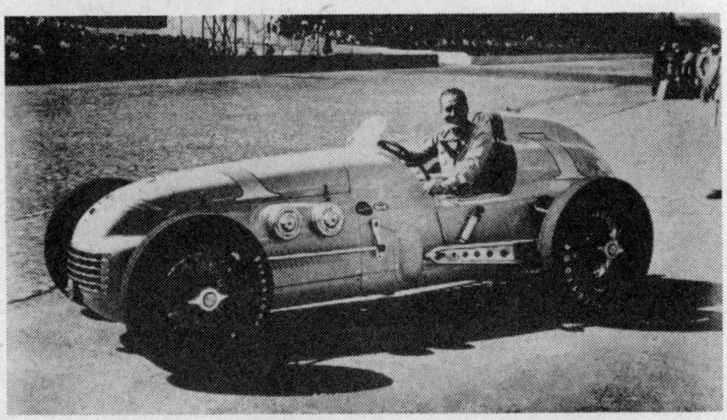

5. ________________

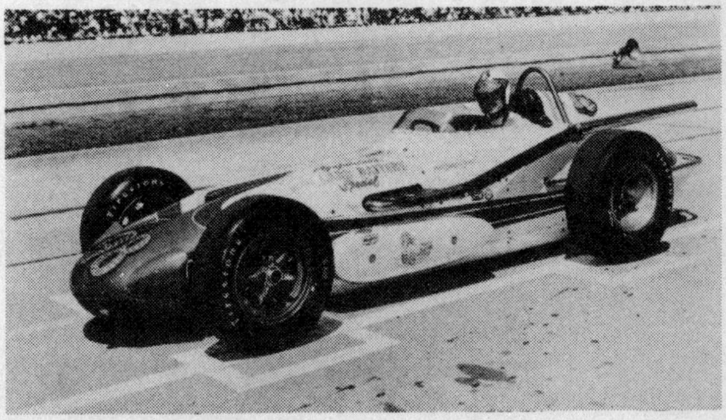

6. ________________

Answers are on page 362

Summer Camp

These six recreational vehicles from years ago are enjoying the great outdoors.
Can you identify the correct year and make for each of these truck/van campers?

1. _____

2. _____

3. _____

4. _____

5. _____

6. _____

Answers are on page 362

Super Highway Stomper Stumper

FoMoCo was envisioning the highways of the future when they premiered this enormous turbine dream truck.

Though this beauty was only a corporate exercise, it was heavily advertised. Search your memory and answer the following questions.

1. What year was this dream truck first introduced?
2. How much horsepower did Ford boast for this supercharged gas turbine engine?
   A. 400   B. 500   C. 600
3. What was the total length of the truck with double trailers?
   A. 55 ft.   B. 90 ft.   C. 115 ft.

ROAD WORK

The type of interchange pictured below has been a part of the American highway system longer than most motorists realize.

1. What is this interchange design called?

2. What state first constructed this type of junction?
   A. New Jersey
   B. Illinois
   C. California

3. What year was it first opened to traffic?

4. What is the name of the highway that first used this design?
   A. Washington Highway
   B. Will Rogers Highway
   C. Lincoln Highway

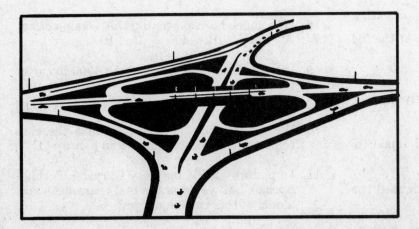

Answers are on page 362

Turbine Teammates

In 1954, Chrysler engineers built a gas turbine engine that could easily fit in their production Plymouth Belvedere with only minor bracket modifications. (Picture A). This started a tradition at Chrysler with newer turbine cars popping up thru the decades.

Can you answer the detail questions about Chrysler turbines listed below?

A.

B.

C.

D.

E.

1. How much horsepower did the 1954 gas turbine engine put out?
   A. 120   B. 140   C. 210

2. What was the idle speed (in rpm) of the '54 turbine?
   A. 5500   B. 15,000   C. 20,000

3. A turbine engine has approximately _____ fewer parts than a piston engine.

4. What year did the car in picture "B" make its debut?

5. Why was the car in picture "B" dubbed the "Engel Bird"?

6. How many units of the "Engel Bird" were built to test consumer driving response?

7. What year, make and model car was the base for the turbine in picture "C"?

8. How much horsepower did this version offer?
   A. 120   B. 140   C. 210

9. What was the top speed of the 4000 lb car in picture "C"?
   A. 95   B. 105   C. 115

10. What year did Chrysler introduce the customized LeBaron turbine car in picture "D"?

11. In picture "E" it may say Chrysler Turbine Special, but we know the real year, make and model of this car—don't we?

Answers are on page 362

Cannibalized Customs # 2

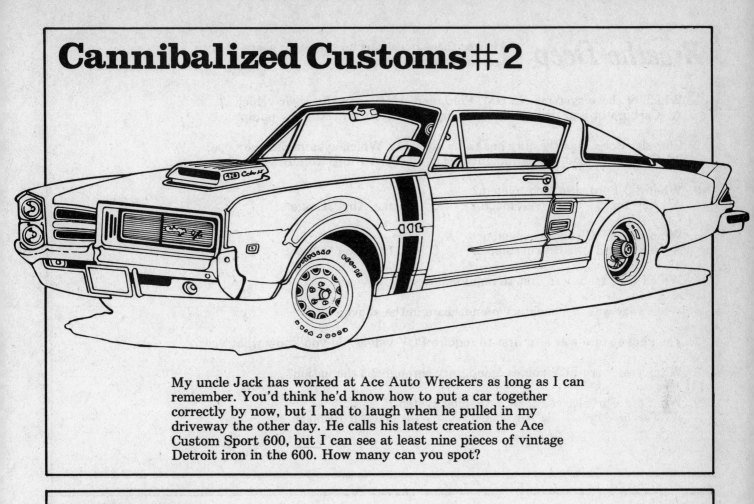

My uncle Jack has worked at Ace Auto Wreckers as long as I can remember. You'd think he'd know how to put a car together correctly by now, but I had to laugh when he pulled in my driveway the other day. He calls his latest creation the Ace Custom Sport 600, but I can see at least nine pieces of vintage Detroit iron in the 600. How many can you spot?

SLANT SIX

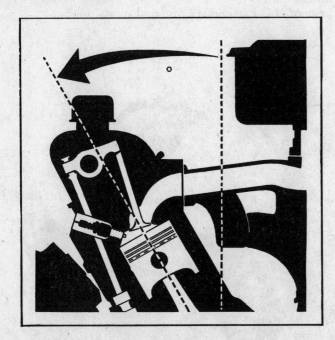

1. What was the first model year Chrysler Corp. offered this unique engine design?

2. The slant six came in two displacement sizes upon introduction, what were they?

3. Fill in the correct incline degree in the illustration above.

4. In what model years was an aluminum slant six available?

Breathe Deep

Answer these questions on the early years of auto emission control systems.

1. Which of these systems did GM, Ford, and AMC adopt for their vehicles?
   A. Carburetor and timing modifications   B. Air injection by pump

2. Chrysler Corp. was the only one to be different. Which system did they use?
   A. Carburetor and timing modifications   B. Air injection by pump

3. What did Ford title their system?
   A. Air Guard   B. Thermactor   C. Cleaner Air Package

4. What did AMC call their system?
   A. Air Guard   B. Thermactor   C. Air Injection Reactor

5. Which U.S. state was first to require anti-smog devices?

6. What year was it mandatory on new cars in the above state?

7. The above state was also first to require PCV valves, do you know what year?

8. What year were PCV valves mandatory throughout the nation?

9. What did Chrysler call their anti-smog system?
   A. Thermactor   B. Air Guard   C. Cleaner Air Package

Surfs Up

This limited-edition eggshell-white Dodge Dart came with red and blue side stripes, orange shag carpeting, and the Beach Boys on the radio.
What is the year of this car and its unusual model name?

128

Answers are on page 362

CAR RAGS #1

The seven artwork examples shown below were the clever headings from different auto-related magazine columns over the past 20 years. Can you name the magazines that used these designs?

POST ENTRY

1. _____

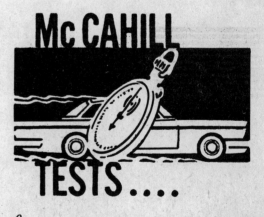
PIT STOP

2. _____

Blowin' Smoke

3. _____

LETTERS

4. _____

Special Delivery

5. _____

McCAHILL TESTS....

6. _____

DETROIT LISTENING POST
By Jim Whipple

7. _____

Answers are on page 362

Junkyard Jumble

From this mountain of metal identify as many crumpled cars as you can by their years and makes.
We can find and name forty. Can you?

FRONT DOOR SERVICE

1. What was the first model year this unique car sold on the American market?

2. What country exported these vehicles?

3. What was the name of the auto company that manufactured them?

4. What was the model name for this car?

5. This car would go how many miles on a gallon of gas?

6. What was the port of entry price the first model year?

Wagons, Whoa!

Heading westward like a wagon train are these six cars from the 1950's and 60's.
Give the correct year and make for each.

1. _____

2. _____

3. _____

4. _____

5. _____

6. _____

Answers are on pages 362-63

Hub Hysteria #1

These 12 different wheel covers and hub designs are laid out for you to identify the cars that wore these chrome creations.

1. _____

2. _____

3. _____

4. _____

5. _____

6. _____

7. _____

8. _____

9. _____

10. _____

11. _____

12. _____

Answers are on page 363

Believe It or Not!

While the average U.S. home uses only 27 light bulbs, the American automobile is a virtual Christmas tree on wheels. Give the total number used on the 1971 AMC Ambassador.

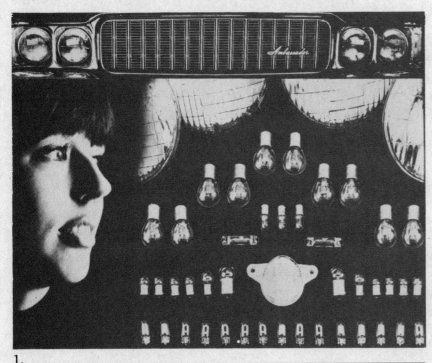

1. _____

INDY 500 PACE CARS 1940~53

World War II interrupted the running of the Indianapolis 500 for four long years, but the prestige of being the "chosen" pace car was alive both before and after the war. Match the correct pacer with its awarded year(s). Note: use Studebaker and Chrysler twice.

1. 1940	A. Lincoln
2. 1941	B. Oldsmobile
3. 1946	C. Studebaker
4. 1947	D. Ford
5. 1948	E. Chrysler
6. 1949	F. Mercury
7. 1950	G. Nash
8. 1951	H. Chevrolet
9. 1952	
10. 1953	

STAR TRUCK?

This picture is a 3/8-inch scale model for a proposed atomic powered vehicle.

NAME _____

YEAR _____

MADE BY _____

Answers are on page 363

RACING LEGENDS

These six faces should be familiar to auto buffs as some of the greatest race car drivers. Can you identify them?

1. _____

2. _____

3. _____

4. _____

5. _____

6. _____

Answers are on page 363

Generation Gap

The top car bears little resemblance to the bottom one, yet they both share the same make and model names.
Fill in the blanks.

Year _____   No. of cylinders _____

Make _____   Horsepower _____

Model _____   Weight _____

Year _____   No. of cylinders _____

Make _____   Horsepower _____

Model _____   Weight _____

What is it?

Auto Be Funny

The illustration below is of the great Groucho Marx.

1. What car brand sponsored both his radio and TV shows? _____

   _____

2. What was the name of his game show? _____

   _____

3. What Cole Porter song was rewritten as an advertising jingle for the car sponsor and premiered on Groucho's show? _____

   _____

Parking Garage of Time

Can you give the correct year and make of cars parked on the three floors of this garage?

1. _____

2. _____

3. _____

Answers are on page 363

"NICE TO MEET YA!" #1

Match the 10 cars listed below to their correct press release date.

DATE	MAKE AND MODEL
1. Oct. 5, 1960	Corvette Stingray
2. Sept. 29, 1961	AMC Javelin
3. Sept. 28, 1962	Ford Maverick
4. Apr. 17, 1964	Chevy II
5. Sept. 29, 1966	Lincoln Versailles
6. Sept. 26, 1967	Buick Special
7. Apr. 17, 1969	Camaro
8. Oct. 1, 1974	Ford Mustang
9. Apr. 15, 1977	AMC Eagle
10. Sept. 27, 1979	Chrysler Cordoba

Electric Hand

What an ominous sounding title for a steering column transmission control. What two car brands offered the "Electric Hand"?

Papal Limousine

Pope Paul VII used this custom limousine during his historic visit to the United States in the 1960's.
Can you answer the following questions on this car?

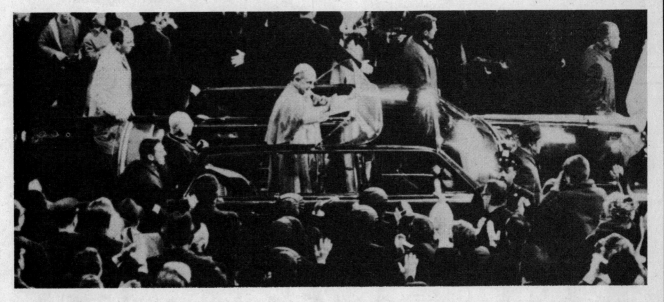

1. What make of car was this limo?

2. What model year?

3. How many feet long was this land yacht?

4. The throne-type rear seat could be elevated how many inches?

Show Car Showdown

Three Chrysler and three Ford show cars from the gutsy sixties are grouped below.
Can you identify the year, make and show name for each?

1. _____

2. _____

3. _____

4. _____

5. _____

6. _____

KEY BOBBERS #2

Can you identify the car brands by their key bob emblem?

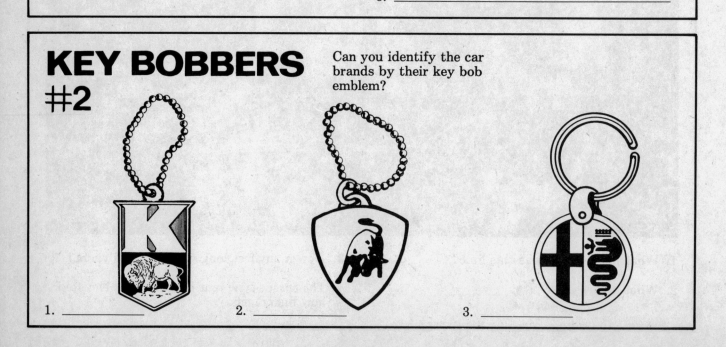

1. _____   2. _____   3. _____

First Impressions

This scene takes place at the "first form press," where flat sheet metal was shaped into front fenders.
Can you recognize the year and make of the car by these parts?

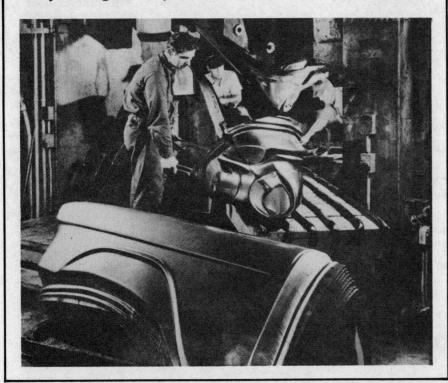

Last of the Mohegans #1

Match the last model year to each of these famous nameplates.

YEARS	CAR/MODEL
1. 1937	DeSoto
2. 1940	Packard
3. 1941	Chevrolet Corvair
4. 1951	Nash Metropolitan
5. 1954	Graham
6. 1957	Plymouth Barracuda
7. 1958	Frazer
8. 1960	Henry J
9. 1961	AMC Marlin
10. 1962	Cadillac LaSalle
11. 1966	Edsel
12. 1967	Dodge Coronet R/T
13. 1969	Pierce-Arrow
14. 1971	Studebaker
15. 1974	Hudson

A Slice of Life

The tree-lined streets are well manicured and all the cars are washed and waxed for another weekend. Identify the year and make of cars.

1. _____

2. _____

3. _____

4. _____

5. _____

HEAVY DUTY TRUCKIN'

Three companies built the 10 heavy truck models listed below. Can you put the correct model under the right manufacturer?

WHITE	GMC	CHEVROLET	MODEL NAMES
			Kodiak
			Turnpike Cruiser
			Payload Special
			Brigadier
			Road Xpeditor
			Astro
			Pappa Bear Bruin
			Road Boss
			Titan 90
			General

School Daze #2

At the top of the class sat four school buses. Identify the brand of truck that powers these kiddy transporters.

1. _____

2. _____

3. _____

4. _____

Answers are on page 364

Birds of Prey #2

Below are quick sketches of four famous winged car emblems. Can you give the correct automobile name for each design?

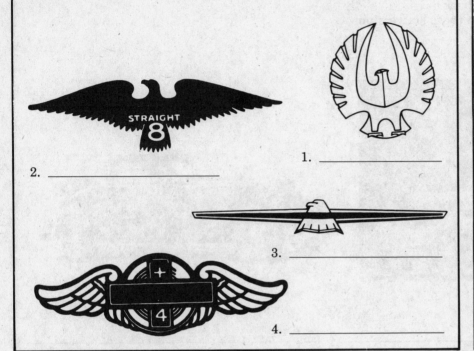

STRAIGHT 8

1. _____

2. _____

3. _____

4. _____

Wild Horses

In 1967 these gutsy horsepower ratings were offered. Match the horsepower to the correct car and engine.

CAR & ENGINE (cu. in.)	HP RATING
1. 289 Ford	A. 200
2. 326 Pontiac	B. 225
3. 383 Dodge	C. 235
4. 427 Ford	D. 250
5. 290 AMC	E. 275
6. 400 Oldsmobile	F. 325
7. 427 Corvette	G. 350
8. 273 Plymouth	H. 360
9. 327 Camaro	I. 400
10. 430 Buick	J. 425

European Titles

The 12 model names listed below are from 20 and 30 years ago. If your memory is up to it, match the model names to the correct car brands and list the country of manufacture.

MODEL NAME	FOREIGN CAR BRAND	COUNTRY
1. Javelin	A. Ford	_____
2. Arondo	B. Hillman	_____
3. Kapitan	C. Borgward	_____
4. Vedette	D. Porsche	_____
5. Princess	E. Panhard	_____
6. Minx	F. Opel	_____
7. Disco Volante	G. Allard	_____
8. Hansa	H. Jewett	_____
9. 375 America	I. Austin	_____
10. 1500 America	J. Alfa Romeo	_____
11. Dyna	K. Simca	_____
12. Monte Carlo	L. Ferrari	_____

COUNTRIES
France—Germany—Great Britain—Italy

Answers are on page 364

Rare Rumblers

The rumble seat is a mystery to car buyers of the 1980's; but looking at the excellent examples pictured below, it might be a fun option to bring back.
Identify the years and makes of these six versions.

1. _____

2. _____

3. _____

4. _____

5. _____

6. _____

Answers are on page 364

Slick Symbols #3

The checkered flag, which symbolizes a winner, appears on each of these four different oil cans.
Can you identify the correct product brand names that belong with these symbols?

1. _____

2. _____

3. _____

4. _____

Queens for a Day #2

In what exotic car are these five beauty queens riding?

_____

T.L.C.

NATIONAL CAR CARE MONTH

1. Which month of the year is officially dedicated to the tender loving care of our favorite set of wheels?

2. Which state was the first to have "Car Care Month"?
   A. New York   B. Ohio   C. California

3. In what year did the above state inaugurate it?
   A. 1978   B. 1980   C. 1982

4. In what year did "Car Care Month" go national?
   A. 1978   B. 1980   C. 1982

Answers are on page 364

HOME SWEET FACTORY #1

Not all car manufacturers during the 1930's and 40's were in Detroit, Michigan. Many companies originated in other Midwest and Eastern cities.
Match the car from the list below to its home base pinpointed on the map.

Dusenberg	Rockne
Jordan	Kissel
Franklin	Willys-Knight
Kaiser	

Southbend, IN

Willow Run, MI

Syracuse, NY

3. _____

4. _____

7. _____

Indianapolis, IN

Toledo, OH

2. _____

5. _____

Hartford, WI

Cleveland, OH

1. _____

6. _____

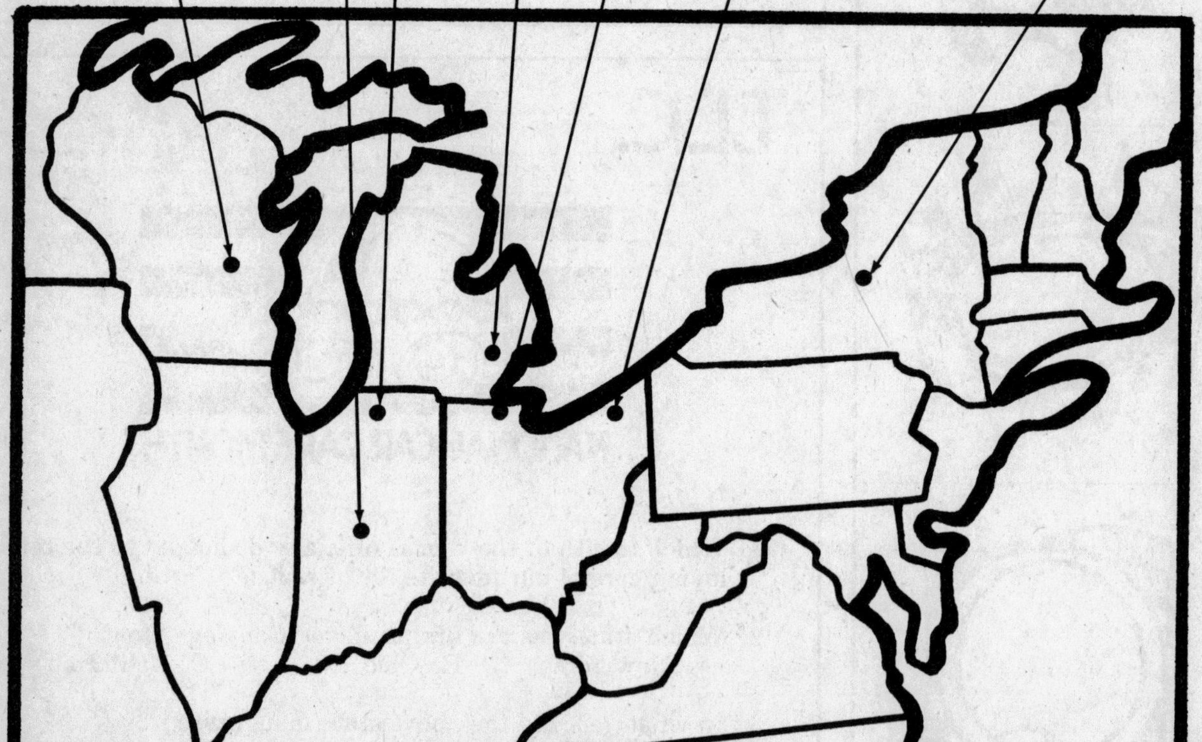

Answers are on page 364

WONDER WILLYS

What model year is each of these five different
Willys designs?

1. _____

2. _____

3. _____

4. _____

5. _____

Answers are on page 364

CONFUSING CONNIES

Talk about mind-boggling subtleties. Correctly match the six years listed below with the Continental grilles.

1962   1963   1964   1966   1967   1968

1. _____

2. _____

3. _____

4. _____

5. _____

6. _____

Answers are on page 364

Prepmobiles

According to preppies around the country, which of these automobiles are acceptable and which are not?

1. AMC Hornet
2. Toyota Land Cruiser
3. Volvo
4. Camaro Z28
5. Peugeot
6. Ford Country Squire Wagon
7. Buick Electra 225
8. Mercedes-Benz
9. Any Italian car
10. International Harvester

A—ACCEPTABLE UN—UNACCEPTABLE

Corporate Giants #1

The four executives pictured below lent their leadership talents to help the survival of various car companies.
Can you identify these gentlemen and the companies they were most associated with?

1. _____

2. _____

3. _____

4. _____

Answers are on pages 364-65

Slick Symbols #4

What product brand names should appear on the oil can art works shown below?

MOTOR OILS

1. _____

MOTOR OIL
Choice of Champions

2. _____

Mileage-Metered
MOTOR OILS
SUPER-REFINED PENNSYLVANIA

3. _____

MOTOR OIL

4. _____

Truly the Triviest #1

1. In which two calendar years in the 1950's did Ford outsell Chevrolet?

2. American-built Rolls-Royces were manufactured in what city and state?

3. What does "Carrera" mean in Spanish?

4. It takes approximately how many hours to completely assemble a new car?

5. What car company used to give out automotive "X-Ray" model comparison books?

6. In what year did the 500,000th Chevrolet Corvette come off the assembly line?

7. How many years did it take Chevrolet to build that half-millionth Corvette?

8. Which Japanese car company used a musical jingle titled "Hello Trees"?

9. What American car manufacturer of 1956 had station wagon models called "Pelham" and "Pinehurst"?

10. What was the name of the woman race driver who had a monthly feature in *Science and Mechanics* magazine, testing new cars?

11. What car brand of 1938 is credited with starting the trend to coil-spring rear suspension?

12. In what country was Louis Chevrolet born?

13. In what country was David Dunbar Buick born?

14. Which two Edsel model names did not survive from the 1958 to the 1959 lineup?

15. What was the name of the 17,500 H.P. Art Arfonz jet car?

16. What 1955 American car brand had L-head engines called "Super Hurricane"?

17. What was the name of the gentleman who started Avanti Motor Corporation and built the Avanti II?

18. What 1967 car brand had a convertible with a unique glass rear window that was hinged in the middle?

19. What famous drag racer used to drive a machine called the "Swamp Rat"?

20. What year did Goodrich Rubber first offer puncture-sealing tubeless tires?

21. What 1930's gangster wrote a thank-you note to Henry Ford for making such great get-away cars?

22. What 1964 car brand had in its glove compartment a slide-out "Beauty Vanity" with pop-up mirror?

23. In what year did Ford celebrate its 50th anniversary?

24. What is the full name of the American genius who taught the Japanese automakers about statistical controls in building quality cars?

Answers are on page 365

Look but Don't Touch #2

While this convertible was revolving on its turntable, the awe-struck crowd was wondering what year and make car was called "Wells Fargo."
Can you help them identify this show car?

Tire Less Travel

Hovering on a cushion of air, this dream car was one vehicle that didn't worry about flat tires.

1. What auto company created this show machine?

2. What was this vehicle called?

   A. Leva Car Mach I
   B. Air-Blast Mach I
   C. Hover Car Mach I

3. What year was it first displayed to the public?

DODGE DESIGNED

These five pickup trucks were all built by Dodge over the years. Can you give the correct year for each design?

1. _____

2. _____

3. _____

4. _____

5. _____

Mystery Car #2

What make and model car does this imaginative word design represent?

FLOW-THROUGH VENTILATION
FRONT DISC BRAKES HEMI ADJUSTABLE STEERING COLUMN UP TO 30 MILES PER GAL.

Answers are on page 365

Tilt for Two

It's been a long time since an American car offered a hood that opens back to front, like the designs shown below.
Can you identify the year and make for both variations?

1. _____ 2. _____

"Leave the Driving to Us"

1. What was the debut year for the famous Greyhound bus design shown above?

2. What did Greyhound name this super bus?

3. Which renowned designer, along with his staff, is credited for this beautiful transporter?

4. How many feet tall does this bus stand?

5. In feet, what is the overall length?

6. What kind of engines originally powered these buses?
   A. dual GM diesels   B. dual 283 Chevy engines
   C. single Chrysler hemi

FLAT TIRE

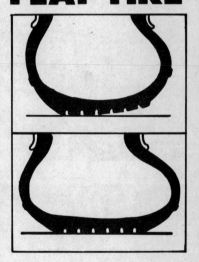

The illustration above shows a conventional tire design and the "Flat Tire" concept for more rubber on the road surface.
What tire company advertised their product as "The Flat Tire"?

_____

Answers are on page 365

Mercury Mug Shots #2

The many faces of the full-size Mercury from the 1960's are
shown below.
Give the correct year for each design.

1. _____

2. _____

3. _____

4. _____

5. _____

6. _____

Answers are on page 365

HUB HYSTERIA #2

One more try. See if you can identify the make of automobile for each of these hubcaps.

1. _____

2. _____

3. _____

4. _____

5. _____

6. _____

SLICK CHARACTER

1. What was the name of this treacherous thug who was the cause of many auto accidents in the 1930's?

2. Which tire company used him in advertisements?

Answers are on page 365

153

Sky Queen

1. Who was this famous woman of the 1930's?

2. What year and make of car does she pose with?

3. The hood side panels indicate whether this car had a six- or eight-cylinder engine; can you tell which powered this model?

4. What size (cu. in.) engine did this model have?

5. What was its horsepower rating?

6. What was the wheelbase for this roadster?

SIGN LANGUAGE #1

Continuing your auto excursion through our national park system, six more recreation symbols need identifying. Can you interpret each?

1. _____

2. _____

3. _____

4. _____

5. _____

6. _____

Symbol Specialist #1

If you're an expert in auto emblems, these four symbols should be easy to identify by brand name.

1. _____

2. _____

3. _____

4. _____

Answers are on page 365

Hood Vents

Buick is famous for body side port holes, but other car makers created their own unique exhaust vent designs, as shown below. Identify each auto by year and make.

1. _____

2. _____

3. _____

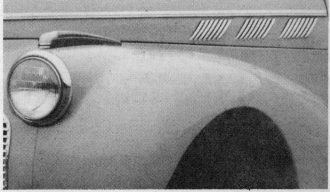

4. _____

5. _____

6. _____

Answers are on page 365

Billboard #2

"IT COSTS $100 LESS THAN I THOUGHT!"

AMERICA'S SMARTEST — LOW PRICED CAR

SEE YOUR NEAREST

Year _____   Make _____

Motor Trend Car of the Year 1959-68

Innovative design and engineering during the 1960's helped a wide variety of makes and models win the prestigious "Car of the Year" award. Match the car with the correct year. Note: use Pontiac GTO twice.

YEAR	CAR
1959	A. AMC Rambler
1960	B. Pontiac Widetrack
1961	C. Buick Special V-6
1962	D. Chevy Corvair
1963	E. Pontiac Tempest
1964	F. Mercury Cougar
1965	G. Ford Division
1966	H. Pontiac GTO
1967	I. Olds Toronado
1968	

What's it Mean?

Look at the strange hieroglyphics on this transmission indicator; can you decipher the meaning behind "HR"?
Give the transmission it came with, plus the year and make of car.

1. _____

2. _____

3. _____

Answers are on page 365

Vette Vents

In these eight views are side scoop and air vent designs from various Chevy Corvettes. Give the correct model year(s) for each design. The hubcaps are free clues.

1. _____

2. _____

3. _____

4. _____

5. _____

6. _____

7. _____

8. _____

Answers are on page 365

MILLIONTH MODEL

The above picture is of the 1,000,000th Lincoln built since its introduction back in September 1920 by Henry M. Leland. What is this model year?

Below are six other auto brands for you to match to their correct millionth model year. Note: use 1950 twice.

AUTO	MILLIONTH YEAR
1. Plymouth	1950
2. Mercury	1934
3. Packard	1935
4. Mustang	1947
5. Cadillac	1966
6. Pontiac	

"TRANS"-LATION #1

Semi- and fully-automatic transmissions came with some wild names during the 1940's and 50's.
What were the eight cars equipped with the transmission names listed below?

1. Dynaflow_____

2. Tip—Toe Hydraulic Shift
_____

3. Electromatic Clutch_____
_____

4. Liquamatic_____

5. Turboglide_____

6. PowerFlite_____

7. Turbo—Matic_____

8. Fluid Drive_____

Billboard #3

IT'S FOR STYLE AND ECONOMY in
PAUL G. HOFFMAN CO *Inc.*
Foster and Kleiser

Year _____   Make _____

LAGER LORRIES

Three cheers for the trucks that have kept us in the "suds" over the past decades.
Can you identify the brand of the tractor portion of the six beer trucks pictured below?

1. _____

2. _____

3. _____

4. _____

5. _____

6. _____

Star Mechanics

Who are these famous mechanics and what is the year and make of car in pictures #1 and #3.

1. _____

2. _____

3. _____

A Rose is a Rose #1

Some model names never die—they don't even fade away, they're just reissued by different manufacturers. Identify the two or more car makers for each name listed below.

1. Citation
_____
_____

2. Phoenix
_____
_____

3. Seville
_____
_____

4. Eagle
_____
_____

5. Regal
_____
_____

6. Celebrity
_____
_____

7. Lark
_____
_____

8. Suburban
_____
_____

9. Hornet
_____
_____

Answers are on page 366

Fairy Tale

Dressed by her new-wave godmother, this modern Cinderella is about to be whisked away to the Royal Ball and Prince Charming in this sleek sports car.
Before this automobile turns back into a bathtub at the stroke of midnight, answer these questions.

1. What is the name for this two-seat car?

2. What model year is shown?

3. The engine had how many cylinders?
   A. 4 cyl.   B. 6 cyl.   C. 8 cyl.

4. How many horses drove Cinderella to the ball?
   A. 125 H.P.   B. 150 H.P.   C. 200 H.P.

5. What name was given to the engine?
   A. Dual Hurricane B. Dual Wildcat   C. Dual Jetfire

6. What was the curb weight of this car?
   A. 2600 lbs.   B. 3000 lbs.   C. 3200 lbs.

Home Away From Home

As you traveled by car back in the 1960's you might have stayed at a motel using this bear as it's symbol.

1. What is the name of this mascot?

2. What is the name of the coast-to-coast motel chain that used him?

FINE FEATHERED FRIENDS

Can you identify the correct "birdie" names that best fit our dictionary meanings?

1. A European bird of the Buick family that is famous for in-flight singing _____
2. A Pontiac species that's also a Baltimore oriole _____
3. An American Indian mythical bird from Ford that can cause rain _____
4. A large AMC bird of prey from the falcon family _____
5. A Plymouth terrestrial cuckoo of America _____
6. A mythical Pontiac bird that rises from the ashes _____

Answers are on page 366

1940s and 1950s

1. A major late-model stock car race was held in Milwaukee on Aug. 22, 1948. Stunt car driver Paul Bjork was declared the winner. He drove a:
   a. Ford
   b. Cadillac
   c. Mercury
   d. Kaiser

2. Who was the first NASCAR Grand National stock car driving champion? (He was crowned after the 1949 season.)
   a. Fonty Flock
   b. Red Byron
   c. Curtis Turner
   d. Tim Flock

3. What two cars did auto writer Tom McCahill use to win flying-mile speed trials back-to-back in 1951 and 1952 at Daytona Beach, Florida?
   a. Both were Oldsmobiles
   b. A Chrysler and a Lincoln
   c. A Chrysler and a Jaguar
   d. An Oldsmobile and a Cadillac

4. Herschel Buchanan won the International Motor Contest Association stock car driving championship in 1950 and 1951. He drove the same make of cars both years. What was the make?
   a. Hudson
   b. Oldsmobile
   c. Chrysler
   d. Nash

5. In 1951, which make didn't win at least one NASCAR Grand National race?
   a. Plymouth
   b. Studebaker
   c. Ford
   d. Nash

6. Who was the first multiple winner of the NASCAR Southern 500 at the Darlington (S.C.) International Raceway? (He won it three times.)
   a. Herb Thomas
   b. Lee Petty
   c. Buck Baker
   d. Fonty Flock

7. In the 1950 Carrera Panamericana (Mexican Road Race), Ray Elliott and Herschel McGriff drove what make of car to victory?
   a. Lincoln
   b. Oldsmobile
   c. Chrysler
   d. Ford

8. Hudson Hornets won more major stock car races than any other make from 1952 through 1954. What kind of an engine did it have?
   a. Overhead-valve V-8
   b. Overhead-valve 6
   c. Flathead or L-head
   d. Flathead or L-head V-8

9. In 1955 the Chrysler 300 took both the NASCAR and AAA (American Automobile Association) stock car circuits by storm. The same company entered the most potent cars on both circuits. What was it?
   a. Chrysler Corporation
   b. Firestone Tire & Rubber
   c. Autolite
   d. Mercury Outboard Motors

10. The last stock car race sanctioned by the AAA Contest Board (Sept. 18, 1955) was won by:
    a. Jim Rathmann
    b. Jack McGrath
    c. Marshall Teague
    d. Frank Mundy

11. The United States Auto Club (USAC) started sanctioning races in 1956. Who was its first stock car champion?
    a. Johnny Mantz
    b. Jimmy Bryan
    c. Frank Mundy
    d. Marshall Teague

12. When the "horsepower race" for domestic cars peaked in 1957, all of the following induction systems were used on cars that raced except:
    a. Supercharging
    b. Fuel Injection
    c. Turbocharging
    d. Multiple carburetion

13. NASCAR had a convertible circuit in 1956. Which make scored 27 wins that year?
    a. Dodge
    b. Chevrolet
    c. Mercury
    d. Ford

14. Who won back-to-back USAC stock car championships in 1958 and 1959?
    a. Tony Bettenhausen
    b. Norm Nelson
    c. Rodger Ward
    d. Fred Lorenzen

15. The son of eventual three-time NASCAR Grand National champion Lee Petty, Richard Petty, started driving on the circuit in 1958. He first drove in a:
    a. Plymouth
    b. Oldsmobile
    c. Dodge
    d. Ford

16. Ford Thunderbirds were allowed to race on the NASCAR Grand National Circuit in 1959. They won six events. What size engine did they have (in cubic inches)?
    a. 352
    b. 390
    c. 406
    d. 430

Answers are on page 366

Rebellious Racer

What is the name of the movie star resting in this picture, and what is the name and model of the car he's leaning against?

Spyder Web

This is a great 3/4 view of a 1964 Corvair Monza Spyder convertible. Can you answer the following questions on this car?

1. What cubic-inch engine was standard with this model?
   A. 140   B. 144.8   C. 164

2. The turbocharged engine put out how many horses?
   A. 110   B. 150   C. 165

3. What was the approximate factory price for this convertible?
   A. $2800   B. $2995   C. $3100

4. Approximately how many 1964 Spyder ragtops were produced?
   A. 4,700   B. 6,700   C. 8,600

5. What was the last model year for the Monza Spyder?

Answers are on page 366

ROLLING RECORDS #1

Side A—"Hey Little Cobra" by _____
Side B—"Tijuana Taxi" by _____

Rhino Riddle

What is the tire company called that used a sophisticated rhinoceros gentleman for an advertising mascot?

To Patrol and Pursue

Track down and capture the correct year and make of these four police cars.

1. _____

2. _____

3. _____

4. _____

Hardtop Heritage

Match the make of cars to their correct hardtop name and their first model year.

MAKE	YEAR	HARDTOP NAME
1. Chevrolet	1949	A. Newport
2. Imperial	1950	B. Hollywood
3. Oldsmobile	1951	C. St. Regis
4. Hudson	1952	D. Country Club
5. Chrysler	1954	E. Holiday
6. Nash	1955	F. Bel Air

JOHN Z.

The four portraits below are of automan John Z. DeLorean. Answer the questions under each photo to discover when they were snapped.

1. What model year Pontiac Grand Prix is Mr. D. standing with?

2. What year did J.Z.D.'s Irish-built sports car reach the showrooms?

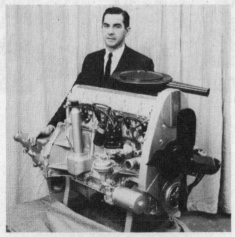

3. A. What engine design was John introducing in this picture?
   B. What model year did Pontiac first use this engine?

4. What Pontiac model was John Z. celebrating in this official snapshot?

Answers are on page 366

Bustle Butts #1

The "trunkback" or "bustleback" design of the 1980 Cadillac Seville and '81 Imperial were inspired by cars of the 1930's. Can you recognize and correctly give the year and make for the five cars below.

1. _____

2. _____

3. _____

4. _____

5. _____

Answers are on page 366

Brotherhood

Can you recognize these sets of famous and inventive auto brothers?

A _____

B _____

There have been many other brother teams that had cars and trucks bearing their family names. Can you match the vehicles to the brothers' given names?

1. Louis, Gaston and Arthur
2. Fred and August
3. Ray, Robert and Joseph
4. Francis and Freelan
5. Windsor, Rollin and Walter
6. George, Carl and Bob
7. August, Charles, William, John and Joseph
8. Henry, Clement, Jacob, Peter and John

A. Hendrickson
B. Stanley
C. Studebaker
D. Chevrolet
E. Mack
F. Graham
G. White
H. Duesenberg

SYMBOL #2 SPECIALIST

The emblems below are a bit harder to recognize than "Symbol Specialist #1." What names would correctly fit these symbols?

1. _____

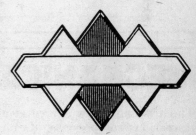

2. _____

3. _____

4. _____

Answers are on page 366

For Law and Order

Whether on traffic patrol or in hot pursuit of bad guys, identify the correct year and model of these four patrol cars.

1. _____

2. _____

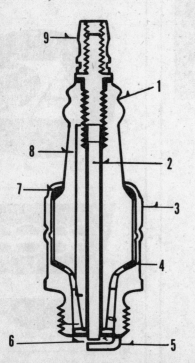

3. _____

4. _____

MECHANICALLY MINDED #2

The drawing below is a cutaway view of a typical spark plug and its various components. Match the identifying terms to the correct parts.

Side electrode
Center seal
Insulator tip
Shell
Terminal
Insulator top
Lower internal gasket
Center electrode
Upper internal gasket

Indy 500 Pace Cars 1930-39

To be chosen the official pace car for the annual Indianapolis 500 Memorial Day race is a great distinction, as well as priceless publicity for car manufacturers.
Match the 1930's pacers with its honored year. Note: use LaSalle twice.

1. 1930	A. Chrysler
2. 1931	B. Ford
3. 1932	C. LaSalle
4. 1933	D. Cord
5. 1934	E. Buick
6. 1935	F. Hudson
7. 1936	G. Lincoln
8. 1937	H. Cadillac
9. 1938	I. Packard
10. 1939	

Answers are on pages 366-67

Stars in Cars #1

Star _____ Year and make of car _____

COUNT THE MONTE CARLOS

There are six different Chevrolet Monte Carlos shown below. Your task is to correctly identify the years.

1. _____

2. _____

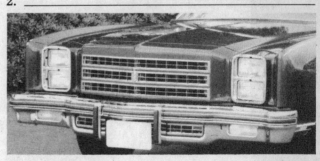

3. _____

4. _____

5. _____

6. _____

Answers are on page 367

Movie Scenes #1

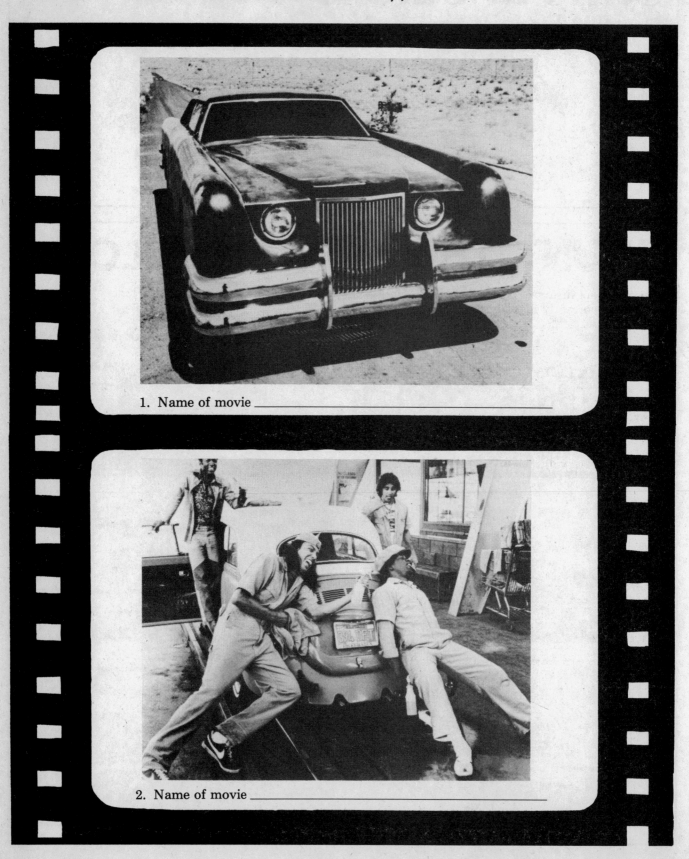

1. Name of movie _____

2. Name of movie _____

Answers are on page 367

More Woody Wonders

Identify the year and make of each of these magnificent wood-body station wagons.

1. _____

2. _____

3. _____

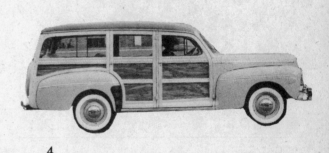

4. _____

Photo Finish

Neck to neck, these two famous racing drivers and their machines battle it out for the USAC checker flag.
Do you know who was behind the wheel in car #15 and car #16?
What is the year and make of cars pictured?

_____   _____

_____   _____

Super Logo

Which aftermarket auto parts manufacturer used this caped super hero symbol?

_____

Problem Solvers

What purpose does each of these wild-looking service station components serve for your automobile?

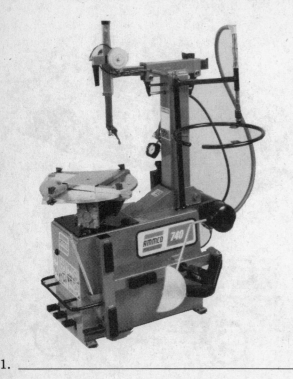

1. _____

2. _____

3. _____

4. _____

Answers are on page 367

UNCLE T

1. Who was this balding, mustached auto tester?

2. Which magazine would you most associate him with?

3. What was the first year he published his car tests for the above magazine?
   A. 1946   B. 1949   C. 1951

Chrome Molars

The gleeming grille air fins of the 50's and 60's were nicknamed "teeth" and became a big styling fad during this era. Match the correct quantity of teeth to each model(s) listed below.

YEAR AND MAKE	NUMBER OF TEETH
1. 1953-57 Corvette	3
2. 1956 Dodge	5
3. 1953 DeSoto	6
4. 1950 Pontiac	7
1954 Chevrolet	
1954 Imperial	
1959 Imperial	
5. 1958-60 Corvette	9
6. 1953 Chevrolet	11
1960 Thunderbird	
7. 1955 DeSoto	13

*Toughie—How many 1″ × 1″ squares fill the grille of the 1958 Buick?

Faraway Places #2

Where in the world do the manufacturers get their car names? The 12 definitions listed below will help you identify the correct model name and location.

1. A Chevy beach area in southern California _____
2. A Pontiac city in northwest France _____
3. A Dodge beach in Florida _____
4. A Buick Mediterranean resort of France and Italy _____
5. An Imperial American seaport _____
6. An Alfa Romeo city in Canada _____
7. A Graham neighborhood in Los Angeles _____
8. A Packard republic in south Central America _____
9. A Chrysler city in Ontario _____
10. A Mercury city in west California _____
11. A Ford city in south Spain _____
12. A Chevy city in north Italy _____

The Cadillac Sixteen

Below are 16 questions to test your knowledge on Cadillac trivia.

1. What was the largest V-8 offered by Cadillac?

2. What was the model year the above V-8 was first offered?

3. What kind of bird graced the hood of the early-1930's Cadillac?

4. What was Cadillac's big engine news in 1930?

5. What was the model year that Cadillac first sold over 100,000 cars?

6. The tailfin first appeared on which Cadillac model year?

7. What new engine design did Cadillac offer for 1931?

8. What was the first model year for the Calais?

9. What was the last model year for the Calais?

10. What year was the futuristic Cadillac Le Mans show car first displayed?

11. What was the debut model year that Cadillac offered a sun roof?

12. What was the last model year for the V-12?

13. Which model year Cadillac had the highest fins in the industry?

14. What model year did Hydra-Matic transmissions become standard equipment on all Cadillacs?

15. What was the debut model year for the Eldorado Brougham?

16. What was the last model year for the V-16?

Muscle Medallions #1

These five designs were symbols of powerful engines during the 1960's. Identify the year and make of car that wore these high-performance emblems.

1. _____

2. _____

3. _____

4. _____

5. _____

Answers are on page 367

Dip-Dip-Dip Boom

Rock 'n' roll music and chrome car side moldings had something in common back in the 50's: they both loved the "Dip."
Identify the 12 model years and cars that wore these similar yet different designs.

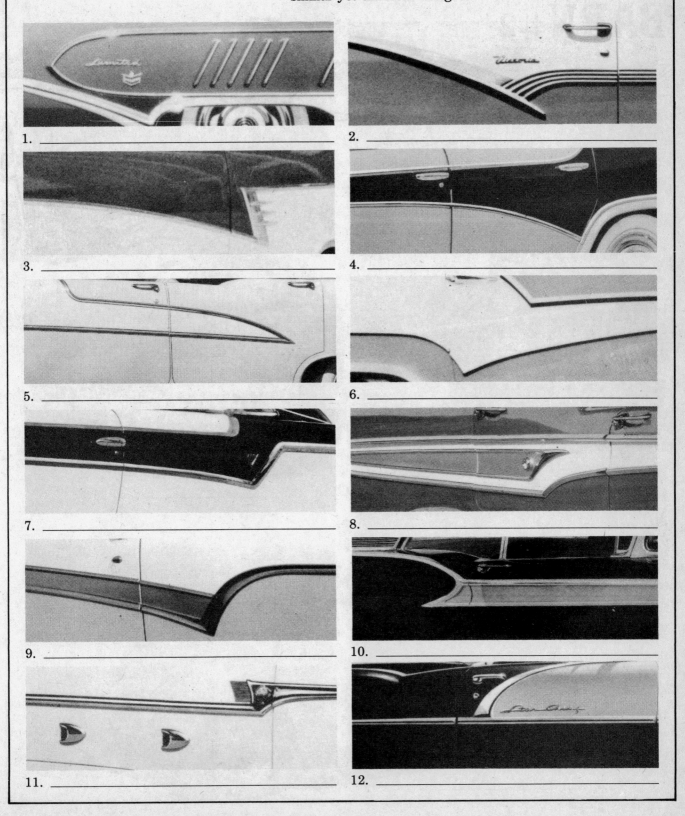

1. _____

2. _____

3. _____

4. _____

5. _____

6. _____

7. _____

8. _____

9. _____

10. _____

11. _____

12. _____

Answers are on page 367

BACK OF THE BARN #2

These three antique cars from the 1930's have been abandoned behind the barn of a country gentleman. He would be glad to give them to anyone who can identify them.
Can you give him the correct year and make for each?

1. _____

2. _____

3. _____

Answers are on page 367

IT'S A GAS

The oil companies over the years have come up with some wild brand names for their gasolines.
Match the oil company with the correct advertised label listed below.

COMPANY	GAS NAME
1. Gulf	A. Sky Chief
2. Sinclair	B. Boron
3. Atlantic	C. Super 5-D
4. Texaco	D. Aviation
5. Cities Service	E. Super No-Nox
6. Phillips	F. Red Crown
7. DX	G. Imperial
8. Kanotex	H. Flite Fuel
9. Conoco	I. Power X
10. Standard	J. Bronze High Test

More Motels!

1. What year did the first Holiday Inn motel open for travelers?

2. Where was the first Holiday Inn located?

3. What year did Howard Johnson's open its first motor lodge?

4. Where was the first Howard Johnson's Motor Lodge located?

STRETCHED STEEL

Answer these simple questions about the elongated Checker airport limousine.

1. What did Checker call this model?

2. Up to how many people could travel in it?

3. What was the curb weight?
   A. 4605 lbs.   B. 5305 lbs.   C. 6305 lbs.

4. What was the incredible headroom for this car (in inches)?

5. In what city and state were these Checker cars built?

Answers are on page 367

CHRYSLER HINDSIGHT

Identify, by their rear-end designs, the year and make of these five different Chrysler Corporation models.

1_____

2_____

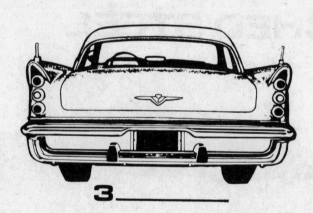

3_____

4_____

5_____

"NICE TO MEET YA !" #2

If you know the original model year for the 10 cars listed below you should be able to match each to their formal introduction date.

First Introduction Date	Car Make and Model
1. Jan. 30, 1958	Front-drive Eldorado
2. Nov. 3, 1960	Mustang II
3. Oct. 6, 1966	Dodge Omni / Plymouth Horizon
4. Sept. 23, 1969	Chevrolet Citation
5. Sept. 21, 1973	Pontiac Tempest
6. Mar. 21, 1975	Ford EXP / Mercury LN7
7. Jan. 16, 1977	Dodge 024 / Plymouth TC3
8. Oct. 5, 1978	Mercury Bobcat
9. Apr. 19, 1979	Rambler American
10. Apr. 9, 1981	Dodge Challenger

Sabotaged

1. What annual nationwide competition did this symbol represent?

2. Who was the perennial sponsor of this event?

3. In what year did this contest first take place?

4. Who were the only eligible contestants?

5. What did a team have to do to win?

Dreams Come True #1

The four dream/show cars featured here all have model names that ultimately became production car titles. Give the year, make and model of each of these fantasy vehicles.

1. _____

2. _____

3. _____

4. _____

Answers are on page 368

Knock Knock

What year and make of car ran this eyebrow-raising ad that "knocks" its own models?

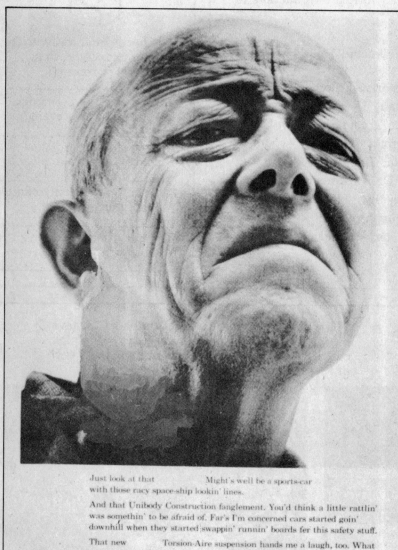

Just look at that   Might's well be a sports-car with those racy space-ship lookin' lines.

And that Unibody Construction fanglement. You'd think a little rattlin' was somethin' to be afraid of. Far's I'm concerned cars started goin' downhill when they started swappin' runnin' boards fer this safety stuff.

That new   Torsion-Aire suspension hands me a laugh, too. What are ye supposed to be doin' anyways—drivin' a car or floatin' on a cloud?

Worst of all's the price. Every whippersnapper under forty can afford one now. And them youngsters put on enough uppity airs already.

If you ask me,   quality's too good fer 'em!

Vintage MGs

Below are some model designations from the MG family tree, plus the years they were produced. Correctly match the model(s) to their years.

PRODUCTION YEARS	MODEL
1. 1926-32	TF
2. 1932-34	MGB
3. 1935-36	PB
4. 1936-49	M
5. 1950-53	MGA
6. 1953-55	TD
7. 1956-62	J 2
8. 1962-67	TA/TB/TC

Answers are on page 368

International Intrigue #1

Five sporty cars from around the world are pictured below. Can you identify these beauties by name and the country they represent?

1. _____

4. _____

2. _____

5. _____

3. _____

Jackrabbit

The compact with the little engine just left the rest of the pack at the light and roared away, just to be first at the next light. Name as many cars in this photo by year and model, and for a toughie, give the range of horsepower ratings each could've had under their hoods.

Name Game #2

Can you identify the correct model names to the car brands listed below?

YEAR AND MAKE	MODEL NAME
1. 1955 Hudson	A. Concours
2. 1946 Chrysler	B. Series 52 Special
3. 1977 Chevrolet	C. Streamliner
4. 1968 Ambassador	D. Italia
5. 1932 Essex	E. Powermaster
6. 1966 Comet	F. Executive
7. 1940 LaSalle	G. Traveler
8. 1953 Desoto	H. Capri
9. 1971 Plymouth	I. Saratoga
10. 1949 Pontiac	J. DPL
11. 1956 Packard	K. Sebring
12. 1951 Kaiser	L. Terraplane

CUSTOM LITE

The above taillight was manufactured by Cal Custom of Los Angeles to be used on customized cars. Of what year and make automobile was this taillight an imitation?

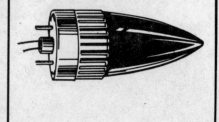

Answers are on page 368

Parting Shots

Eight taillight designs from three different decades are grouped below. Identify the year, make and model car for each.

1. _____

2. _____

3. _____

4. _____

5. _____

6. _____

7. _____

8. _____

Answers are on page 368

Dealer Displays #2

Back in the 1930's, new-car dealers would decorate their
showroom windows with seasonal displays, hoping to attract new
car buyers.
Identify the year and make of the cars in these beautiful
examples.

1. _____

2. _____

3. _____

4. _____

Answers are on page 368

Secret Compartment

"Only car in its field with 'Center-fill' fueling"

1. What car make used the above artwork and statement in their advertising?

2. What was the first model year for this car to offer the filler cap behind the license plate?

3. Where were the gas tank filler caps hidden on the cars listed below?
   A. 1954 Nash _____
   B. 1955 Imperial _____
   C. 1956 Chevrolet _____
   D. 1958 Pontiac _____
   E. 1963 Corvette _____

BIG BLOCKS

Can you match these 1933 car brands with the correct engine displacement they offered that year?

CAR BRANDS	CUBIC INCHES
1. Duesenberg	A: 384.8
2. Packard	B: 391.1
3. Chrysler	C: 419.7
4. Lincoln	D: 447.9
5. Auburn	E: 452.0
6. Marmon	F: 455.5
7. Cadillac	G: 462.0
8. Pierce-Arrow	H: 471.0
9. Cunningham	I: 490.8

Key Bobbers #3

Which car brands used the three key bobs pictured below?

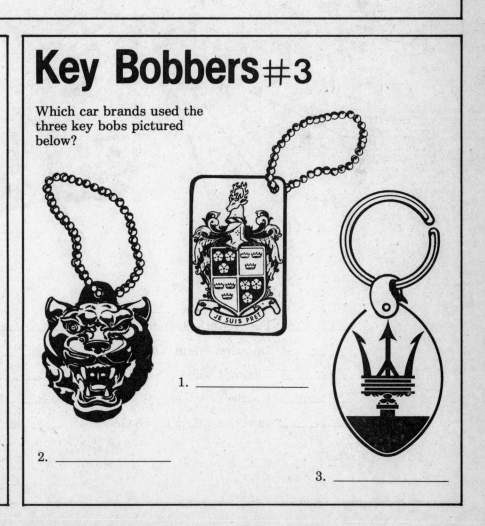

1. _____

2. _____

3. _____

Diesel

This engine cutaway view is of a 1978 General Motors Diesel. Can you match the labels below to the 10 different parts indicated by the arrows?

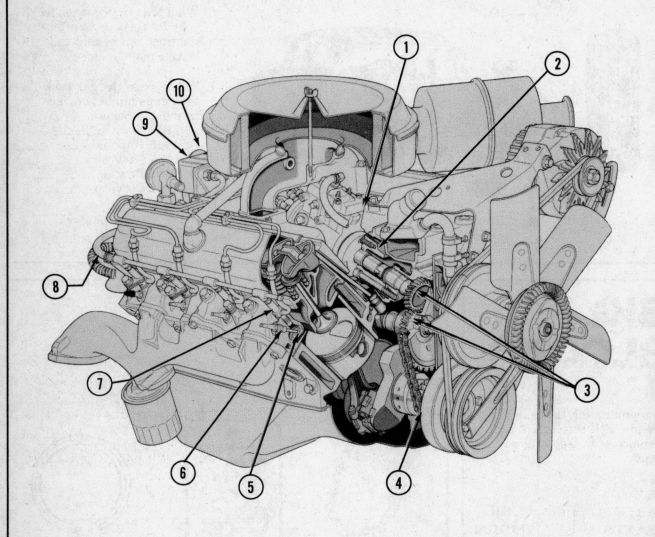

_____ Fuel Return System

_____ Injection Pump Adapter

_____ Timing Chain

_____ Nozzle

_____ Injection Pump Drive Gears

_____ Vacuum Pump

_____ Fuel Filter

_____ Injection Pump

_____ Glow Plug

_____ Prechamber

Answers are on page 368

Chevy Fronts

The similarity in these six Chevrolet front ends may make it difficult for you to give the correct model year to each.

1. _____

2. _____

3. _____

4. _____

5. _____

6. _____

Outdoor Ads #2

Fuel injected was here.

1. Year _____ Make _____

2. Year _____ Make _____

3. Year _____ Make _____

Answers are on page 368

American Ruling Class #1

Match these eight "Noble" models to their correct make.

MODEL NAME	MAKE
1. Marquis	A. Lincoln
2. Boss	B. Studebaker
3. Star Chief	C. Chevrolet
4. Commodore Eight	D. Mustang
5. Commander	E. Mercury
6. Premiere	F. Packard
7. Master 85	G. Pontiac
8. Patrician	H. Hudson

Life Like Logos #2

OK, all you part freaks: can you identify the company that used this logo?

Kiddy Cars

Can you identify the year and make of cars that these junior versions represent?

1. _____

2. _____

3. _____

4. _____

Answers are on pages 368-69

Johnnies Come Lately

All the cars shown below sport model names that were famous during the muscle car era of the 1960's.

Your task is to identify the correct year for these "in name only" models from the mid- to late 1970's.

1. _____

2. _____

3. _____

4. _____

5. _____

        Answers are on page 369

Easy Pickups #2

Match the pickup makes to the correct model names.

MAKES	MODELS
1. Chevrolet	A. Rampage
2. Dodge	B. Honcho
3. Studebaker	C. Scout Terra
4. Ford	D. Gentleman Jim
5. International	E. Scamp
6. Jeep	F. Apache
7. GMC	G. Courier
8. Plymouth	H. Champ

TAILOR~MADE

The great American pasttime of driving an automobile was possible for returning World War II veterans whose wounds had cost them the use of arms, legs, hands, or feet. The auto industry created "tailored-to-measure" control modifications for amputees. Can you describe what function each of the arrows are pointing to? Bonus: What kind of car is pictured?

A _____   F _____
B _____   G _____
C _____   H _____
D _____   I _____
E _____

Muscle Medallions #2

During the 1960's car emblems relating to engine size became symbols of power and prestige. Name the make of cars that proudly wore these badges.

1 _____

2 _____

3 _____

4 _____

5 _____

6 _____

STOP LIGHT

Quick: While these cars are stopped for a red light, identify the correct year and make of each.
Bonus: What make truck is the delivery van?

Answers are on page 369

Cannibalized Customs #3

My uncle Jack has worked for Ace Auto Wreckers for 25 years. Yesterday he drove home in this car. In the last 10 years he had carefully collected enough parts from hundreds of different makes and models of cars to build the car you see below. It sure looked like a crazy conglomeration, but the thing ran and got great mileage to boot! I enjoyed trying to identify the different cars from which each part had been salvaged. So far, I've come up with 16 different cars. How many can you find? _____

Wood'nt Rust

This wooden pickup truck is 16 feet long and has a full-scale wood engine, instrument panel and exhaust system.
Can you identify the correct year and make of this duplicate truck?

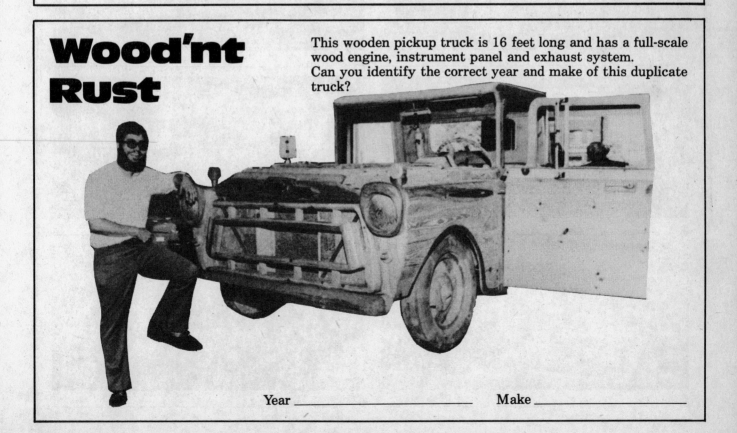

Year _____   Make _____

Answers are on page 369

What is it? #2

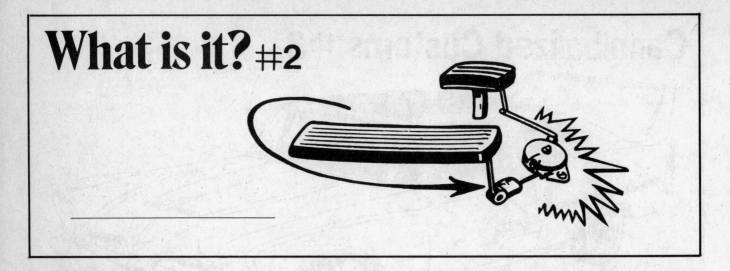

_____

Firebird Fronts #2

The split grille design continued on all Firebird models from 1974 through 1979. Some of these years have minor mind-racking differences while others show drastic revisions. Give the correct year for each front end.

1. _____

2. _____

3. _____

4. _____

5. _____

6. _____

Answers are on page 369

Green House #1

With just the roof section as your clue, can you identify the correct year and make for the six designs shown below.

1. _____

2. _____

3. _____

4. _____

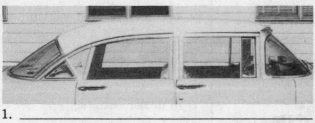

5. _____

6. _____

Motor Trend Car of the Year 1949-58

Motor Trend began awarding their revered "Car of the Year" prize to American auto manufacturers back in 1949; however, not every year during the 1950's had an honoree. Think carefully, because the 10 years listed below can be matched year by year to the five answers.

1949	A. Chrysler Corporation
1950	B. Cadillac Division
1951	C. Ford Thunderbird
1952	D. No Award
1953	E. Ford Division
1954	
1955	
1956	
1957	
1958	

So Sensitive

What purpose did this auto exterior micro-control device have for the special 1958 Cadillac Eldorado Biarritz convertible?

Answers are on page 369

Auto Parts #1

Can you correctly name the four after-market auto parts manufacturers simply by their graphic logos?

1. _____

2. _____

3. _____

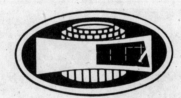

4. _____

Dealer's Choice—Trucks

It's unbelievable, the number of new truck dealers located in these United States.
Listed below are 10 truck brands to choose from. Match them to their correct number of dealer outlets.

NUMBERS OF DEALERS	TRUCK BRAND
1. 5155	A. Dodge
2. 4783	B. Jeep
3. 2838	C. Iveco
4. 2452	D. Chevrolet
5. 1540	E. Freightliner
6. 885	F. GMC
7. 230	G. FWD
8. 205	H. Ford
9. 172	I. Mack
10. 70	J. International

FIRST OF ITS KIND

This homely little car was built in a General Motors plant halfway around the world from Detroit. Actually it was the first car this distant country produced after World War II. Can you identify the year and make of car and the country where it was manufactured?

_____

_____

Answers are on page 369

DECAL DISGUISE #2

FoMoCo offered the above Pinto, Maverick, and Mustang with a special trim package that included red and blue stripes plus American flag decals.
What was this optional package called, and what model year are the three Fords?

Slogans of the Fifties #1

Auto advertising played a big part in a car maker's image during the 1950's. Identify the car brands that proclaimed these phrases.

1. THE HOT ONE'S EVEN HOTTER _____

2. AMERICA'S ACCELERATION CHAMPION _____

3. BUILT TO BETTER THE BEST ON THE ROAD _____

4. AMERICA'S MOST POWERFUL CAR: 375 H.P. _____

5. TREAT YOURSELF TO A TRIGGER-TORQUE TEST DRIVE _____

6. THE 100-MILLION-DOLLAR LOOK _____

7. THE AIR BORN B-58 _____

8. FIRST OF THE DREAM CARS TO COME TRUE _____

9. THE BIG M _____

10. SUDDENLY IT'S 1960 _____

Answers are on page 369

THOSE MISCHIEVOUS GREMLINS

These Gremlin roof indentations plus their stripe configurations require serious consideration in giving the correct year identification.

1. 197____   2. 197____

3. 197____   4. 197____

5. 197____   6. 197____

1. _____

2. _____

3. _____

4. _____

5. _____

6. _____

Answers are on page 369

The Hornets' Nest

This quiz may prove a "stinger" in your attempt to match the correct year to each of the four Hornet and four Concord grilles pictured below.

1970   1972   1973   1975   1978   1979   1980   1981

1. _____

2. _____

3. _____

4. _____

5. _____

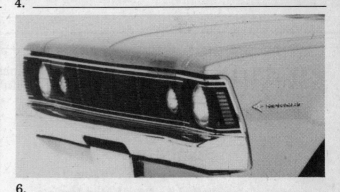

6. _____

7. _____

8. _____

Answers are on page 369

Cars from Crops?

1. Who is this auto "farmer"? _____

2. What year is this experimental car? _____

3. What material is the body made of? _____

4. What surprising ingredient is in the body material?

_____

Mission-"Initials"

Your assignment, if you choose to accept it, is to decipher the full meaning behind the sometimes cryptic muscle car initials listed below.

1. Dodge R/T

2. Camaro RS

3. Oldsmobile 4-4-2

4. "H" in Shelby GT-350H

5. Buick GS

6. Pontiac Fiero 2M4

7. Pontiac GTO

8. American Motors AMX

9. Chevrolet SS

10. "KR" in Shelby GT-500KR

'84 Liters

Cubic inches has turned into liters as a way of describing engine sizes. Be careful, as this is a tricky match-up between correct engine and car name.

ENGINE SIZE	CAR MODEL
1. L4—1.6 FI optional	A. Lincoln Mark VII
2. L4—1.8 FI standard	B. AMC Eagle 6
3. L4—2.0 FI standard	C. Buick Riviera Turbo
4. L6—2.4 FI optional	D. Ford EXP Turbo
5. L4—2.6 optional	E. Cadillac Cimarron
6. V6—3.8 FI optional	F. Chevrolet Corvette
7. L6—4.2 standard	G. Dodge 600
8. V-8—5.2 standard	H. Cadillac Limousine
9. V-8—5.7 FI standard	I. Buick Skyhawk Turbo
10. V-8-6-4—6.0 FI standard	J. Chrysler Fifth Avenue

Answers are on page 370

Devious Dodges

It may prove tricky, but give the year for each of the front views displayed below of late 1940's to mid-50's Dodges.

1. _____

2. _____

3. _____

4. _____

5. _____

6. _____

7. _____

8. _____

Answers are on page 370

Don't Let it "Bug" You

These two views of the Volkswagen Bug are actually composites
of the various subtle styling and mechanical changes that
occurred during its long evolution.
Can you give the correct model year for each "innovation"
pointed out in these sketches?

1. Wolfsburg crest added to
   front hood 19____ and
   dropped 19____

2. Front turn signal lights
   moved to top of fenders—
   19____

3. Fabric sunroof—19____

4. Adjustable head
   restraints—19____

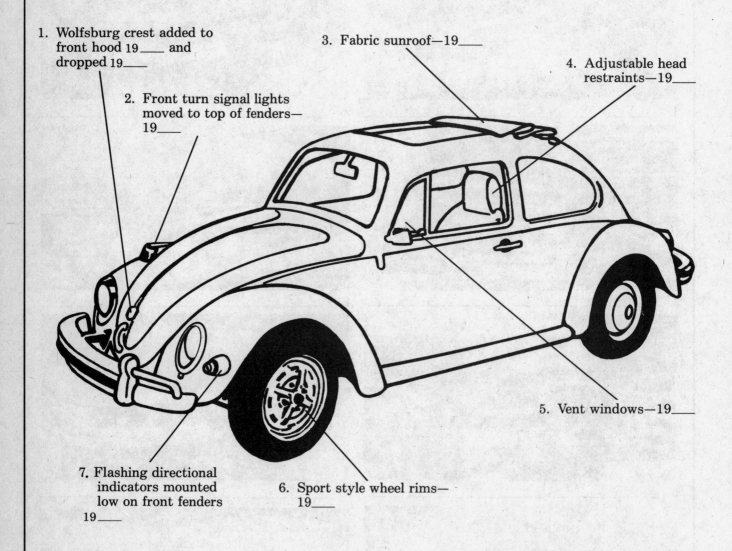

5. Vent windows—19____

6. Sport style wheel rims—
   19____

7. Flashing directional
   indicators mounted
   low on front fenders
   19____

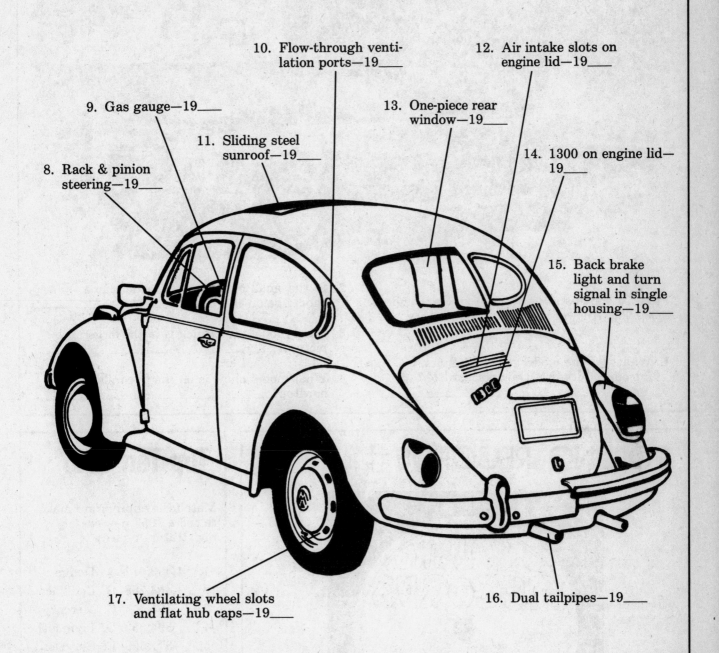

10. Flow-through venti-
    lation ports—19____

12. Air intake slots on
    engine lid—19____

9. Gas gauge—19____

13. One-piece rear
    window—19____

11. Sliding steel
    sunroof—19____

14. 1300 on engine lid—
    19____

8. Rack & pinion
   steering—19____

15. Back brake
    light and turn
    signal in single
    housing—19____

17. Ventilating wheel slots
    and flat hub caps—19____

16. Dual tailpipes—19____

Five~Millionth Hardtops

Pictured above are Buick hardtops no. 1 and no. 5,000,000. Answer these related questions.

1. What was the model year that Buick introduced its first two-door hardtop? _____

2. In the small picture, what model name should be on this design? _____

3. What model year Buick is in the larger picture? _____

4. What model name is on the five-millionth hardtop? _____

ROLLING RECORDS #2

SIDE A:
Mustang Sally
by _____

SIDE B:
Drag City
by _____

Top Ten 1957

Match the appropriate make to these 1957 new-car registration figures.

1. __ 1,493,617   A. Dodge
2. __ 1,456,288   B. Cadillac
3. __   595,503   C. Mercury
4. __   394,553   D. Plymouth
5. __   371,596   E. Chrysler
6. __   319,719   F. Chevrolet
7. __   260,573   G. Pontiac
8. __   257,488   H. Ford
9. __   141,209   I. Oldsmobile
10. __ 106,436   J. Buick

Bonus: Who was in 11th place? _____

Answers are on page 370

Charger Choices

Choose the correct model year for each of the six gutsy-looking Dodge Charger grille designs from the 1970s.

1970 1971 1972 1975 1976 1977

1. _____

2. _____

3. _____

4. _____

5. _____

6. _____

Pickups to Ponder

You may have to contemplate awhile before you guess the correct year and make of each pickup truck shown below.

1. _____

2. _____

3. _____

4. _____

6. _____

5. _____

206

Answers are on page 370

Memories #2

Can you name the country and auto company that in 1959 imported this four-wheel drive vehicle to America? What company name appeared on this gasoline sign?

Call Me by My First Name

Below are the first and last names of famous automobile pioneers. The problem is that they're not synchronized. Can you correctly match the first and last names?

FIRST NAME	LAST NAME
1. John North	A. Benz
2. Louis	B. Buick
3. Fred O.	C. Daimler
4. Karl	D. Marmon
5. Charles Stewart	E. Packard
6. David Dunbar	F. Paige
7. Harry C.	G. Pierce
8. Gottlieb	H. Renault
9. James Ward	I. Rolls
10. Howard C.	J. Royce
11. George N.	K. Stutz
12. Frederick Henry	L. Willys

Symbol Specialist #3

You may have to really think hard before you can name these four car emblems. Bonus: Name the make and model for #1 and #4.

1. _____

2. _____

3. _____

4. _____

Name Game #3

Match the correct model name to the car company. The years will help you.

Car Brands	Model Names
1. '52 Henry J	A. Barcelona
2. '61 Mercury	B. Coronado
3. '84 Buick	C. Bermuda
4. '76 AMC Matador	D. Cruiser
5. '70 Mustang	E. Meteor
6. '55 DeSoto	F. Statesman
7. '77 Pontiac	G. Maverick
8. '64 Studebaker	H. Vagabond
9. '60 Dodge	I. Can AM
10. '58 Edsel	J. T-Types
11. '59 Jeep	K. Seneca
12. '51 Nash	L. Grandé

See No Evil Hear No Evil

The above automobile accessory had dual purposes. Can you name both?

_____

SPEED WEEK

This wild race car was one of the factory experimental entries at a NASCAR "speed week" event that took place at Daytona Beach several decades ago.

1. What year, make and model car is this NASCAR racing machine?_____

2. What reason was given for the single rear fin?_____

3. Which stock engine block was modified?
   A. 368 cu. in.   B. 390 cu. in.   C. 430 cu. in.

4. Which special type of fuel feeders topped off this engine?
   A. Paxton Supercharger   B. Offenhauser Dual Quads   C. Hilborn Injectors

Answers are on page 370

Parking Garage of Time

What year and make of cars are parked on the three floors of this garage?

Movie Scenes #2

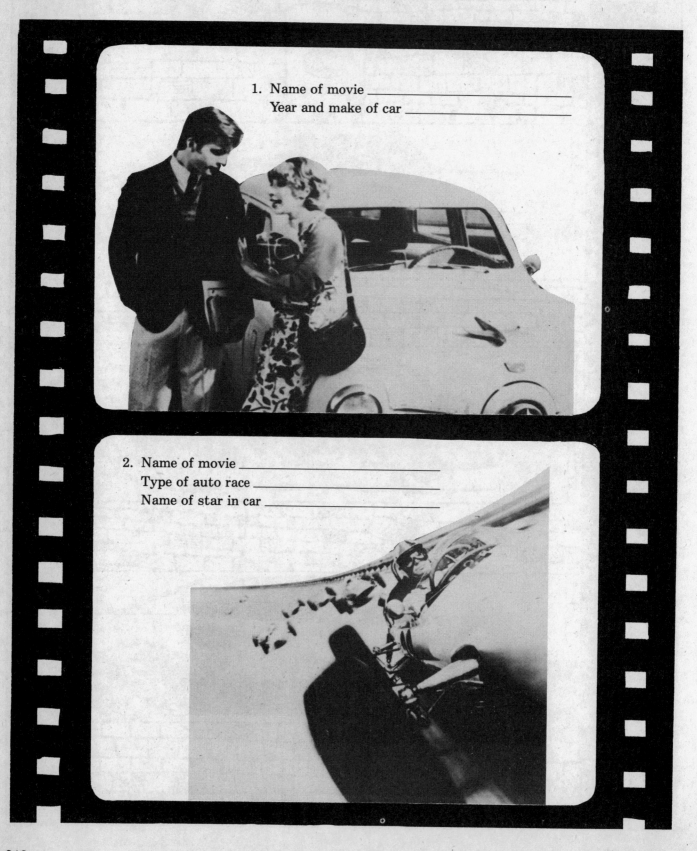

1. Name of movie _____
   Year and make of car _____

2. Name of movie _____
   Type of auto race _____
   Name of star in car _____

Answers are on page 370

Pierce-Arrow Club Page

The following 12 questions were compiled by the Pierce-Arrow Society to test your knowledge on this prestigious automobile.

1. Where would you find the words "Tireur d'arc" on a 1933 Pierce-Arrow?

2. Endurance speed records were set by Pierce-Arrow V-12 cars in three consecutive years. What were the years, and what were the average speed marks attained for the 24-hour runs?

3. The taillight assembly of most Pierce-Arrows from 1925 to 1933 consisted of three individual drum-shaped units. On the 1930 models, what was the color of the glass lens and the purpose of the *innermost* light?

4. What large automobile manufacturing concern held a controlling interest in Pierce-Arrow from 1928 to 1933?

5. What was George N. Pierce's middle name?

6. Body styles were identified by a letter of the alphabet stamped on a metal tag affixed to each car. What body style did the letter "N" represent?

7. What does the slang term "frog eyes" refer to?

8. Name two products (other than vehicles) made by Pierce.

9. One 1930 Pierce-Arrow town car had all its brightwork gold-plated. For whom was it built?

10. The largest of the three Pierce Travelodge trailer models for 1937 was the Model C.   True or false?

11. The five 1933 Silver Arrow show cars were originally painted tan and brown.   True or false?

12. After Pierce-Arrow was liquidated in 1938, what vehicle company continued to make and use Pierce V-8 and V-12 engines for over 20 years?

Rail-Car

The Missouri, Kansas and Texas Railroad bought this automobile for their president to use for his inspection trips over the line. What year, make and model car is pictured here with the steel flanged wheels?

Answers are on pages 370-71

Big Impressions

This Goodyear tire is claimed as the world's largest. Answer these questions on "big tire."

1. How tall does this rubber giant stand?
   A. 10 ft.
   B. 12 ft.
   C. 13½ ft.

2. What is the weight of this tire?
   A. Nearly one ton
   B. Exactly two tons
   C. Nearly three tons

3. How many passenger car tires can be made from the rubber of this single tire?
   A. Exactly 225
   B. Over 300
   C. Over 400

4. What kind of vehicles would use this type of tire?

Postwar Output

The figures listed below represent the total production run for the top 10 car brands of 1947. The figures are from January 1 to December 31 and usually include the output for two model years. Correctly rank the car name that matches the units produced.

RANK	CAR	OUTPUT
1	Buick	695,986
2	Plymouth	601,665
3	Ford	350,327
4	Mercury	267,830
5	Dodge	232,216
6	Pontiac	223,015
7	Chevrolet	191,454
8	Studebaker	144,490
9	Oldsmobile	124,612
10	Kaiser-Frazer	123,642

A Pat on the Back

Pontiac awarded itself this medal to celebrate its first twenty-five years of car production.
What numbers appeared on this medal to make up the correct silver anniversary combination?

Answers are on page 371

Passion Pits

Under the starry skies of summer you've got a set of wheels, a hot date, and a speaker that doesn't work. What great memories. Can you identify the year and makes of cars in front of you at the local drive-in?

MAN & MACHINES

Each of the individuals listed below were associated with different muscle cars during the mid-1960's. Correctly match the man with his machine.

1. Richard Petty
2. Carroll Shelby
3. Mark Donohue
4. The Beach Boys
5. John Delorean
6. Lee Iacocoa
7. Andy Granatelli
8. Dan Gurney
9. Hayden Proffitt
10. Craig Breedlove

A. Pontiac
B. Studebaker
C. Plymouth
D. Cougar
E. Cobra
F. AMX
G. Rambler
H. Javelin
I. Mustang
J. Chevy 409

Answers are on page 371

Playmate Cars

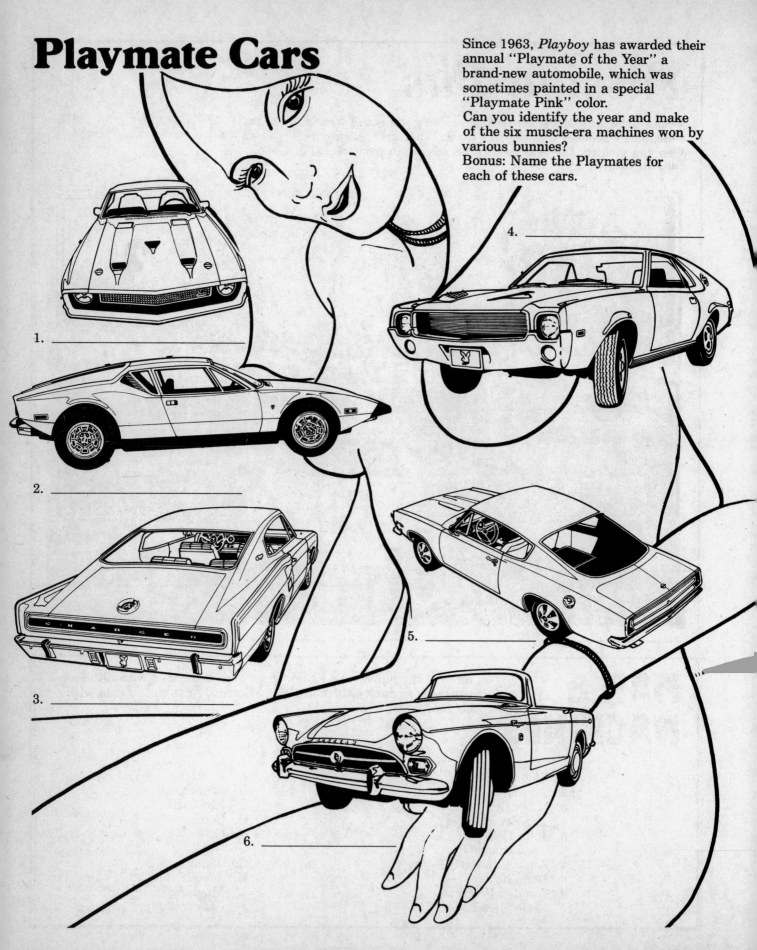

Since 1963, *Playboy* has awarded their annual "Playmate of the Year" a brand-new automobile, which was sometimes painted in a special "Playmate Pink" color.
Can you identify the year and make of the six muscle-era machines won by various bunnies?
Bonus: Name the Playmates for each of these cars.

1. _____

2. _____

3. _____

4. _____

5. _____

6. _____

Answers are on page 371

Name that State #2

Can you identify the states that used these slogans on their license plates in the mid-1950's?

The number combination on each plate represents an engine size offered by a car maker for the 1958 model year. Identify the brand by the cubic inches.

VISIT 8·392 **55**

V 8 Colorful 383 '55

1. _____

2. _____

55 V·371 PEACH STATE

19 '55 V8·289 WATER WONDERLAND

3. _____

4. _____

Battery Bafflers

A battery may look like a one-piece unit from the outside, but it is actually made of many different parts.

Can you match the component terms listed below to the correct arrows?

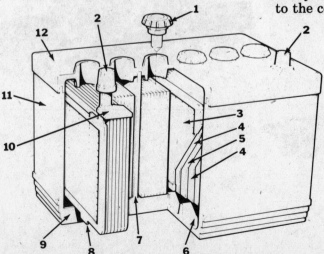

TERMS

_____ Case

_____ Cell partition

_____ Cover

_____ Element rests

_____ Negative plate

_____ Plate feet

_____ Positive plate

_____ Post strap

_____ Sediment space

_____ Separator

_____ Terminal Post

_____ Vent cap

Answers are on page 371

FORD DREAMING

The fertile imagination of FoMoCo car stylists over the years have produced these mild to wild dream/show machines.
Identify the year each was first shown and its full name.

1. _____

2. _____

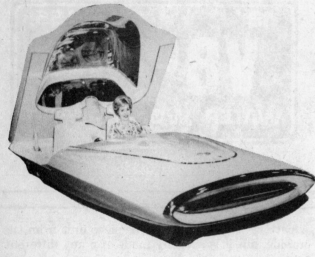

3. _____

4. _____

5. _____

6. _____

Answers are on page 371

Opera Windows

Give the year and make of cars for each of these opera window designs.

1. _____

2. _____

3. _____

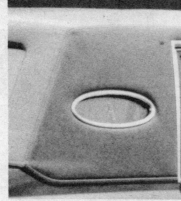

4. _____

5. _____

6. _____

Long and Short of it!

Match the correct overall length to each of the 1965 cars listed below.

1. Chevy Corvair
2. AMC Ambassador
3. Dodge Monaco
4. Rambler American
5. Imperial LeBaron
6. Cadillac Series 75
7. Pontiac Bonneville
8. Chevy Corvette
9. Plymouth Barracuda
10. Ford Thunderbird

A. 175.1 inches
B. 177.3 inches
C. 183.3 inches
D. 188.2 inches
E. 200.0 inches
F. 205.4 inches
G. 212.3 inches
H. 221.7 inches
I. 227.8 inches
J. 243.8 inches

Slick Symbols #5

The symbol below represents what oil company?

REG. U.S. PAT. OFF.

WAX FREE OIL

Find the Differences

In picture #1 is a Buick Century two-door hardtop ad from 1956. Can you find the 10 slight changes in picture #2?

WHO'S GOT THE GREATEST GETAWAY IN 1956 ?

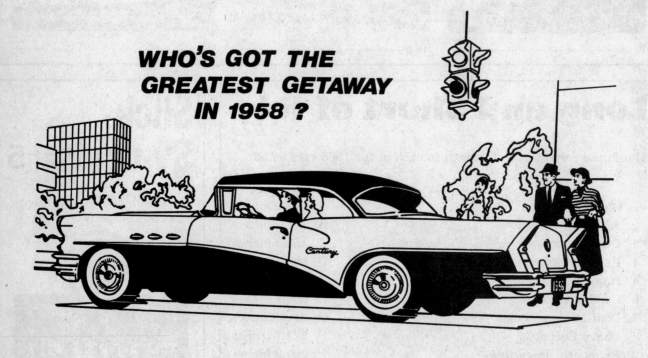

WHO'S GOT THE GREATEST GETAWAY IN 1958 ?

Answers are on page 371

American Ruling Class #2

Identify the "commanding" model names for the cars on which they appeared.

MODEL NAME	MAKE
1. Crown Victoria	A. Plymouth
2. Road King	B. Mustang
3. King Cobra	C. Nash/AMC
4. Royal Lancer	D. Chevrolet
5. Le Baron	E. Studebaker
6. Ambassador	F. Dodge
7. Champion	G. Ford
8. Stylemaster	H. Imperial

Slick #6 Symbols

The symbol below represents what oil company?

DASH, DANG~IT

That's what you might be cursing when you try to identify the correct year and make of car that used these six dashboard designs.

1. _____

2. _____

3. _____

4. _____

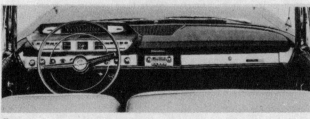

5. _____

6. _____

Answers are on page 371

Quiz Delivery Van

ACROSS

1. British Body-Ford Powered
4. Spanish Explorer
6. Kilometers Per Hour
10. 1959 Compact Car
12. American Motors Two Seater
14. If You're Scared, You've Got The _____
15. Limited (Abbr.)
18. European _____ Cars
19. Speed of Sound (2 Wds.)
20. A French Race
24. Grand Touring (Initials)
25. Dragsters Favorite Engine
26. AMC Ghosts
27. American Symbol
30. French Female Dodge
33. Joisting Weapon
35. Gallant _____ of Olds
36. Quarter Mile Strip
37. Cartoon Character Car
39. Service Island
40. Tiger Paws
42. Merged With Nash
43. Engine Size in Three Letters

DOWN

1. Shelby's Given Name
2. _____ Without a Cause
3. Limited Mustangs
5. Chrysler _____ and Country
7. Rapid Transit Cars
8. English Pub Game
9. Mad Scientist Muscle Car Company
11. Dodge In Two Letters
13. Cyclone Company
16. 340 Cubic Inch Devils
17. Scat Pack Car
21. Henry's Son
22. Horse Race
23. Largest Auto Manufacturer (initials)
28. Sour Car
29. Feathered Pontiac
31. Italian for "Forward"
32. Type of Swordfish
33. Singing Studebaker
34. Oil and Gas Container
36. Ambassador in 3 Letters
38. Car Cover
41. Super Sport (Abbr.)

Answers are on page 372

Name that State #3

Can you name the states that used these slogans or symbols on license plates back in the 1950's?

The number combination that's on each plate represents an engine size offered by a car make for the 1960 model year. Identify the brands by their cubic inches.

19° 8·250 °55
THE CORN STATE

1. _____

1955 8·401
LAND OF OPPORTUNITY

2. _____

8 317
19 · · 55

3. _____

10,000 LAKES
8·390
19 · · 55

4. _____

Corvair Club Page

The Corvair Club of Cincinnati, Ohio, challenges your knowledge about its favorite special interest automobile, the Chevrolet Corvair.

1. What day, month and year was the first Corvair sold, and to whom?

   _____

2. What Corvair body style continued into 1965 unchanged? _____

3. What was the first model year factory air conditioning was offered on Corvairs?

   _____

4. What model years had the exact same taillights? _____

5. What model year had a hand choke?

6. What was the model year that first offered FM stereo?

   _____

7. Which model out-sold the convertible, but was not produced after 1967?

   _____

8. What was the first model year for a turbo charged Corvair?

   _____

9. What U.S. President's daughter had a Corvair, and what year and type was it?

   _____

10. What was the body style of the last production Corvair?

    _____

Cannibalized Customs #4

You'd never know it now, but when this beauty arrived at Ace Auto Wreckers it had a badly mangled front end. My Uncle Jack, Ace's expert body and fender man, decided to save a few bucks by using old parts to repair the damage. He entered it in an old car show recently and the judges didn't know how to classify it. I've found parts from at least nine different makes in Jack's latest effort. How many can you spot?

Name Game #4

Correctly match the model name to the year and make shown below.

'65 Pontiac	Rallye 350
'70 Buick	Corsa
'63 Studebaker	GTX
'65 Corvair	GTS
'70 Olds	GSX
'69 Plymouth	Eliminator
'67 Rambler	Rallye
'73 Challenger	2 + 2
'67 Cougar	Hawk
'67 Dart	Rogue

Answers are on page 372

FASTBACK FOOLERS

Eight slick, windswept roof designs from three different decades are shown below. Identify these "fastbacks" by their year, make and model.

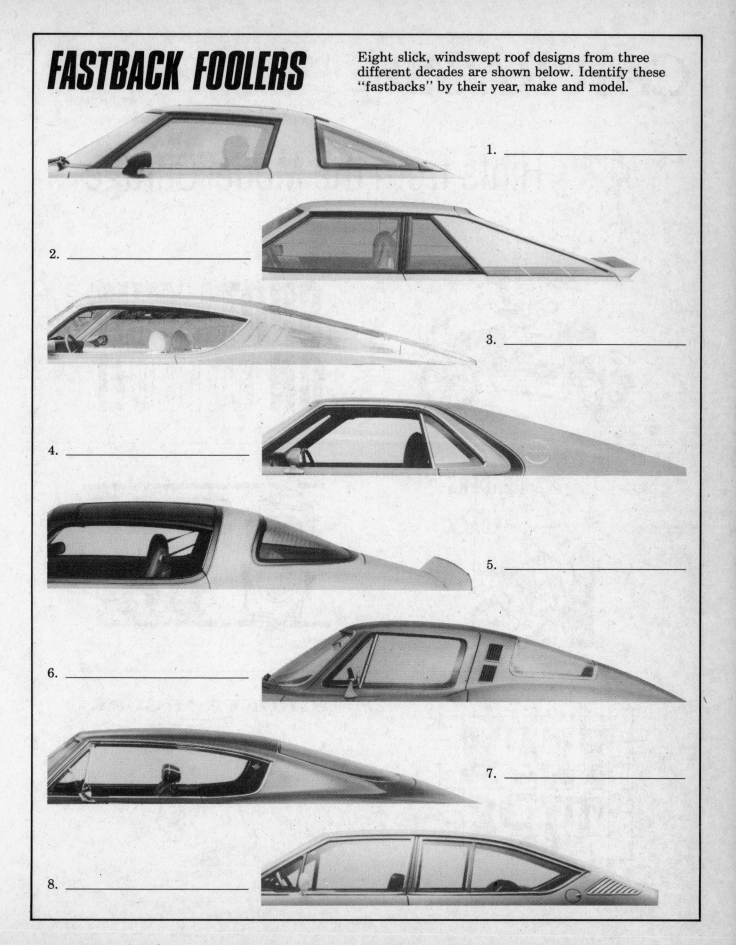

1. _____

2. _____

3. _____

4. _____

5. _____

6. _____

7. _____

8. _____

CAR RAGS #2

Can you name the seven magazines that featured the headings pictured below for their monthly columns?

 Hints from the Model Garage

1. _____

2. _____

SPOTLIGHT ON DETROIT

3. _____

READERS TALK BACK

4. _____

STOP And GO

5. _____

TECH TIPS

6. _____

STROKER McGURK

7. _____

Answers are on page 372

Once Upon a Time...

These three little princesses introduced the brand-new model names for the car behind them.
What are the three names, and the year and make of the car?

1. _____ 2. _____ 3. _____

Nice to Meet Ya! #3

The dates below were the coming-out parties for the 10 cars listed.
Match the brand names to their original debut dates.

First Introduction Date	Car Make and Model
1. Oct. 21, 1955	Buick Riviera
2. Oct. 15, 1957	Cadillac Seville
3. Oct. 4, 1962	Dodge Charger
4. Sept. 26, 1963	Packard Hawk
5. Oct. 14, 1965	AMC AMX
6. Jan. 1, 1966	Oldsmobile Omega
7. Feb. 24, 1968	Chevrolet Monte Carlo
8. Sept. 18, 1969	Continental Mark II
9. Sept. 21, 1972	Oldsmobile Toronado
10. May 1, 1975	Chevrolet Chevelle

Answers are on page 372

International Intrigue #2

What are the brand names for the six imports pictured below? Bonus: What is the model name for picture #1 and who is sitting in car #2?

2. _____

1. _____

4. _____

3. _____

6. _____

5. _____

Answers are on page 372

Name Game #5

Car model names come and go at a very fast pace in the auto world. Can you match the year and make to the correct model?

YEAR AND MAKE	MODEL NAME
1. 1946 Nash	Medalist
2. 1952 Studebaker	Jetfire
3. 1953 Kaiser	Sizzler
4. 1954 Hudson	600
5. 1956 Mercury	Cricket
6. 1963 Oldsmobile	MPG
7. 1967 Jeepster	Dragon
8. 1971 Plymouth	State Starliner
9. 1971 Dodge Demon	Commando
10. 1976 Mercury Bobcat	Jet-Liner

Mystery Car #3

Answer the following questions about the sleek sports car shown here.

1. What is the full name for this two-seater?

2. What was the first year this car was offered to the American market?

3. What three companies and their countries collectively made this car possible?

4. What size engine (in liters) was under the hood?

5. How many cylinders?

6. What was the horsepower rating?

Muscular Massage

TOUGH but oh so Gentle

1. What company does this bruiser symbolize?

2. What is his name?

3. Which of the company's many products is he promoting in this sketch?

4. What is he tough on, and what is he gentle on?

Bird Colors

From 1977 to 1980 the Firebird Esprit was offered in a limited-edition model with the above emblem.
What were the three different colors offered over the years?

Answers are on pages 372-73

Movie Scenes #3

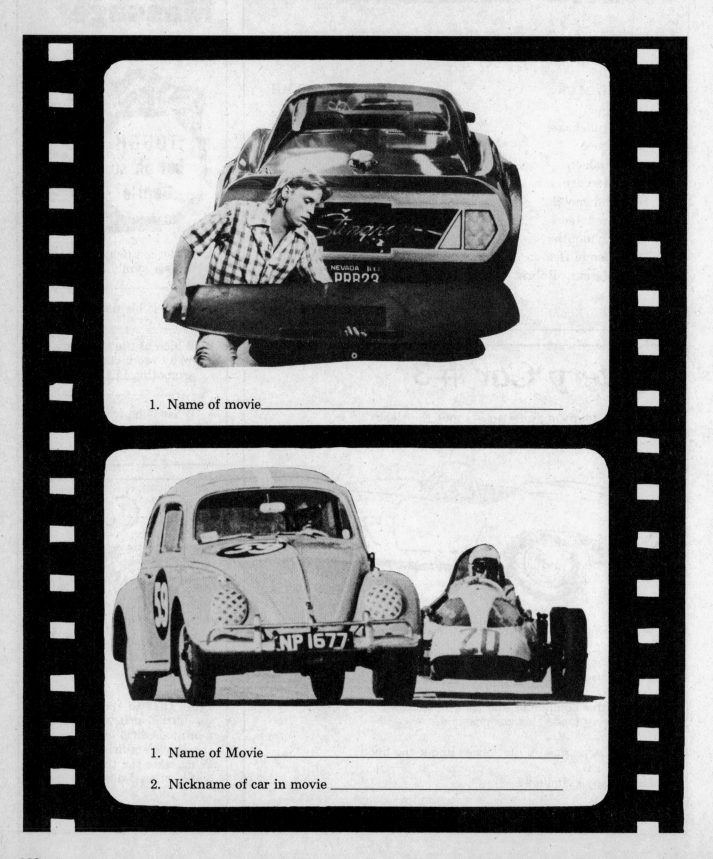

1. Name of movie_____

1. Name of Movie _____

2. Nickname of car in movie _____

Answers are on page 373

EXPOSED

These seven cut-away views span many decades, and uncover major design and construction differences.
Be the first on your block to identify the correct year and make for each vehicle.

1. _____

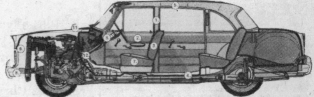

2. _____   3. _____

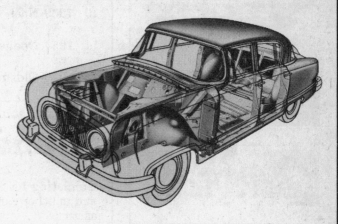

4. _____   5. _____

6. _____   7. _____

The Hole Truth

Yes we want the truth and nothing else, so fess-up and correctly identify the nine different years for these Buick fender porthole designs.

1. _____

2. _____

3. _____

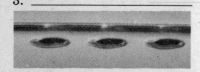

4. _____

5. _____

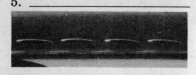

6. _____

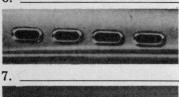

7. _____

8. _____

9. _____

Name Game #6

Match the correct model names to the auto brands listed below.

YEAR AND MAKE	MODEL NAME
1. 1977 Pontiac	A. Caliente
2. 1940 Hudson	B. Royal
3. 1958 Desoto	C. Concord
4. 1949 Kaiser	D. LaFayette
5. 1964 Comet	E. Fireflite
6. 1951 Plymouth	F. Super
7. 1959 Buick	G. Astre
8. 1942 Chrysler	H. Invicta
9. 1956 Clipper	I. Meadowbrook
10. 1939 Nash	J. Big Boy
11. 1954 Dodge	K. Futuramic 76
12. 1949 Oldsmobile	L. Virginian

Grandpa Duke

Emulating his kin, grandpa's car goes up and over a high bush and another car to cover a total of 80 feet before plumping to earth.
Can you identify his airborne auto by year, make and model?

_____ _____ _____

Answers are on page 373

PLYMOUTH
PICTURE PUZZLERS

Plymouth had a wide variety of front-end designs during the
1960's. Shown below are eight of them.
Can you easily identify the correct year for these Mopars?

1. _____

2. _____

3. _____

4. _____

5. _____

6. _____

7. _____

8. _____

Sky Light

Car designers back in the 1960's literally "raised the roof" on two station wagon models.
Answer these questions about this unique feature.

1. What were the two makers that offered this type of roof?
   _____
   _____

2. What were the model names for each make?
   _____
   _____

3. What was the first model year for this design?
   _____

4. How many inches did this roof section rise above the normal car top?
   _____

5. What was the last model year for this roof design?
   _____

Drive~in Quickies

1. What is the correct month and year that the first drive-in theater opened?

   A. June 1933
   B. July 1938
   C. May 1946

2. Which city and state has the honor of the location for the first drive-in?

   A. Lombard, IL
   B. Camden, NJ
   C. San Diego, CA

3. What was the all-time high number of drive-in movies in this country?

   A. 4,000
   B. 5,000
   C. 6,000

4. As of 1982, how many outdoor theaters were still open for business?

   A. Under 1,000
   B. 2,000
   C. Over 3,000

Auto Language #1

Can you unscramble the eight automotive terms and match them to their correct meanings?

1. ZEEBL
2. IDDOE
3. LOCI
4. NONPII
5. GEANILK
6. KRAPS
7. BINGERA
8. HYELLEW

A. An electrical current that jumps from one conductor to another
B. A part in which a pivot turns or moves
C. A part of the alternator
D. A part in which energy is absorbed and stored
E. A piece surrounding a gauge
F. A part of the ignition system
G. Rods used to transmit motion from one unit to another
H. The smaller of two gears

Answers are on page 373

STOCK STARS

Six wild and wooly stock car machines are shown below, blasting their way around the race tracks of time.

What is the year and make for each car, and the size engine under their hoods? Extra credit: Can you name the drivers associated with these autos?

1. _____

2. _____

3. _____

4. _____

5. _____

6. _____

Answers are on page 373

MOTOR PSYCHO

The scene shown above is from Alfred Hitchcock's 1960 movie *Psycho*.

1. Janet Leigh leaves town with the stolen money in what year and make of car? _____

2. What state and letter/number combination does the highway patrolman see on the above car? _____

3. What was the year and make of the patrol car? _____

4. Miss Leigh trades in her first car for what year and make of car? _____

Original Rough Riders

1. What car brand used the above symbol? _____

2. What auto company manufactured them? _____

3. What model year was this car brand introduced? _____

4. This car was advertised as "the world's first straight-eight" for under what price?
   A. $600
   B. $1000
   C. $2000

5. What year was this car brand dropped?

Auto Language #2

Eight automobile terms are listed below with their definitions. Can you unscramble the words and match them to their correct meaning?

1. REBO
2. CLOW
3. TENJORIC
4. QUOTER
5. LAVVE
6. SUPHORD
7. LEID
8. HADS

A. A steel rod between valve lifter and rocker arm
B. An effort devoted toward twisting or turning
C. Engine operating, but vehicle not in motion
D. The diameter of a cylinder
E. A partition between the driver and the engine
F. A portion of body between the engine and driver
G. A device for opening and sealing an aperture
H. A pump to inject fuel

Answers are on page 373

Mopar Fins

Can you identify the year and make of the Chrysler Corp. cars that proudly wore these fins?

1. _____

2. _____

3. _____

4. _____

5. _____

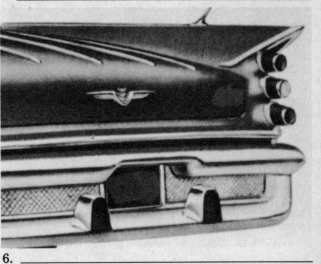

6. _____

Answers are on page 373

Piston Poppers

Round and round they go,
where they'll stop,
we'll never know.

What is the year, make and model of these racing cars,
and the size engine they used?
Bonus: Can you name the driver most associated with
each of these cars?

1. _____

2. _____

3. _____

4. _____

5. _____

6. _____

Answers are on page 373

SECRET AGENT

Like a Dick Tracy combatting public enemies, this special agent was assigned the duty of stopping a gang of engine-robbing mugs. Fill in the name of the product on the dotted line, and you'll know who this square-jawed enforcer works for. Match the correct names to the cartoon characters.

1. _____ 2. _____

3. _____ 4. _____

A. Blackie Carbon   C. Sticky Valves
B. Dirty Sludge   D. Gummy Rings

Nick Names

Do you know the nicknames of these drag racing kings of the 1960's?

1. Don "_____" Prudhomme   A. Snow Man
2. Bill "_____" Jenkins   B. Dyno
3. "_____" Tommy Ivo   C. Big Daddy
4. Tom "_____" McEwen   D. Grumpy
5. Gene "_____" Snow   E. The Snake
6. Don "_____" Garlits   F. TV
7. "_____" Don Nicholson   G. The Mongoose

Engine Abbreviations

Can you decipher these abbreviations for valve and cylinder arrangements?

1. IL_____
2. VO_____
3. VHV_____
4. IO_____
5. VL_____

HALF DOZEN INDY'S...

...is what these two brothers have won between themselves at the 500-mile classic.
Can you identify these amazing drivers and the three years they each won?

1. _____

2. _____

Car Tunes #1

1. What was the title of the Beach Boys song of 1964 about a girl and her T-Bird?

_____

2. In 1960, Charlie Ryan had a minor hit called "Hot Rod Lincoln." Another artist in that same year had an even bigger hit with "Hot Rod Lincoln," name him?

_____

3. What make of car is mentioned in Chuck Berry's 1955 hit "Maybellene"?

_____

4. What group named after a GM luxury car had 1955-56 songs called "Speedo" and "Zoom"?

_____

LOVE THOSE 8's

What the future holds for production of eight-cylinder engines is uncertain, but luckily we can still drive excellent examples like those shown here.
Identify the make of car(s) that used these V-8 and straight-8 designs.

1. _____

2. _____

3. _____

4. _____

5. _____

6. _____

T-Bird Teaser

These six Ford Thunderbirds may all look alike, but in fact they have many subtle design differences. Name the years.

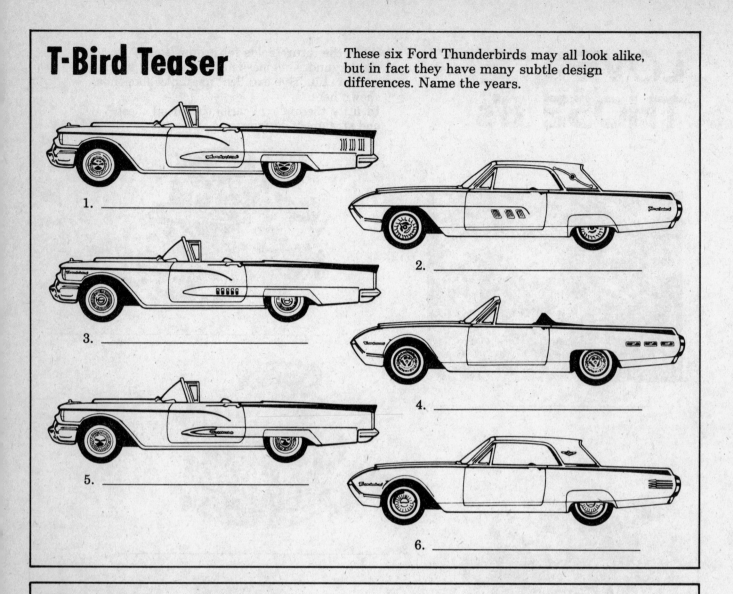

1. _____

2. _____

3. _____

4. _____

5. _____

6. _____

Engine Specs

1. What was the first model year that all car companies had to have exhaust emission controls on their engines?
   A. 1967   B. 1968   C. 1969

2. In cubic inches, what was the engine size of the 1948 Tucker?
   A. 335   B. 279   C. 351

3. Chrysler first offered its five-year/50,000-mile engine warranty for which model year?
   A. 1962   B. 1965   C. 1963

4. The original Lincoln Zephyrs came with which engine configuration?
   A. L-Head V-8   B. Flathead V-8   C. L-Head V-12

5. Which company in 1964 offered America's only passenger cars with overhead-cam engines?
   A. Pontiac   B. Jeep   C. Studebaker

6. What car company offered an enormous 472 cu. in. V-8 engine in 1968?
   A. Cadillac   B. Lincoln   C. Imperial

7. In 1930, which major car corporation was the first to adopt downdraft carburetors?
   A. Graham   B. Chrysler   C. Buick

8. What year did Ford build its 30-millionth V-8 engine?
   A. 1952   B. 1962   C. 1972

Answers are on page 374

ASSEMBLY LINES #2

Before the era of robotics, it was men and women who physically assembled all our favorite automobiles.

Identify the year and make of the cars in these six factory scenes.

1. _____

2. _____

3. _____

4. _____

5. _____

6. _____

Grand Prix Game

Below are eight Grand Prix front and rear designs. Can you match them up and give their correct years?

1. _____

2. _____

3. _____

4. _____

5. _____

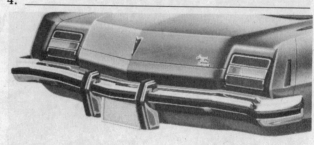

6. _____

7. _____

8. _____

242

Answers are on page 374

HOME SWEET FACTORY #2

The eight cities listed on the map below were the original factory sites for different car companies of the past. Match the car from the list below to its home base located on the map.

Crosley   Marmon
Durant   Pierce-Arrow
Elcar   Peerless
Essex   Viking

Lansing, MI

3. _____

Indianapolis, IN   Detroit, MI   Buffalo, NY

1. _____   4. _____   7. _____

Elkhart, IN   Cincinnati, OH   Elizabeth, NJ

2. _____   5. _____   8. _____

Cleveland, OH

6. _____

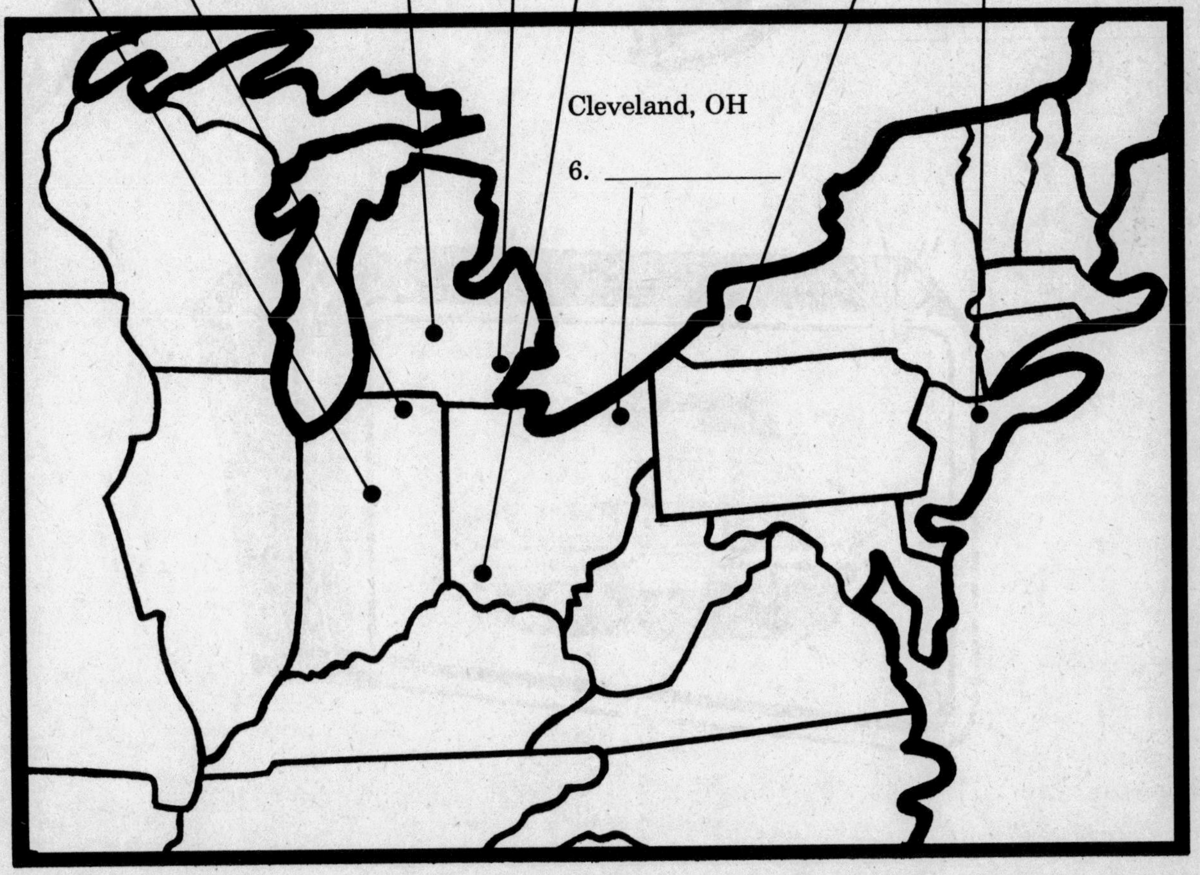

Past Reflections

Give the correct year and make of car reflected in these three side view mirrors.

1. _____

2. _____

3. _____

Answers are on page 374

AMX Club Page

The Classic AMX Club International of Arvada, Colorado,
compiled these trivia questions about their favorite automobile.

1. How many two-seat AMXs were built for 1968-70?
   A. 19,134   B. 32,651   C. 50,406

2. What years did AMX offer the over-the-roof optional racing stripes?

3. Dual exhaust and tachometer were popular options. True or false?

4. What model year AMX did not have AMC's traditional reclining seats?

5. Of the three years the AMX was offered as a two-seater, which was the best selling year?
   A. 1968   B. 1969   C. 1970

6. The circle insignia on the left quarter panel of the 1968-70 AMX cleverly concealed the gasoline filler cap. True or false?

7. What was the name of the V-8 mid-engine limited production car built by AMC, and how many were built?

8. What noted U.S. Senator is an original owner of an AMX?

9. For what country did AMC build 24 AMXs with right-hand drive?

10. A stock 390 cu. in. AMX could run the quarter mile in which elapsed time range?
    A. 13.99-14.49 sec.   B. 14.50-14.99 sec.   C. 15.00-15.49 sec.

11. The AMC 390 cu. in. block was actually built by Ford. True or false?

12. Can you name four other AMC models that offered the AMX as a trim package and the years?

Do-it-Yourself Key

Which 1971 make and model automobile offered this ingenious key with the built-in emergency tool kit?
Can you identify the six different tools?

Name Sakes

The nine distinguished gentlemen pictured below all built automobiles bearing their names. Can you recognize these auto giants?

1. _____

2. _____

3. _____

4. _____

5. _____

6. _____

7. _____

8. _____

9. _____

Answers are on page 374

Bustle Butts #2

Six more "trunkback" cars from the 1930's. Identify their years and models.

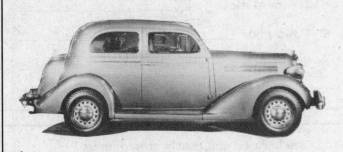

1. _____

2. _____

4. _____

3. _____

6. _____

5. _____

More El Camino/Ranchero

1. What model year did the Ranchero change to the compact Falcon body?_____

2. What was the first model year for the Chevelle-based El Camino? _____

3. What model year did the Ranchero switch to the Fairlane body style?_____

4. What was the last model year that Ford produced a Ranchero model?_____

Slick Symbols #7

Can you name the oil company that this graphic symbol represents?

_____

Answers are on page 374

"TRANS"-LATION #2

What eight cars came equipped with the semi- or fully automatic transmissions listed below?

1. Vacamatic _____

2. Flightomatic _____

3. Cruise-O-Matic _____

4. Triple-Turbine Transmission

_____

5. Drive-Master _____

6. Hydra-Matic _____

7. Powerglide _____

8. TorqueFlite _____

Open Season

All the tops are lowered and neatly stored under their boots. But before you peel away into the sun, identify the year, make and model of these six convertibles.

1. Year _____ Make _____ Model _____   2. Year _____ Make _____ Model _____

3. Year _____ Make _____ Model _____   4. Year _____ Make _____ Model _____

5. Year _____ Make _____ Model _____   6. Year _____ Make _____ Model _____

Answers are on page 374

Movin' Mascot

Name the cartoon characters shown below and the after-market parts company each represented.

1. _____

2. _____

RAINY DAY RAGTOPS

Inclement weather means the fold away soft tops come out of hiding, giving the convertible a totally different look. Identify the six handsome examples below by year and make.

1. _____

2. _____

3. _____

4. _____

5. _____

6. _____

This Must Be "Z" Car

One of the most popular and collectible Oriental cars is the
Datsun Z series.
Can you answer "Z" simple questions below?

1. The picture above is of the Japanese version of the Z. What is it called?_____

2. What was the first model year for the imported 240Z?_____

3. What size engine (liters or cubic inches) powered the original 240Zs?_____

4. The 240Z body was made of fiberglass. True or false?_____

5. What auto magazine named the 240Z its "Car of the Year"?_____

6. How many 240Zs were sold in its first three years in the U.S.A.?
   A. 100,000   B. 130,000   C. 165,000

7. Which was the only model year for the 260Z?_____

8. How many more "cc's" did the 260Z engine have over the 240Z version?
   A. 200 cc   B. 350 cc   C. 400 cc

9. What was the first model year for the fuel-injected 280Z?_____

10. What was the first model year for the luxury 280ZX?_____

Bonus: What was the model name for Toyota's two-seat sports car of the mid '60's?

_____

Answers are on page 375

Sports Car Silhouettes

These six silhouettes appeared in an ad for Castrol Oil back in September 1957.
Can you identify each sports car just by the blacked-out profiles?

2. _____

1. _____

4. _____

3. _____

6. _____

5. _____

Answers are on page 375

Underwater Dreams

Years back, after just being handformed in Italy, this tasty dream car was crossing the Atlantic Ocean when the ocean liner it was traveling in sunk.

Identify this "lost dream" by its year, make and model name and the ship's name.

Year _____

Make _____

Model _____

Ship's Name _____

Chevy Blocks

What was the correct model year for each of these Chevrolet engine milestones?

1. Four-cylinder replaced by six-cylinder_____

2. "Blue-Flame" six cylinder _____

3. 265 cu. in. V-8_____

4. 283 cu. in. V-8_____

5. 327 cu. in. V-8_____

6. 396 cu. in. V-8_____

7. 409 cu. in. V-8_____

SYMBOL SPECIALIST #4

Are you an expert at recognizing automobile brands simply by their symbols?
Name these four as a sampler.

3. _____

1. _____

2. _____ 4. _____

Answers are on page 375

Pickups of the Past

Pickup trucks from various decades are shown below. Can you identify the correct year and make of each?

1. _____

2. _____

3. _____

4. _____

5. _____

6. _____

War Years

The auto companies halted their civilian car production in 1942 and started full-time manufacturing of war supplies.
Answer the following war-years questions.

1. What name should appear in the above picture?_____

2. What month in '42 did all companies stop normal car production?_____

3. In 1944, basic ration books were cut to how many gallons per week?
    A. 2 gallons   B. 3½ gallons   C. 4 gallons

4. What company in 1941 achieved mass production of tanks?
    _____

5. What kind of aircraft engines did Packard build during the war?
    A. Rolls-Royce   B. Pratt & Whitney   C. Briggs & Stratton

6. In what war year was the national speed limit cut to 35 M.P.H.?
    A. 1941   B. 1942   C. 1944

7. What was the popular name for the WWII amphibious trucks?
    _____

8. In what year did Willys begin delivery of the famous "Jeep," to the military?_____

9. Besides Willys, what other two manufacturers made bids for the government contract on Jeeps?_____

10. In what year did civilian vehicle production begin again?
    _____

Last of the Mohegans #2

What was the final model year for car production with these famous nameplates.

YEAR	CAR/MODEL
1. 1931	Nash Statesman
2. 1934	Buick Invicta
3. 1937	Hudson
4. 1941	Terraplane
5. 1952	Plymouth GTX
6. 1955	Ford Model A
7. 1957	Willys
8. 1961	AMC Gremlin
9. 1962	Franklin
10. 1965	Crosley
11. 1963	Ford Falcon
12. 1970	Pontiac GTO
13. 1971	Dodge Custom 880
14. 1974	Hupmobile
15. 1978	Chrysler Windsor

Mystery Emblem

1. What car brand used the above emblem?

2. In what country was this car built?

3. Which American dealer network sold and serviced this car?

Answers are on page 375

Parking Garage of Time

Identify the year and make of cars parked on the three floors of this garage.

1. _____

2. _____

3. _____

PASS WITH CARE

Looking at these side view mirrors, can you recognize the year and make of cars trying to pass you by?

1. _____   2. _____

Name Game #7

Test your memory and match the year and make cars to their correct model name listed below.

YEAR AND MAKE	MODEL NAME
1. 1954 Lincoln	A. Skyway Champion
2. 1940 Graham	B. Mirada
3. 1969 Plymouth	C. Pacemaker
4. 1983 Pontiac	D. Vista Cruiser
5. 1946 Studebaker	E. Cosmopolitan
6. 1950 Hudson	F. Fleetline
7. 1931 REO	G. Corsair
8. 1980 Dodge	H. VIP
9. 1963 Checker	I. Royale
10. 1948 Chevrolet	J. Superba
11. 1966 Oldsmobile	K. Hollywood
12. 1952 Henry J	L. 1000

Wild Horses #2

In 1967, these gutsy horsepower ratings were offered. Match the horsepower to the correct car and engine.

HORSE-POWER RATING	CAR AND ENGINE (cu. in.)
1. 200	A. Ford—289
2. 225	B. Pontiac—326
3. 235	C. Dodge—383
4. 250	D. Ford—427
5. 275	E. AMC—290
6. 325	F. Oldsmobile—400
7. 350	G. Corvette—427
8. 360	H. Plymouth—273
9. 400	I. Camaro—327
10. 425	J. Buick—430

Answers are on page 375

Tail~End of Trivia

Recognize the six different taillight assemblies shown below, then give the correct year and make of car for each design.

1. _____

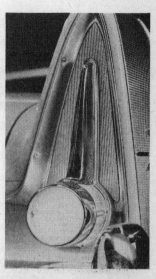

2. _____ 3. _____

4. _____ 5. _____ 6. _____

7. _____ 8. _____

Lengthy Limos

These luxurious limousines span
many decades. Can you identify each
by year and make?

2. _____

1. _____

4. _____

3. _____

6. _____

5. _____

Answers are on page 375

Wild Horses 1958

Eight car makes and their 1958 carburetion are listed below. Your task is to match them correctly with their horsepower ratings.

MAKE AND CARBURETION	H.P. RATING
1. Plymouth / two four-barrel	A. 250
2. Edsel / four-barrel	B. 275
3. Chevrolet / four-barrel	C. 300
4. Chrysler / two four-barrel	D. 305
5. Mercury / four-barrel	E. 330
6. Packard / two-barrel	F. 345
7. Pontiac / three two-barrel	G. 360
8. Thunderbird / four-barrel	H. 380

SLICK SYMBOLS

The oil symbol below represented what oil comany?

_____

Flying Car Facts

Know anything about flying cars? If not, then just take educated guesses and fill in the blanks below.

Wingspan

_____

Make of Aircraft Engine

_____

Horsepower Rating

_____

Horsepower Rating

_____

Make of Car Engine

_____

Fin Fun

Eight of the best Cadillac tailfin designs are pictured below. Identify the correct year for each.

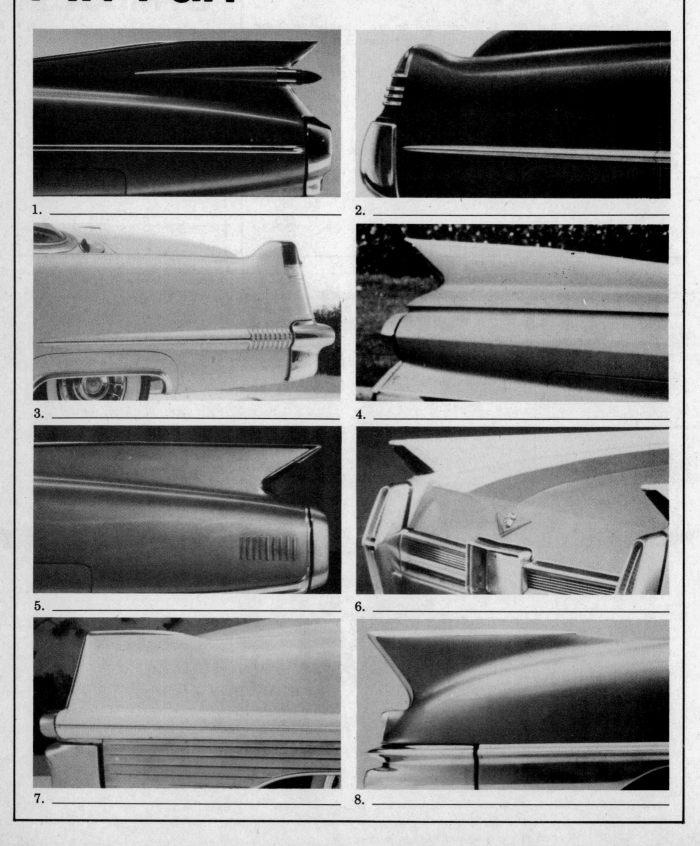

1. _____

2. _____

3. _____

4. _____

5. _____

6. _____

7. _____

8. _____

Answers are on page 376

Body Builders

There are few photos that exist of all seven brothers whose last name has become synonymous with cars built by General Motors. Can you identify any of them by their given names, or even just their last?

FoMoCo First

Give the correct model year for these 12 debuts by Ford Motor Company.

1. First Mercury produced _____

2. Ford-O-Matic transmission introduced _____

3. Debut of plexiglass Crestline Skyliner hardtop _____

4. Intro of woody Sportsman convertible _____

5. First Ford Falcon _____

6. Arrival of the DeTomaso Pantera _____

7. The first flathead V-8 _____

8. T-Bird Sports/Roadster available _____

9. Ford Victoria hardtop debuts _____

10. First Galaxie 500XL _____

11. Two-piece vee windshield that opens outward _____

12. Introduction of retractable Fairlane 500 Skyliner convertible _____

Flattery

The classic "coffin nose" Cord front-end design from 1937 has been imitated by several other car brands over the decades. Can you identify the year and make for each car?

1. _____

2. _____

3. _____

4. _____

Answers are on page 376

'Lil' HUSTLER

Which car/truck manufacturer offered a pickup model named "Lil' Hustler"?

Exotic GT Sports

Can you correctly match the model name to each of these 10 off-shore cars?

CAR MAKE	MODEL
1. Lamborghini	Alpine
2. Bentley	Eclat
3. Maserati	Interceptor
4. Aston Martin	Khamsin
5. Jensen	Lagonda
6. Lancia	Mondial
7. Alfa Romeo	Mulsanne
8. Ferrari	Spider
9. Renault	Urraco
10. Lotus	Zagato

Zealous Patriot

This suburban housewife always goes grocery shopping dressed as the Statue of Liberty, and her husband as Uncle Sam. They just love America.
In what year and make antique auto are they being chauffeured?

Year _____   Make _____

Answers are on page 376

263

Dreams Come True #2

These four automotive fantasies have model names that eventually were used on production cars. Identify these "dream machines" by year, make and model.

1. _____

2. _____

3. _____

4. _____

Badge Brainbusters

The clever emblem designs shown below symbolize five different auto models. Name the models and makes they represent.

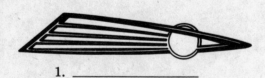

1. _____

2. _____

3. _____

4. _____

5. _____

Answers are on page 376

Rear View

The variety of mid-60's rear designs is clearly illustrated by the six tail views shown below. Correctly give the year and make for each car.

2. _____

1. _____

3. _____

4. _____

6. _____

5. _____

"Shifty" Hurst

1. What model year and make of car first offered Hurst shifters as optional factory equipment?

2. What was the first model year that Oldsmobile and Hurst teamed up on a production car?

3. What year did Hurst first offer their "Hurst Hatch" T-Tops?

4. What make and model car was the Hurst "Rescue System 1" vehicle?

5. What model year was the limited-edition Hurst Chrysler 300?

6. What is the real name of "Miss Hurst Golden Shifter" pictured above?

7. What model year is the SSJ Grand Prix she is standing in?

8. The 1966 "Hairy Olds" was powered by what unique engine set-up?

9. Who is known as the Hurst "Shifty Doc"?

10. What model year Barracuda bodyshell was first used for the famous "Hemi-Under Glass"?

Billboard #4

Year _____

Make _____

Number of cylinders _____

EASY TO LOOK AT
··· EASY TO OWN

$1165

AT DETROIT FACTORY
TAXES EXTRA

J. E. COBERLY, Inc.   Distributor   1357 N. VINE & 827 S. FIGUEROA, LOS ANGELES

1966~70 Toronado Front Ends

These first-generation Toronado front-end designs include some mighty "macho" grilles. Give the correct year for each.

1. _____

2. _____

3. _____

4. _____

5. _____

TV..."And Now a Word From Our Sponsors!"

Match the car brand to the correct TV show it sponsored.

CAR	TV PROGRAM
1. Chevrolet	A. Howdy Doody Show
2. Dodge	B. Maverick
3. Edsel	C. Mr. Ed
4. Ford	D. Sing Along with Mitch
5. Jeep (Kaiser-Jeep)	E. Jerry Lewis
6. Oldsmobile	F. Bonanza
7. Pontiac	G. Lawrence Welk
8. Studebaker	H. Dragnet

TREE~MENDOUS

Which auto company used this sturdy "tree of knowledge" symbol during the early 1930's?

MOTORS · STANDARDIZED QUALITY ·

Answers are on page 376

Silhouettes #2

Cars of the 60's and 70's came in all shapes and contours. Give the correct year(s), make and model for the six cars shown in profile below.

1. _____

2. _____

3. _____

4. _____

5. _____

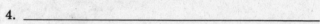

6. _____

STAR SHIP COMMANDER

Who is the fellow in the driver's seat, and what year and make of dream machine is he piloting?

Answers are on page 376

Grille Greats #1

What a wild variety of aggressive-looking front ends. These six pictures cover three decades. Give the year, make and model for each design.

1. _____

2. _____

3. _____

4. _____

5. _____

6. _____

Answers are on page 376

SUPER BIRD

Fill in the dimensions and engine blanks on the 1970 Plymouth Road Runner Superbird, and also the correct answers to the questions below.

1. How many model years was this model offered?_____

2. What did Dodge name its version of this design?_____

3. Was the angle of the rear wing adjustable?_____

4. Three engines were available on the Superbird. Which was *not* offered by Dodge?_____

5. Which of the Superbird's seven colors was named after a famous race driver?_____

His & Hers

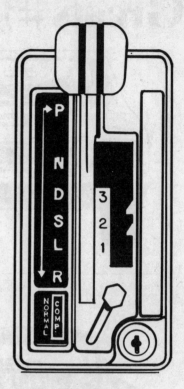

1. What aftermarket company offered this innovating transmission control gimmick?

   _____

2. What was this system named?_____

3. What was the "her" feature?_____

4. With the turn of a key you had the "His" feature. What did this allow you to do?_____

5. What two car models were advertised as being the first to offer this special shifter, and what car company was to follow shortly?_____

Answers are on page 376

Show Girls

Live, on stage, at the annual auto show, are these
12 stylish bodies.
Identify the year and make of cars behind each
smile.

1. _____

2. _____

3. _____

4. _____

5. _____

6. _____

License to Quiz #2

1. Which state had a grapefruit on its plate back in 1935? _____

2. What was the first year the shape of the state of Kansas appeared on its plate? _____

3. Which state had a bison's skull imprinted on a license plate? _____

4. What presidents appear on the South Dakota plate? _____

5. What's the motto for Wyoming plates? _____

6. The motto: "Funnel For World Commerce," appears on the plate of what U.S. Territory? _____

Toronado Fronts

These second-generation Toronado front-end designs are quite similar in appearance, making your task of identifying the correct year for each that much harder.

1. _____

2. _____

3. _____

4. _____

5. _____

6. _____

272

Answers are on page 377

VETTE QUICKIE #2

Four more Corvette front views that need to be correctly identified by their years.

1. _____

2. _____

3. _____

4. _____

Official Results

In the 1958 Mobilgas Economy Run, 29 new stock cars were driven 1,883 miles from Los Angeles to Galveston. Below are six of those contenders. Can you correctly match them to their surprising MPG?

MAKE	MPG
1. Chevrolet V-8	20.8
2. Dodge	20.5
3. Edsel	19.2
4. Ford 6	18.7
5. Imperial	18.0
6. Lincoln Continental	17.8

Answers are on page 377

Five Generations

Five different Mercedes-Benz models are displayed below. To the best of your ability, identify the years each was produced, and the model number(s) as sold in the U.S.

1. From ___ to ___

   Model #___SL

2. From ___ to ___

   Model #_ /_ /_ SL

3. From ___ to ___

   Model #_ / _ SL

4. From ___ to ___

   Model #___SL roadster

5. From ___ to ___

   Model #___SL coupe

Mystery Hubcaps

What make of car offered these six full-cover hubcaps, and can you give the correct model year for each design?

1. _____

2. _____

3. _____

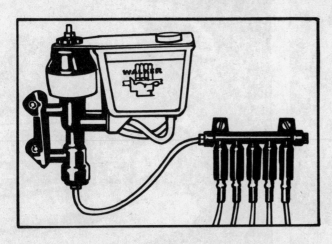

4. _____

5. _____

6. _____

What is it? #4

Looking like a cow milking machine, this $24.95 device was to provide what type of full-time automotive service?

_____

Heavy Traffic MPG

The six 1951 auto brands listed below were all tested for their fuel consumption while driven in heavy traffic.
Take a guess and match the car make to the miles per gallon rating it reached during the rush hour tests.

CAR MAKE	MPG RATING
1. Packard	A. 9.6
2. Mercury	B. 11.3
3. Chrysler	C. 12.8
4. Henry J	D. 13.4
5. Hudson Hornet	E. 14.8
6. Buick	F. 23.2

Answers are on page 377

Gimmicks and Gadgets #3

There are six auto novelties shown in the photos below. Can you describe what they are? Give the year and make for each picture.

1. _____

2. _____

3. _____

4. _____

5. _____

6. _____

Answers are on page 377

Sign Language #2

Driving your favorite set of wheels through a federal park, you are confronted by six recreation symbols that need identification. Do you know what each of these signs stand for?

1. _____

2. _____

3. _____

4. _____

5. _____

6. _____

As the World Turns

Buick Riviera and Oldsmobile Toronado offered auxiliary turn signals as standard equipment back in the 1970's.

1. For what model year did Olds introduce this safety-minded gimmick?

2. How many model years after Olds did Buick first offer this novel idea?

3. What was the last model year that Buick offered this lighting system?

4. What was the last model year for Oldsmobile's auxiliary turn signals?

TIRELESS TYCOONS

We who love to cruise around in cars owe a lot to these two geniuses. Can you identify them?

1. _____

2. _____

Rubber Man

You've seen this character on TV, billboards, in newspapers and magazines. Can you answer these simple questions?

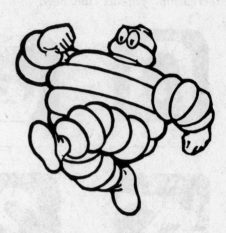

1. What company does he represent?

2. What is his full name?

3. What do his friends call him?

4. How old is he?
   A. Nearly a century old   B. 125 years old
   C. 133 years old

Prototype

Which car brand considered these far-out designs for its proposed 1962 model?

278

Answers are on page 377

Knudsen Kar

Semon E. "Bunkie" Knudsen was the spearhead behind Pontiac's dramatic transformation from dull to dynamic back in the Mid-1950's. One of his first contributions was this limited-production convertible.

1. What is the year and model name for this car?

2. How many units were built the first year?
   A. 630   B. 1000   C. 2300

3. What cubic-inch block was standard under the hood?
   A. 327   B. 347   C. 370

4. What kind of fuel feeders sat on top of this engine?
   A. Tri-power   B. Fuel Injection
   C. Dual Quads

5. What was the average miles per gallon rating on this muscle machine?
   A. 11-13 mpg   B. 14-16 mpg   C. 17-18 mpg

6. What was the retail price?
   A. $3,988   B. $4,685   C. $5,782

7. What was the Hydra-Matic transmission name?
   A. Strato-shift   B. Turbo-strato
   C. Strato-Flight

8. Where on the exterior body of this model is the Pontiac name plate?

GAS WAR

When this picture was taken in Los Angeles on February 20, 1950, a consumers dream was spreading across America—a gas war!

Can you come within 3¢ of the retail prices shown on the sign?

Lil' Ramblers

The Rambler American/Rogue front 3/4 views from the 50's and 60's have such sly differences that they may prove difficult when you try to identify the correct model year.

1. _____

2. _____

3. _____

4. _____

5. _____

6. _____

7. _____

8. _____

Answers are on page 377

Birth Announcement

How many seconds are shown on the sign above this computerized tabulator, which appeared at the Chicago Auto Show in the mid-1960's?

EVERY ___ SECONDS A CAR IS BORN

73527082

UNITED STATES MOTOR VEHICLE POPULATION

_____

Star Endorsement

The lists below are of six famous celebrities and the year and make car they endorsed at one time. Can you match the star with the car?

STAR	CAR
1. Jack Dempsey	A. 1936 Dodge
2. Bob Hope	B. 1937 Studebaker
3. Ted Williams	C. 1938 DeSoto
4. Charlie Brown and Snoopy	D. 1939 DeSoto
5. Walt Disney	E. 1951 Dodge
6. Shirley Temple	F. 1962-65 Ford Falcon

Key Bobbers #4

Which three car brands used the key bob emblems below?

1. _____

2. _____

3. _____

Can't Dodge 'Em

Supply the correct model year for these four designs from Dodge.
Bonus: What model is #4?

1. _____

2. _____

3. _____

4. _____

Stars in Cars #2

Star _____ Make of car _____

Answers are on page 377

CODE 7

These off-duty policemen are impressing the pretty show girls with their vintage patrol car.
Can you identify the year and make of this automobile and the eight differences between pictures #1 and #2?

_____ _____
_____ _____
_____ _____

BEACH PARTY BAFFLE

These new-wave teenagers are on their way to pick up Annette and Frankie for some surfing at Malibu Beach. In what year and make woody do they cruise in?

Year _____   Make _____

A Rare Sight

Quick, in your side view mirror there is an oldie, but very rare goodie.
Can you identify the year and make of this car?

Year _____

Make _____

Sounds Good

The picture above is of the first commercially successful car radio.

1. What year was this radio introduced?

   _____

2. What is the famous brand name for this early radio?

   _____

3. Who was the man most responsible for its creation?

   _____

Answers are on page 378

SPEEDWAYS

Not all racing tracks are ovals, as these eight plans from the 1960's demonstrate.
Can you match the raceway names to their unique configuration?

Bridgehampton   Indianapolis   Langhorne   Mexican Grand Prix
Elkhart Lake   Laguna Seca   Marlboro   Phoenix

1. _____

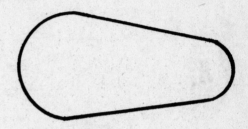

5. _____

2. _____

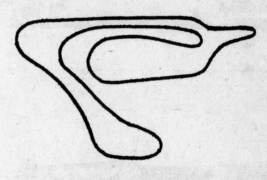

6. _____

3. _____

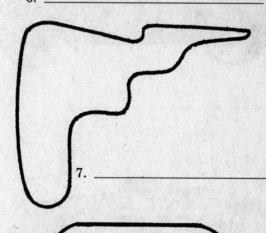

7. _____

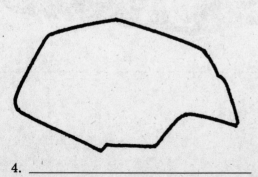

4. _____

8. _____

Answers are on page 378

Top These #2

Six dynamite convertibles are shown below. Identify the correct model year and car brand of each ragtop.

2. _____

1. _____

4. _____

3. _____

6. _____

5. _____

Answers are on page 378

Indy Trilogies

A racing car driver would have to be blessed with enormous talent, incredible endurance, and a little luck in order to win the Indy 500 three times.
Pictured below are four men who have accomplished this amazing feat. Can you identify them and give the triple years each won?

1. _____

2. _____

3. _____

4. _____

Rolling Records #3

SIDE A:
Three Window Coupe

by _____

SIDE B:
Little Deuce Coupe

by _____

Horse Racing 1954

1954 was the last year before the industry-wide V-8 boom and horsepower battles that lasted into the 1970's.
Match the correct car make to the maximum horsepower it offered that year.

CAR BRAND	HORSE POWER
1. Cadillac	A. 100
2. Ford	B. 125
3. Buick	C. 130
4. Lincoln	D. 150
5. Plymouth	E. 200
6. Chrysler	F. 205
7. Chevrolet	G. 230
8. Dodge	H. 235

Answers are on page 378

Bewildering Bumpers #1

It may prove tough, but can you identify the year and make of cars simply by their front bumpers and a section of grille?
Live dangerously and try to recognize the eight designs shown below.

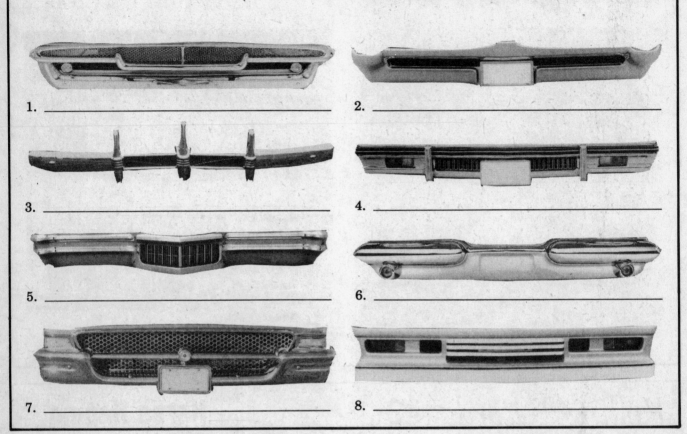

1. _____

2. _____

3. _____

4. _____

5. _____

6. _____

7. _____

8. _____

FIRST PRIZE

This great outdoor billboard won many artistic and commercial grand prize awards.
Can you guess the correct model year this artwork was advertised?
Hint: It was Buick's first year for eight-cylinder engines.

"Boy...that's travelin'!"

BUICK VIII

Hey, Sport Fans!

What was America's favorite spectator sport in 1930?
Well, correctly match the crowd attendance to these five events and you'll know.

EVENT	CROWD
1. Horse Racing	64,000
2. Auto Racing	85,000
3. Baseball	116,000
4. Football	145,000
5. Boxing	163,000

Answers are on page 378

Dagmars

The similarity between the missle-shaped Cadillac bumperettes and a buxom, tight-sweatered blonde comedienne of the early 50's is all in the eye of the beholder.
Can you name the year for these six sets?

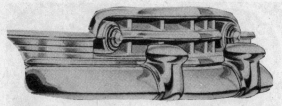

1. _____

2. _____

3. _____

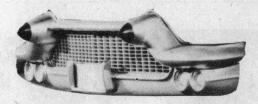

4. _____

5. _____

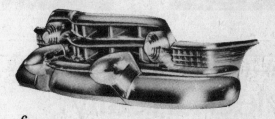

6. _____

Gallant Men?

Dr. Oldsmobile, the mad car scientist from the 1960-70 muscle era, had a performance committee that included some bizarre individuals.
Can you fill in the full names for Dr. Old's top five assistants?

1. _____ _____ Ernie

2. _____ Sidney

3. _____ _____ Waldo

4. _____ Fernhill

5. HY _____

Answers are on page 378

HUB HYSTERIA #3

Hubba hubba, here we go again trying to test your wheel cover/hub knowledge.
What make of cars used the eight designs laid out below?

1. _____

2. _____

3. _____

4. _____

5. _____

6. _____

7. _____

8. _____

Mechanically Minded #3

Can you unscramble these nine component names and match them to the correct differential parts illustrated below?

6. _____

1. _____

2. _____

8. _____

7. _____

TO DRIVE SHAFT

3. _____

9. _____

4. _____

5. _____

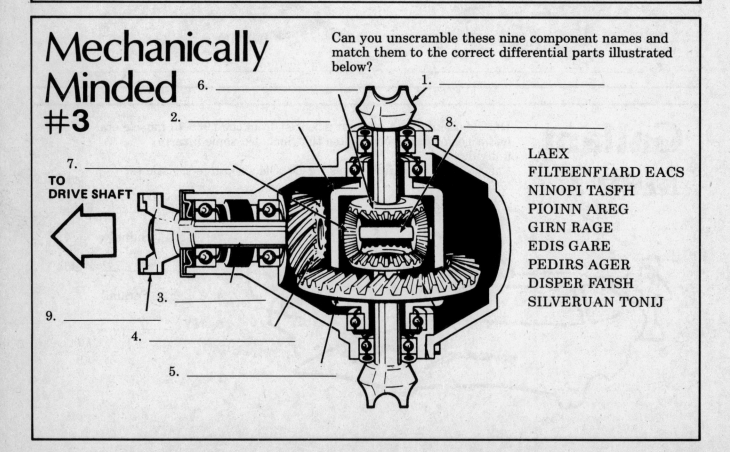

LAEX
FILTEENFIARD EACS
NINOPI TASFH
PIOINN AREG
GIRN RAGE
EDIS GARE
PEDIRS AGER
DISPER FATSH
SILVERUAN TONIJ

Answers are on page 378

DREAM STAR

The experimental car shown has racked up quite a career since its introduction. If you feel educated enough, take this brief history test on "Dream Star."

1. Name this show car._____
2. What year did it debut?_____
3. Horsepower rating?_____
4. In what movie did it co-star with Debbie Reynolds?_____
5. What two functions did the free standing disk mounted on the trunk lid serve?_____

6. Where and how did you shift the automatic transmission? _____
7. What was the overall length and height?_____
8. What famous TV car did "Dream Star" become after a radical customizing?_____

Answers are on page 378

Pontiac Pickers

Below are eight Pontiac front ends. Can you match the full-size design on the left to the same model year compact version on the right?

FULL SIZE

COMPACT

1. _____

2. _____

3. _____

4. _____

A.

B.

C.

D.

Answers are on page 378

Dreams Come True #3

All of the machines shown below have model names that were eventually used on production cars. Identify these dream cars by their year, make and model.

1. _____

2. _____

3. _____

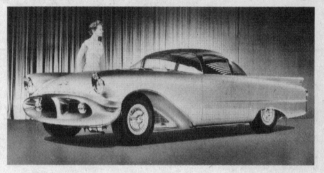

4. _____

Six Cylinder Quickies

1. Which car make had a standard 90 H.P. six-cylinder F-head engine?
   A. Oldsmobile   B. Nash   C. Aero Willys

2. In what year did Oldsmobile discontinue six-cylinder engines?
   A. 1946   B. 1950   C. 1955

3. In 1932, who used the ad slogan "Six Cylinders—No More, No Less"?
   A. Chevrolet   B. Hudson   C. DeSoto

4. Plymouth received its first six-cylinder engine in which year?
   A. 1930   B. 1933   C. 1939

5. Which car came equipped with a 235 cu. in. six with three side-draft carburetors?
   A. Corvette   B. Packard   C. Graham

6. What was the first model year for Buick's V-6 engine?
   A. 1961   B. 1962   C. 1963

SMILEAGE

Which tire company urged you to "stop at the sign of the smiling tire"?

_____

Stars in Cars #3

Star _____

Year and make of car _____

FARAWAY PLACES #3

You can travel the world just on the model names used for cars through the years. Give the correct name that fits each definition.

1. A Chrysler city in southern Spain _____

2. A Packard sea between South and Central America _____

3. A Cadillac city in southwestern France _____

4. An AMC capital of New Hampshire _____

5. A Mercury that's an island off western Italy _____

6. A Chrysler New England town _____

7. A Buick street in New York city _____

8. A Lincoln city in northern France _____

9. A Pontiac salt flat in Utah _____

10. A Chevrolet town outside of Los Angeles _____

11. A Dodge principality on the Mediterranean _____

12. A Pontiac island off southern California _____

Car Tunes #2

1. What model year is mentioned in the hit song "Mustang Sally"?

2. In 1954, there was a song titled "Buick 59." What group recorded it?

3. What was the luxury car Janis Joplin asked the Lord for?

4. In the song "Beep Beep," what make of car is stuck in second gear, and what make of car did it race?

Passing Dreams #2

Identify these fleeting visions of the future as they flick their tail ends at you. Give the year, make and model.

1. _____

2. _____

3. _____

4. _____

5. _____

6. _____

Answers are on page 379

TAIL WATCHING

Pictured below are the southern exposures of eight northbound American cars. As dramatically different as these taillights are, can you still identify the year, make and model of each design?

1. _____

2. _____

3. _____

4. _____

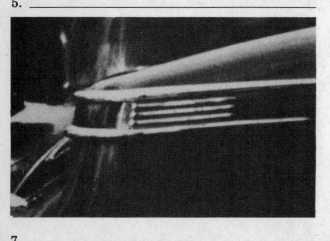

5. _____

6. _____

7. _____

8. _____

Answers are on page 379

Engine Weight

Can you match the approximate weight in pounds to these six different engines?

CAR MAKE AND ENGINE	ENGINE WEIGHT
1. Rambler 327 cu. in.	A. 330 lbs
2. Oldsmobile 394 cu. in.	B. 465 lbs
3. Chrysler 392 cu. in.	C. 530 lbs
4. Valiant 170 cu. in.	D. 600 lbs
5. Buick 215 cu. in.	E. 715 lbs
6. Chevrolet 283 cu. in.	F. 765 lbs

Look but Don't Touch #3

Roped in so as not to be soiled by fingerprints, this experimental sports car was trimmed in copper, brass, and bronze.

1. What year was this sexy-looking machine first displayed?

2. What was its hyphenated name?

3. What make of V-8 engine powered this two-seater?

4. How many cubic inches?

5. Who had this vehicle built for promotional purposes?

CB Lingo

What do each of these CB terms really mean?

1. Tijuana taxi

2. Six-wheeler

3. Pregnant roller skate

4. Smokey with ears

5. Kenosha Cadillac

6. Bodacious

7. Catch you on the old flip/flop

8. Hammer

9. Train station

10. Green Stamps

11. Shake the leaves

12. Two-wheeler

13. Wrapper

14. Picture taker

15. Seat covers

16. Back door

17. Chicken coop

18. Keep the greasy side down and the shiny side up

Raindrops
Keep Falling

Keeping the elements out of your convertible can take on various
styles of coverings.
Identify the six cars shown below by year and make.

1. _____

2. _____

3. _____

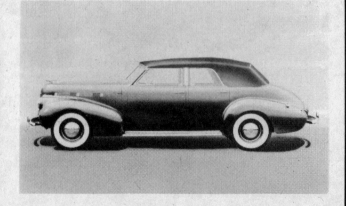

4. _____

5. _____

6. _____

Answers are on page 379

Suspension Quickie

WHEEL
TO
WHEEL
SECURITY

1. What steering and suspension parts manufacturer used this symbol? _____

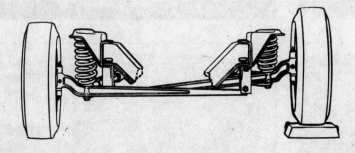

2. A. Which truck manufacturer used this independent front suspension on their pickups? _____

   B. What was the first model year for this design? _____

   C. What was the advertised name? _____

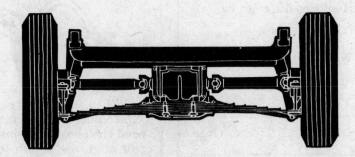

3. What American car make used this independent rear suspension? _____

Here Today, #1 Gone Tomorrow

What was the single model year for the eight cars listed below?

1. 19_____ Olds 4-4-2 four-door Sedan

2. 19_____ Packard Hawk

3. 19_____ Dodge Charger Daytona

4. 19_____ Pontiac Trans-Am Convertible

5. 19_____ Edsel Citation

6. 19_____ Mercury Cyclone Spoiler II

7. 19_____ Plymouth Barracuda Gran Coupe convertible

8. 19_____ Corvair Monza Wagon

How Much?

This service station manager had a tire sale going on when this picture was snapped on June 9, 1950.
Can you guess the unbelievable price he was asking per tire?

Dashing Designs

Six different dashboard and steering wheel configurations are grouped below.
Identify the correct year and make of car that used these instrument panels.

1. _____

2. _____

3. _____

4. _____

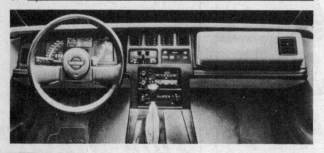

5. _____

6. _____

DUAL PERSONALITIES

What three individual auto pioneers have had two different car brands named after them?

NAME

A. _____

B. _____

C. _____

CAR NAME SAKE

1. _____
2. _____

1. _____
2. _____

1. _____
2. _____

Steer Clear

Which auto manufacturer used the above drawing of a pair of gloves, a shift lever, and a very unusual steering wheel in their ads?

_____

Answers are on page 379

TV Car #2

1. What is the name of the television program that stars the custom Trans-Am shown above?_____

2. What is the name of this computerized car in the show?
   _____

3. This name stands for what?_____

High Octane

In 1969 you could have pumped one of these super gasolines into your muscle machine for a performance boost.
Can you match gas brand to the correct octane rating?

BRAND	OCTANE
1. Amoco Super Premium	A. 98.7
2. Blue Sunoco 260	B. 99.4
3. Cities Service 100 Plus	C. 100.4
4. Pure Firebird Super	D. 101.7
5. Super Shell	E. 101.8

Hood Winked

What year and make of automobile sported these sleek hood ornaments?

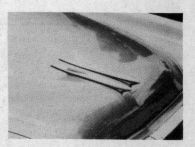

1. _____

2. _____

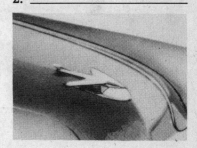

3. _____

4. _____

Falcon Fronts

The skill of the auto designer is evident by the clever interpretations of the same basic design. Give the appropriate year to these six similar Ford Falcon front ends.

1. _____

2. _____

3. _____

4. _____

5. _____

6. _____

Answers are on page 379

Safe Steering

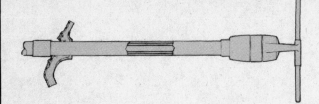

In picture 1 you see the old traditional steering column design. Picture 2 is of a safer steering column created to meet government regulations. What was the first model year that the newer design was required?
What were its two characteristics?

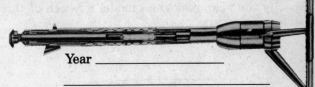

Year _____

_____

Chrysler–300 Word Quiz

Sometimes there can be much confusion concerning Chrysler 300s, especially with the mixing of the letter series and the normal line of 300 models. The 12 questions in this quiz touch on some of the significant details that highlight the reign of this milestone car.

1. The first year the high performance Chrysler 300 was offered to the power hungry public was in nineteen _____.

2. When Chrysler chose the name "300," it was in honor of the fact that this model was the first production car to have an engine with _____.

3. The last Chrysler 300 to come with tailfins was the letter series _____, which was the nineteen _____ model.

4. The first year you could purchase a muscular 300 as a convertible model was in nineteen _____.

5. The Chrysler 300 became a full-line series, along with the letter models, beginning with the nineteen _____ cars.

6. Two of the letter series did not offer a convertible model. They are the letter _____ in nineteen _____ and the letter _____ in nineteen _____.

7. Pushbutton transmission first came with the nineteen _____ model, and was last used on the nineteen _____ version.

8. The last year for the full-line Chrysler Three Hundred was in nineteen _____.

9. The wedge-shaped Mopar engine replaced the celebrated hemi-head design beginning with letter _____ for nineteen _____.

10. The final letter year for the Chrysler 300 was in nineteen _____ with the letter _____.

11. Bob Rodger is considered by many experts to be the _____ of the powerful three hundreds.

12. A limited edition in the Chrysler Cordoba series was the reintroduced 300 model in nineteen _____.

Answers are on pages 379-80

GRILLE GREATS #2

There are six cars from the mid-60s shown below, but only by their front-end designs.
Specify the year, make and model for each of these performance cars.

1 _____

2 _____

3 _____

4 _____

5 _____

6 _____

Answers are on page 380

Leapin' Logos

What a strange-looking symbol this running/jumping character with the horns and tail made back in the 1960's, but the product name is even wilder.

1. What was the macho name for the aftermarket product that used this logo?

   _____

2. What kind of product was it?_____

3. Who was the manufacturer?_____

Corporate Giants #2

These four portraits are of auto executives whose talents gave needed leadership to various car companies. Name these men and the auto companies they commanded.

1. _____

2. _____

3. _____

4. _____

INDY 500 PACE CARS 1954-64

The 1950's and 1960's marked the high-performance age for most production cars. The brands picked to pace the Indianapolis 500 were excellent examples from that era. Match the correct pacer with its awarded year.

1. 1954	A. Chrysler
2. 1955	B. Pontiac
3. 1956	C. Ford
4. 1957	Thunderbird
5. 1958	D. Studebaker
6. 1959	E. Oldsmobile
7. 1960	F. Dodge
8. 1961	G. Ford Mustang
9. 1962	H. Chevrolet
10. 1963	I. Buick
11. 1964	J. Mercury
	K. DeSoto

Answers are on page 380

PANEL PLEASERS

Six excellent panel designs are pictured below
and require you to deliver their correct year and
make.

2. _____

1. _____

3. _____

4. _____

6. _____

5. _____

306

Answers are on page 380

Bird's-Eye-View #3

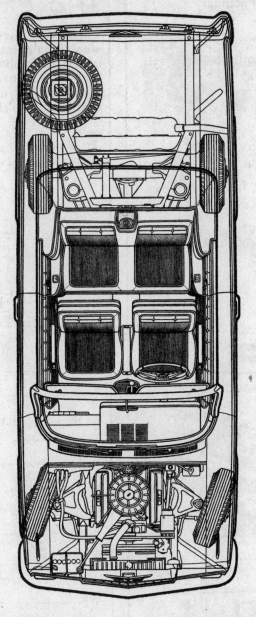

Like Superman, you are able to fly above this car and with X-ray vision see right through it.
Clark Kent can answer these questions. Can you?

1. What make of car is pictured above?_____

2. What model year is it?_____

3. In cubic inches, what were the three V-8 engine blocks offered on this model? _____

4. The largest V-8 with dual quads and solid lifters put out how much horsepower?_____

Smilin' Symbol

1. Which oil company used this happy little gas drop character as its logo?
_____

2. What word is needed under "Happy" to finish the motto?_____

Slick Symbols #9

Can you name the oil company that this graphic symbol represented?

_____

Answers are on page 380

All Wheel Drive

Can you give the correct make for each of these popular four-wheel drive vehicles?

1. _____

2. _____

3. _____

A Rose is a Rose #2

There must have been something special in the model names shown below, because they were all used by two or more different manufacturers. Can you name them?

1. Matador
   _____
   _____

2. Executive
   _____
   _____

3. Skylark
   _____
   _____

4. Corsair
   _____
   _____

5. Super Sport
   _____
   _____

6. Daytona
   _____
   _____

7. GTO
   _____
   _____

8. Concord
   _____
   _____

9. Falcon
   _____
   _____

10. Cavalier
    _____
    _____

Answers are on page 380

Memories #3

1. What single letter belongs on this winged gasoline station sign? _____

2. What make of truck is filling the station's underground tanks? _____

3. How many gallons of gas could the above truck carry?
   A. 25,000   B. 36,000   C. 42,000

Indy 500 Pace Cars 1965-1975

Muscle cars were kings during these 11 years and the Indy 500 pace cars included some of the best.
Match the 11 pace cars with the correct year(s). Note, use Chevrolet Camaro and Hurst/Olds twice.

1. 1965	A. Oldsmobile 4-4-2
2. 1966	B. Ford Torino
3. 1967	C. Buick Regal
4. 1968	D. Hurst/Olds
5. 1969	E. Plymouth Sport Fury
6. 1970	F. Cadillac Eldorado
7. 1971	G. Mercury Comet Cyclone
8. 1972	H. Chevrolet Camaro
9. 1973	I. Dodge Challenger
10. 1974	
11. 1975	

Hubba Bubba

What was the first model year that some car makers offered optional air cushion restraint systems?

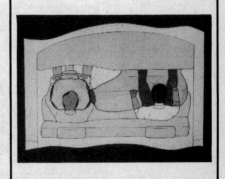

Answers are on page 380

HUB HYSTERIA #4

Around and around you'll go trying to identify the correct makes that wore the 12 steel hub or wheel cover designs shown below.

1. _____

2. _____

3. _____

4. _____

5. _____

6. _____

7. _____

8. _____

9. _____

10. _____

11. _____

12. _____

Answers are on page 380

Trivial Twenty

1. What were the first and last model years for factory-built Cadillac Eldorado convertibles? _____

2. Checker cabs from 1965 to 1982 have been powered by what other manufacturer's six and V-8 engines?_____

3. In what month and year did Chevrolet build its last Corvair? _____

4. What was so unusual about the driver's side-rear passenger door on the 1949 Kaiser Traveler?_____

5. Which car brand in 1960 offered three engines named Turbo-Flash, Mark I, and Ram Charge?_____

6. For how many model years did Ford offer a hardtop with a transparent plexiglass roof panel?_____

7. Ford named its transparent-roof hardtop Skyliner. What did Mercury call its version? _____

8. In what year did American Motors acquire the Kaiser-Jeep Corporation?_____

9. What kind of car did Richard Nixon give to USSR's Leonid Brezhnev in 1972?_____

10. What was the full official name of the 1939-40 Continental built by Lincoln?_____

11. Which car company is credited with the introduction of fender skirts?_____

12. For what model year were fender skirts first offered?_____

13. "Square Bird," refers to which three-year Thunderbird design?_____

14. In what year did George Romney resign as president and chairman of American Motors because he was elected governor of Michigan?_____

15. For how many consecutive years did Buick offer cars styled with Ventiport holes on their front fenders?_____

16. What was the name of the *nine*-passenger DeSoto for 1946-48?_____

17. What name did Ford give its 289 cu. in. engine in the original Mustangs?_____

18. In what model year did the public first have "Dodge Fever"?_____

19. What did Hudson call its new compact car for 1953?_____

20. What foreign country used the Kaiser body dies to manufacture cars called "Carabella" in the late 1950's?_____

American Ruling Class #3

Majestic-sounding names have appeared on various cars through the years. Match the correct make to each model name.

MODEL NAME	MAKE
1. President	A. Buick
2. Chieftain	B. Chrysler
3. Diplomat	C. Chevrolet
4. Fleetmaster	D. Pontiac
5. Roadmaster	E. Mercury
6. Powermaster	F. Studebaker
7. Monarch	G. Dodge
8. Windsor	H. DeSoto

Slick Symbols

Can you name the oil company that this graphic symbol represented?

The Lower Forties #2

Unbelievable, but you lucked out again and found Old Macdonald's brother and his field of vintage cars. Can you identify the correct year and make for each automobile?

1. _____

2. _____

3. _____

4. _____

5. _____

6. _____

Answers are on page 381

Guilt Trip

Don't get paranoid, but check your side view mirror. What year and make cop car is following you?

What's Up, Doc?

What three-word professional-sounding title should be on the coat patch of this sincere spokesperson? What aftermarket company did he represent?

Mystery Car

Can you answer the following questions on the three-wheel four-passenger car illustrated below?

1. What was the name of this vehicle? _____

2. What size engine powered it? _____
_____

3. What was the horsepower rating? _____

4. What was the: wheelbase in inches, height in inches, and curb weight in pounds? _____

Club Page
Kaiser-Fraser-Willys

The following 20 questions were compiled by the International Kaiser-Frazer Owners Club to test your knowledge on these automobiles.

1. Who is responsible for the body design of the 1947 Kaiser and Frazer and the 1951 Kaiser?

2. What was the only difference between the 1954 and 1955 Kaiser styling?

3. Who designed the Willys Aero?

4. In what years were Kaiser-Darrins built?

5. Which figure represents total Willys Aero production?
   A. 513,721   B. 92,036   C. 37,908   D. 1,075,436

6. Who built the Woodill Wildfire?

7. Kaiser-Frazer was known for color-coordinated interiors and exciting fabric designs. Who was the man responsible for the interior design?

8. For what model years were Henry Js built?

9. How many production Henry Js were equipped with Hydra-Matic transmissions?

10. What was the name of the badge-engineered Henry J marketed through Sears & Roebuck stores?

11. Kaiser-Frazer introduced the first fiberglas-bodied car to the American public, beating the Corvette into production by half a year. What was the name of the car?

12. For what model years were Allstates built?

13. After production ended in the U.S.A., Willys built cars in South America. With what country was it associated?

14. In the 1960's, Kaiser and Willys assembled European cars in South America under license and marketed them under their own names. What cars were used and what were they called?

15. Who styled the South American Willys Aero models in the early 1960's?

16. There was something special about the original Kaiser prototype shown at the Waldorf-Astoria in 1946. What was it?

17. In 1951, a flashy, top-of-the-line Kaiser with special vinyl upholstery was introduced. The car was named after the vinyl. What was the name of both?

18. A later edition of this vinyl upholstery was issued. What was it called?

19. For what model years were Willys Aeros built?

20. Both Kaiser and Willys built taxicabs. True or false?

Answers are on page 381

So Surrey

Just for the frill of it, answer the following questions under each picture.

PICTURE 1

A. In what model year did Willys Motors introduce the Jeep Surrey?_____

B. The candy stripe top could be trimmed in one of three color selections. What were the choices?_____

C. What was the primary purpose behind these fun vehicles?_____

PICTURE 2

A. What auto manufacturer produced this compact surrey car?_____

B. What was this vehicle's happy-sounding model name?_____

PICTURE 3

A. What is the year, make and model of this four-doorless wagon?_____

B. What ABC TV series did the car star in?

_____

Answers are on page 381

Truly the Triviest #2

1. For what model year did front seat belts become standard equipment on all U.S. cars?

2. What was the first model year for seat belts as standard on Corvettes?

3. How much does a gallon of gasoline weigh?

4. What city and state installed the first parking meter?

5. What year was the first parking meter installed?

6. What is the name for the famous Indy 500 portrait trophy?

7. Which ex-GM executive co-authored *On a Clear Day You Can See General Motors*?

8. In what year did the first drive-in church open?

9. What city and state did the first drive-in church open in?

10. Which of the Smothers Brothers is a race car enthusiast?

11. What was Plymouth's humorous Latin name for its cartoon Road Runner bird?

12. Dustin Hoffman was the on camera spokesman for which 1964 automobile?

13. For what year did Ford introduce a reversible key?

14. What year did Firestone drop out of auto racing sponsorship?

15. What do the initials SAE stand for on auto related products?

16. Which car is credited with introducing the first automatic cruise control, and for which model year?

17. When was Volkswagen's best sales year?

18. In what year did all states adopt 12×6-inch size license plates?

19. Which 1966 American car had a split transmission using chain drive?

20. Cardmembers of which company could once order through a catalog a 24-karat goldplated $85,000 DeLorean?

21. What make of car was the first to be awarded to a Playboy "Playmate of The Year"?

22. The last car to be manufactured in Chicago was built back in 1930. What make was it?

23. What American auto corporation was the exclusive distributor of Mercedes-Benz motor cars in 1958?

24. It takes an average of how many parts to build an automobile?

Answers are on page 381

International Intrigue #3

Six cars from around the globe are assembled below.
Identify their make, model and country.

1. _____

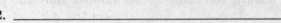

2. _____

3. _____

4. _____

5. _____

6. _____

Answers are on page 381

Rush Hour

These early-morning motorists make their way to work or school back in the mid-1950's.
Identify as many cars as you can by their year and make.

1. _____
2. _____
3. _____
4. _____
5. _____
6. _____
7. _____
8. _____
9. _____
10. _____
11. _____
12. _____

Four Eyes

1957 and 1958 were the years for the introduction of dual headlights on most major car brands.
Separate the 10 names listed here and place under either 1957 or 1958.

1957	1958	CAR MAKE
		Cadillac
		Continental
		Buick
		DeSoto
		Imperial
		Lincoln
		Mercury
		Nash
		Packard
		Rambler

EASY RIDER

Which year and make of automobile offered the radically new "Rhythmic Ride," featuring knee-action suspension?

REVOLUTIONARY NEW
RHYTHMIC RIDE!

BASED ON
1. QUADRI-COIL SPRINGING!
2. 4-WAY STABILIZATION!
3. KNEE-ACTION WHEELS!

Year_____ Make_____

Daydreams #4

Show cars from the distant past would cause "daydreaming" among car lovers. They would have visions of cruising in similar machines with eye-catching styling and advanced engineering. Give the correct year, make and model name for each of these one-of-a-kinds.

1. _____

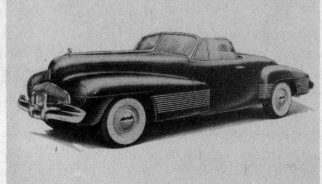

2. _____

3. _____

4. _____

5. _____

6. _____

Answers are on page 381

FRAMED

The automobile frame design shown in this illustration is very unusual for an American car.
What make of car created this plow-shaped safety frame?

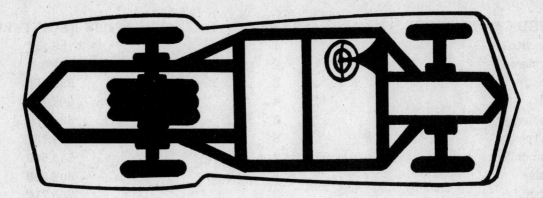

NAME GAME #8

There are four decades of car model names mixed-up below, and your task is to match them to the correct year and car company listed next to them.

CAR BRANDS	MODEL NAMES
1. '76 Dodge Dart	A. Commuter
2. '52 Kaiser	B. Signet
3. '67 Mercury	C. Lite
4. '57 DeSoto Fireflite	D. Conestoga
5. '71 Ford Maverick	E. Fleetline
6. '69 Plymouth Valiant	F. Rallye
7. '54 Studebaker	G. Virginian
8. '42 Hudson	H. Hotshot
9. '73 Dodge Challenger	I. Rally 350
10. '51 Crosley	J. Shopper
11. '70 Oldsmobile	K. Commodore
12. '48 Chevrolet	L. Grabber

Commercial Cutie

In the 1960's this petite spokesperson for a major car brand charmed us in TV and radio commercials. Can you answer the following questions?

1. What car name do you associate her with?
2. What was her name in the commercials?
3. What is this actress's real name?

Answers are on page 381

Top Ten '66

Correctly unmix the car names listed below and put them in correct order to match their sales rank for 1966.

MIXED CAR BRANDS	RANK	UNITS REGISTERED
Plymouth	1	2,158,811
Chrysler	2	1,991,520
Buick	3	830,856
Ford	4	598,160
Rambler	5	580,550
Chevrolet	6	569,131
Oldsmobile	7	543,560
Pontiac	8	308,049
Mercury	9	265,712
Dodge	10	230,182

Call Me a Cab

Cab driver: What can I do for you, Mac?
You: Can you identify the year and make of the four taxicabs pictured below?
Cab driver: Only while the meter's ticking.

1. _____

2. _____

3. _____

4. _____

Answers are on pages 381-82

Roof Relics

#1

The eight roof designs from the 1950's and 60's shown below need to be identified by their year and make. Warning—proceed with caution.

1. _____

   _____

2. _____

3. _____

   _____

4. _____

   _____

5. _____

6. _____

   _____

7. _____

   _____

8. _____

   _____

Answers are on page 382

Open for Business!

Identify each of these six cavernous station wagons by their year and make.

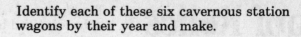

1. _____

2. _____

4. _____

3. _____

5. _____

6. _____

Answers are on page 382

Show Time

Identify the year and make of cars presented by these lovely ladies at the annual auto shows.

1. _____   2. _____

3. _____   4. _____

5. _____   6. _____

Happy Anniversary

To celebrate their maker's 40th anniversary these two cars got together for a family portrait.
Can you identify the years and make of these automobiles?

Years _____   Make _____

MULTI-CARBS

1. What was the first model year that Buick offered its dual-quad 425 cubic-inch engine?
   A. 1959   B. 1963   C. 1969

2. In 1961 and '62, Chevrolet had a dual-quad engine. Do you know the cubic-inch size of this V-8?
   A. 327   B. 348   C. 409

3. In what single year did Oldsmobile have a "tri-power" 400 cu. in. engine?
   A. 1966   B. 1968   C. 1971

4. What year did Ford offer an OHV-6 with three single-barrel carburetors?
   A. 1958   B. 1960   C. 1963

5. How many cubes was the 1965-67 dual quad Shelby V-8 engine?
   A. 390   B. 427   C. 428

6. What was the first year Dodge offered dual quads?
   A. 1952   B. 1954   C. 1956

7. Packard had a dual-quad engine way back in 1956. How many cubic inches was it?
   A. 374   B. 352   C. 289

8. What were the two years that Mercury sold the "406" engine with tri-power?
   A. 1955-56   B. 1959-60   C. 1962-63

The Man Behind

The man behind the Stutz automobile was this distinguished-looking gentleman.
Who was he?

A. Charles S. Schwab
B. Alfred Sloan Jr.
C. Henry LeLand

Life Like Logos #3

Can you identify the company that used this logo?

Answers are on page 382

Perplexing Pontiac Pictures

Below are six faces that Pontiac wore during the 1950's. Can you identify the correct year for each design?

1. _____

2. _____

3. _____

4. _____

5. _____

6. _____

Answers are on page 382

Roof Relics #2

Identifying car makers just by their roof designs might prove difficult for the novice, but if you look carefully you can easily name the year and make of these eight "greenhouses."

1. _____

_____

2. _____

_____

3. _____

_____

4. _____

_____

5. _____

_____

6. _____

_____

7. _____

_____

8. _____

_____

Answers are on page 382

Green House #2

From these 3/4 views can you recognize the car brand and model name for each of the roof designs shown below?

1. _____

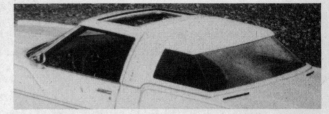

2. _____

3. _____

4. _____

5. _____

6. _____

Rolling Records #4

ROLLING RECORDS

SIDE A:
The Little Old Lady (from Pasadena)
by_____

SIDE B:
Sting Ray
by_____

Rising Sun

Below are Japan's top 10 auto markets. Can you match the correct country to its ranking?

RANK		COUNTRY
1.	A.	West Germany
2.	B.	Malaysia
3.	C.	Canada
4.	D.	Saudi Arabia
5.	E.	U.S.A.
6.	F.	Holland
7.	G.	Indonesia
8.	H.	Australia
9.	I.	Thailand
10.	J.	United Kingdom

Answers are on page 382

Topless Models

OK, drool over these gorgeous bodies, but before you soak the page identify the year and make of each.

1. _____

2. _____

3. _____

4. _____

5. _____

6. _____

Answers are on page 382

Color Me Wild

Fill in the full name for the late sixties/early seventies exterior paint jobs offered by these five cars.

CAR MAKE	SPECIAL COLOR
1. Pontiac GTO Judge	Orbit _____
2. AMC Javelin	_____
	Big Bad _____
	_____
3. Ford Maverick	Anti-Establish _____
	Hulla _____
	Freudian _____
	Thanks _____
	Original _____
4. Dodge	Citron _____
	_____ Crazy
	_____ Go
5. Plymouth	Vitamin _____
	_____ Light
	_____ Twist
	Tor _____

Top Secret Initials

The gentleman shown below was the next president of Chrysler Corp. after Walter P. retired.
His name was K. T. Keller, and to 99% of the automobile trade he kept his initials a top secret.
Are you one of the selected few that know the names behind the initials K. T.?

F.O.B. Factory

Each of the nine 1937 autos listed below had a lowest to highest model price range. Try to match the correct prices to the car names.
Bonus—what does F.O.B. stand for?

MAKE	RANGE
Packard	1. $ 510-$ 680
Terraplane	2. $ 525-$ 685
Plymouth	3. $ 595-$ 745
Chrysler Custom Imperial	4. $ 665-$1065
Pierce-Arrow	5. $ 765-$1995
Studebaker	6. $ 795-$5900
Chevrolet	7. $1445-$1945
Cadillac	8. $2060-$2160
Buick	9. $3195-$5795

Woody Wonders

The beauty of wood accents on car bodies from different decades is shown in the station wagons pictured here.
Can you identify the year and make of each car?

2. _____

1. _____

3. _____

4. _____

Key Bobbers #5

Can you identify the car brand by their key-bob emblem?

1. _____

2. _____

3. _____

Answers are on page 382

Bug Bus

When Volkswagen introduced their van/bus/station wagon vehicle years ago there was nothing like it being offered by any other manufacturer—it was quite an original approach. Can you answer any or all of the questions listed below?

A.

B.

1. What was the first year these VW vehicles came off the Wolfsburg assembly line?_____

2. What was Volkswagen's official designation for this transporter?_____

3. Because of its resemblance to a specific canine, what nickname was given to the vehicle?_____

4. How many cylinders did the original engine have?_____

5. What was the original horsepower rating?
   A. 25 HP   B. 30 HP   C. 45 HP

6. How tall was the original station wagon/bus?
   A. 66½″   B. 75″   C. 80″

7. What was the overall length?
   A. 141½″   B. 151½″   C. 161½″

8. The load space measured how many cubic feet?
   A. 162   B. 169   C. 175

9. Picture A is of the second-generation model with new slide door feature. What model year did this design first appear?_____

10. The third-generation design is shown in picture B. What model year did this VW first appear?_____

1930 Word Search #2

Find all the car brands that started and/or ceased production in the 1930's as contained within this automobile shape. The words can be found horizontally, vertically, or diagonally. They may read backwards or forwards.

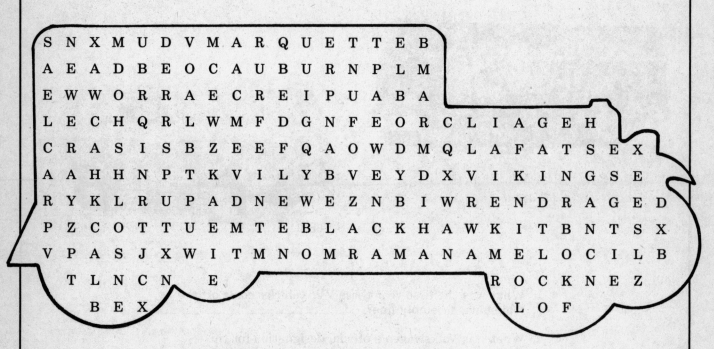

```
S N X M U D V M A R Q U E T T E B
A E A D B E O C A U B U R N P L M
E W W O R R A E C R E I P U A B A
L E C H Q R L W M F D G N F E O R C L I A G E H
C R A S I S B Z E E F Q A O W D M Q L A F A T S E X
A A H H N P T K V I L Y B V E Y D X V I K I N G S E
R Y K L R U P A D N E W E Z N B I W R E N D R A G E D
P Z C O T T U E M T E B L A C K H A W K I T B N T S X
V P A S J X W I T M N O M R A M A N A M E L O C I L B
  T L N C N   E                     R O C K N E Z
    B E X                           L O F
```

ACME
AUBURN
BLACKHAWK
CLINTON
COLEMAN
DERR
DEVAUX
DOBLE
ELCAR
ESSES

GARDNER
LA FAYETTE
MARMON
MARQUETTE
NEW ERA
PIERCE-ARROW
ROCKNE
STUTZ
VIKING
WHIPPET

Answers are on page 383

Cuda-Dragin'

Answer the following questions about these four drag racing Barracudas.

1

3

2

4

1. What model year is picture #1?

2. What is the second racing partner's name that's missing on the door in pictures #1 and #3?

3. What is the model year of the 'Cuda in picture #2?

4. What two names are missing from the door in picture #2?

5. What model year is in picture #3?

6. What model year is the fastback in picture #4?

NAME GAME #9

How well do you remember car model names from the past 30 years? Match year and make to correct model.

YEAR AND MAKE	MODEL NAME
1. 1951 Packard	Roundup
2. 1953 Kaiser	Pioneer
3. 1953 Oldsmobile	Talladega
4. 1958 Edsel	Mayfair
5. 1960 Dodge Dart	Scamp
6. 1964 Studebaker	Can Am
7. 1969 Ford Torino	Stallion
8. 1971 Plymouth Valiant	Carolina
9. 1976 Ford Mustang II	Fiesta
10. 1977 Pontiac	Challenger

Up in Smoke

1. What unusual automobile accessory is shown in the above illustration?

2. What make of car offered this on their models in 1961?

Answers are on page 383

MOVIE SCENES #4

1. Name of movie _____
    Year and make of car _____

2. Name of movie _____

Answers are on page 383

More Munchin Motorists

1. What year did Ray Kroc open his first McDonald's _____

2. In what city and state was it located? _____

3. What was the name for the little hamburger man that was McDonald's original symbol? _____

4. What was the first year you could buy a Burger King hamburger? _____

5. Denny's started out as a doughnut road stand. Do you know what year it opened? _____

6. What food franchise opened the first U.S. turnpike restaurant? _____

7. What year did this turnpike restaurant open? _____

8. Name the turnpike. _____

Classic Continentals

Continentals show a heritage of clean, elegant lines, but these Connies become tricky when guessing the correct series number. Six excellent examples are shown below. Your task is to fill in the correct model year and series number for each distinctive design.

1. _____

2. _____

3. _____

4. _____

5. _____

6. _____

MOVIE SCENES #5

1. Name of movie _____
   Year and make of car _____

2. Name of movie _____
   Year, make and model of car _____

338

Answers are on page 383

Family Resemblance

What is the year and make of the dotted line car and its long-lost relative in the background? Can you fill in the correct numbers to the blanks below?

OLDER CAR		DOTTED LINE CAR
_____ inches	Wheelbase	_____ inches
_____ inches	Overall length	_____ inches
_____ inches	Height	_____ inches
_____ inches	Width	_____ inches
_____ lbs	Weight	_____ lbs

Rolling Records #5

ROLLING RECORDS

SIDE A: 409

by_____

SIDE B: Beep Beep

by_____

Secret Symbol/ Slogan

Can you name the car that used the symbol below and its "three S" slogan?

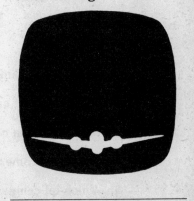

_____

Answers are on page 383

Tourist Info

Three world travelers parked their cars in front of a famous slogan, obviously taking the message literally, so answer the following questions.

1.

2.

3.

1. What is the name of cars number 1, 2, and 3 and the country each comes from?

2. Which car had an air-cooled two-cylinder engine?_____

3. Which car was not front-wheel drive? _____

4. Which car came with a twin overhead-cam four-cylinder engine?_____

5. Which oil company used the above slogan? _____

Answers are on page 383

Hub Hysteria #5

We don't easily give up trying to stump you. Identify the correct car make for each of the wheel/hubcap designs grouped below.

1. ______________

2. ______________

3. ______________

4. ______________

5. ______________

6. ______________

7. ______________

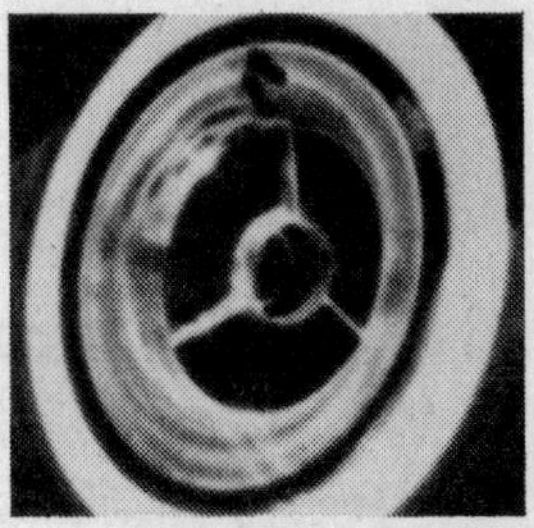

8. ______________

Independent Quickie

1. Who is that man and why is he smiling? ______________

2. What's the name and year of the car? ______________

Car Phones

Decode the telephone numbers listed below, and you'll know the unlisted numbers of eight past and present American cars.

687-8264 ______________

722-5273 ______________

527-2553 ______________

276-7539 ______________

748-4372 ______________

726-2537 ______________

267-8247 ______________

766-8422 ______________

Answers are on page 383

Grand Prix Grilles

Six different Grand Prix front ends are shown below. Identify each design by its correct model year.

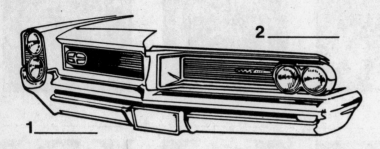

2 _____

1 _____

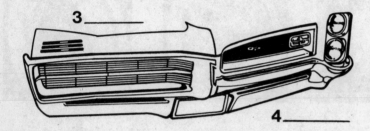

3 _____

4 _____

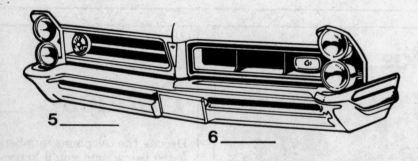

5 _____

6 _____

Here Today, Gone Tomorrow #2

What was the single model year for these cars, offered in the 1950's to the 1970's?

1. 19___ Plymouth Superbird
2. 19___ Chevy Monza Mirage
3. 19___ AMC The Machine
4. 19___ Pontiac Can Am
5. 19___ Chevy II Nova Super Sport Convertible
6. 19___ Ford Galaxie retractable hardtop
7. 19___ Chevy Impala two-door sedan
8. 19___ Ford Talladega

SYMBOL SPECIALIST #5

Quite a few decades are covered with these four emblems. Can you identify the car make for each?

1. _____

2. _____

3. _____

4. _____

Answers are on pages 383-84

"Honest Ingines"

The heart and spirit of any automobile is its well-tuned engine, no matter the configuration. Answer all three questions beneath each of the six engines shown here.

1. Make of car _____
   Number of cylinders _____
   Era of engine _____

2. Make of car _____
   Number of cylinders _____
   Era of engine _____

3. Make of car _____
   Number of cylinders _____
   Era of engine _____

4. Make of car _____
   Number of cylinders _____
   Era of engine _____

5. Make of car _____
   Number of cylinders _____
   Era of engine _____

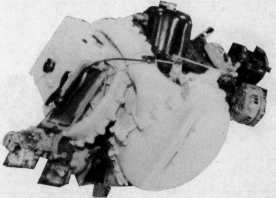

6. Make of car _____
   Number of cylinders _____
   Era of engine _____

Answers are on page 384

"Home, James"

Your driver, who's asleep, is waiting to pick you up in your black 1936 Cadillac Town Car with the convertible chauffeur's quarters. The problem is that you've wined more than dined and there in the drive-up lane are six 1930's-era "cabriolet" style Cadillacs. A bit befuddled, you identify the correct year for each car to find your vintage model.

1. _____

2. _____

3. _____

4. _____

5. _____

6. _____

Answers are on page 384

Prehistoric Power

1. What was the name of the gasoline station chain that used the above symbol?_____

2. What was the advertised name of this gigantic mascot? _____

3. What year did he become extinct as a company representative? _____

4. What new name does this oil company go by today?_____

Ten Little Indians

During the 1950's and 60's Pontiac introduced these 10 names into their tribe of full-production cars.
Can you give the correct model year that each of these names made their debut.

1. Bonneville_____
2. Catalina 2 + 2_____
3. Firebird_____
4. Firebird Trans Am_____
5. Grand Prix_____
6. GTO_____
7. GTO "The Judge"_____
8. Safari_____
9. Star Chief_____
10. Tempest_____

Side Swipe #2

The side decorations of six different cars are pictured below. Do you know the year and make of car that used these designs.

1. _____

2. _____

3. _____

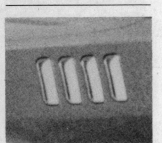

4. _____

5. _____

6. _____

Answers are on page 384

Fantastic Fin-Fad

Thanks to Harley Earl, Virgil Exner, and all the other talented stylists that gave us the fabulous fins from the past. Can you identify the year and make of the cars that sported the six designs pictured below?

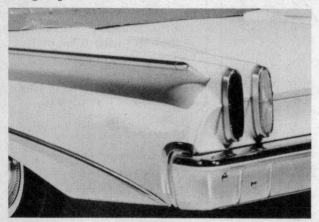

1. _____

2. _____

3. _____

4. _____

5. _____

6. _____

346

Answers are on page 384

English Eagle

1. What was the full name and title of this British world speed champion?
   _____

2. What was the name of his famous land racer?
   _____

3. What year and make of car is he standing with?
   _____

Spark Art

The artwork shown here represents two spark plug companies' approaches to representing themselves. Match each company with their symbols.

1. _____

2. _____

Nostalgic Unscrambler

The scrambled words listed below are all well-known car companies from the 1940's. Rearrange their letters to discover who they are.

1. OLYCERS
   _____

2. ZARRFE
   _____

3. MAGHAR
   _____

4. DUOSHN
   _____

5. CETRUK
   _____

6. LIYWSL
   _____

7. POULIHEMB
   _____

8. KRADCAP
   _____

9. DRATUBEEKS
   _____

10. HANS
    _____

Cover Quiz

Can you correctly identify all of the auto
related images that were designed into the
front and rear covers of this trivia book?

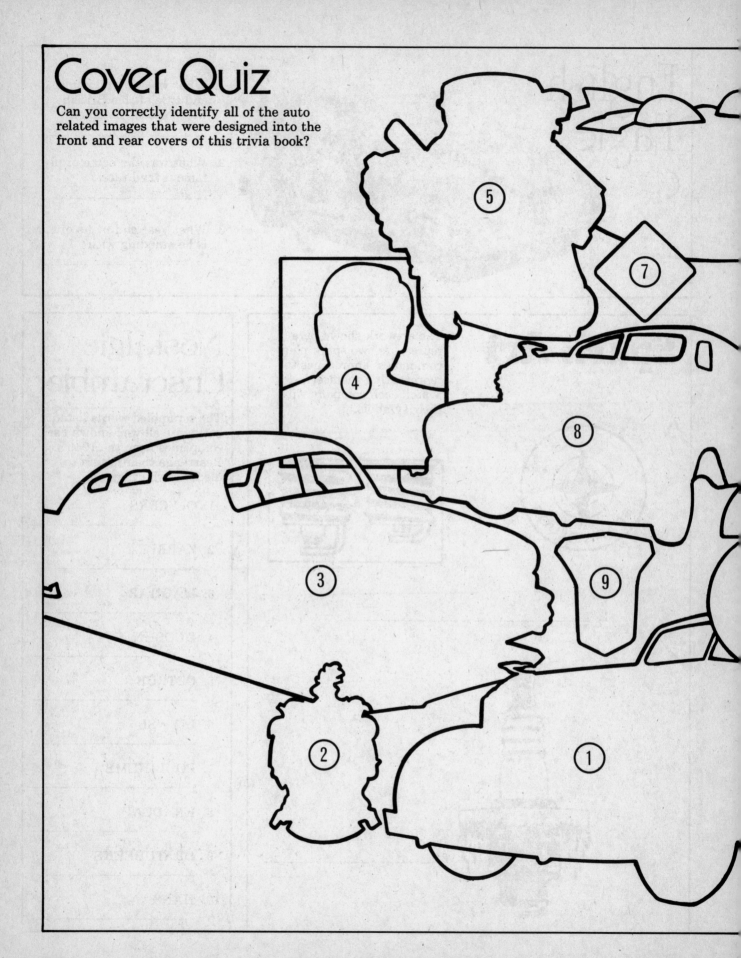

1. _____
2. _____
3. _____
4. _____
5. _____
6. _____
7. _____
8. _____

9. _____
10. _____
11. _____
12. _____
13. _____
14. _____
15. _____

Motor Trend Car of the Year 1969-78

The auto manufacturers were going through some turbulent times during the seventies, and it was getting harder to pick outstanding autos to receive the respected "Car of the Year" award. One year a French make even beat out all American brands.

Match the various car names listed below to the correct year in which they won.

1969	A. Chevrolet Vega	1974	F. Citroen S.M.
		1975	G. Dodge Omni/ Plymouth Horizon
1970	B. Plymouth Road Runner		
1971	C. Chevy Monte Carlo	1976	H. Chevrolet Caprice
1972	D. Dodge Aspen/ Plymouth Volare	1977	I. Ford Mustang II
		1978	J. Chevrolet Monza 2+2
1973	E. Ford Torino		

Back in the USSR

While you're driving through the Soviet Union you might ask the comrade that owns one what this Packard-inspired car is—or do you already know?

_____

Seeing-Eye Symbol

1. What famous auto racing equipment company name goes with this symbol?

_____

2. What is this symbol called?

_____

3. Do you know the first and last name of the man who started this company?

_____

Answers are on page 384

ANSWERS

FIN FEVER
1. 1963 Mercury Meteor
2. 1960 DeSoto
3. 1960 Plymouth
4. 1961 Ford
5. 1960 Lincoln
6. 1959 Rambler

GET A HORSE
1. A. Pinto, Maverick and Mustang II
   B. Stallion
2. Arnolt-Bristol
3. Ferrari
4. Ford Country Squires
5. Pegaso

DOUBLE YOUR PLEASURE
1. Rambler
2. Twin-Stick Floor Shift with Instant Overtake
3. Five

SLICK SYMBOLS #1
Pure Oil Co.

IDENTIFY THE IMPERIALS #1
1. 1975
2. 1971
3. 1973
4. 1982
5. 1974
6. 1972
7. 1970
8. 1969

MERCURY MUG SHOTS #1
1. 1949
2. 1956
3. 1955
4. 1950
5. 1957
6. 1954
7. 1952
8. 1959

THE TAXIS THAT HURRIED
1. 1938 Chevrolet
2. 1949 Checker
3. 1940 Plymouth
4. 1965 Dodge

BIRD'S-EYE VIEW
1. Pierce-Arrow Silver Arrow
2. 1933
3. 12
4. 175 H.P.
5. 139
6. $10,000

OUTDOOR ADS #1
1. 1955 Plymouth
2. 1968 Dodge Charger
3. 1960 Chrysler

TURBINE TRUCK TEST
1. Turbo Titan III
2. 1965
3. 280 H.P.
4. Automatic
5. Six-speed
6. Two small wheels in place of conventional steering wheel

DEALER'S CHOICE (IMPORTS)
1. E
2. I
3. B
4. D
5. J
6. G
7. F
8. C
9. H
10. A

SLICK SYMBOLS #2
Marathon

DON'T TAILGATE
1. '67 Pontiac
2. '55 Dodge
3. '66 Plymouth Barracuda
4. '81 Imperial
5. '57 DeSoto
6. '74 Chevrolet
7. '61 Chevrolet Corvette
8. '57 Pontiac

LICENSE TO QUIZ
1. Arizona
2. Florida
3. Idaho
4. Indiana
5. Montana
6. Manitoba

WOODY WAGONS #1
1. 1941 Chrysler
2. 1960 Mercury
3. 1978 Chrysler
4. 1940 Oldsmobile
5. 1933 Ford
6. 1949 Ford
   Real wood—#'s 1, 4, 5

TOP THESE
1. 1940 Mercury
2. 1965-69 Excalibur SSK
3. 1968 Plymouth Barracuda
4. 1954 Ford
5. 1947 Oldsmobile 98
6. 1957 Mercury

MOVIE CAR TRIVIA #1
1. 1975-77 AMC Pacer
2. 6.6 Liter
3. 1973 Ford
4. 1977-78
5. Mercedes-Benz 4.5
6. 1959 Cadillac
7. DeLorean and Maserati
8. Rolls-Royce

CORNER STATION
Car on the left is a 1938 Hupmobile
Car on the right is a 1939 Pontiac
Mobilgas Socony—Vacuum
Pegasus

FIREBIRD FRONTS #1
1. 1969
2. 1972
3. 1967
4. 1970
5. 1973
6. 1968

"STOCK" STUMBLERS
1. 1965 Plymouth—426 Hemi—Jim Hurtubise
2. 1964 Ford—427 cu. in.—Marvin Panch
3. 1967 Dodge—426 Hemi—Marty Robbins (country music singer)
4. 1957 Pontiac—347 cu. in.—Ernie Derr
5. 1971 Mercury—429 cu. in.—David Pearson

ORIENTAL ROOT QUICKIES

1. Dat Division of the Motor Industry, Ltd.
2. 1933
3. 1934
4. Toyota Automatic Loom Works
5. 1933
6. 1937

PAST SHADOWS

1. 1959 Chevrolet
2. 1975 Lotus Elite
3. 1951 Cadillac
4. 1959 Plymouth
5. 1956 Pontiac
6. 1968-73 Corvette

SCRAMBLED SUSPENSION

1. Ball Joint
2. Steering Knuckle
3. Frame
4. Upper Control Arm
5. Coil Spring
6. Lower Control Arm
7. Shock Absorber

BY THE SEAT OF YOUR PANTS

1. Foam rubber
2. 1939 Hudson
3. Chrysler Corp.
4. 1959
5. 1961
6. Five
7. Hudson
8. 1948

PASSING DREAMS #1

1. '63 Corvair Monza GT
2. '68 Ford Techna
3. '60 Plymouth XNR
4. '54 DeSoto Adventurer II
5. '51 Plymouth Explorer
6. '61 Dodge Flitewing

SHORT CUT

1. 1953 Kaiser Manhattan
2. B
3. No (1954)
4. A

TV CAR

Route 66
Corvettes

MUSCLE CAR UNSCRAMBLE

1. Camaro
2. Judge
3. Javelin
4. Dodge
5. Pontiac
6. Mustang
7. Torino
8. Cougar
9. Wildcat
10. Monza
11. Starfire
12. Shelby

TRUCKIN' SPIRITS

1. White
2. Mack
3. Federal
4. International
5. Diamond T.
6. Dodge

SINK OR SWIM

1. Amphicar
2. C
3. 1961
4. A
5. A
6. A
7. Land—Approx. 90 mph
   Water—Approx. 10 mph
8. B

WHAT'S IN A NAME?

1. Her first name
2. Mercédès Jellinek
3. Spanish
4. "Mercy"
5. Austrian

AUTO ASSOCIATIONS

1. American Automobile Association
2. Association of American Battery Manufacturers, Inc.
3. Automotive Electric Association
4. Automotive Engine Rebuilders Association
5. Automotive Parts Manufacturers Association
6. American Society of Mechanical Engineers
7. Motor and Equipment Wholesalers Association
8. Motor Vehicle Manufacturers Association
9. National Automobile Dealers Association
10. National Automotive Parts Association

CUDAS AND CHALLENGERS

1. 1970 Challenger
2. 1971 'Cuda
3. 1974 Barracuda
4. 1970 Barracuda
5. 1972 Challenger
6. 1971 Challenger

IDENTIFY THE IMPERIALS #2

1. 1957
2. 1962
3. 1963
4. 1958
5. 1968
6. 1960
7. 1967
8. 1961

TV SCREAMER

1. The Monkees
2. 1966
3. Monkey Mobile

DEANS OF DESIGN

1. C and G
2. F and K
3. E and H
4. A and I
5. D and L
6. B and J

PORSCHE PAGE

A. 1954
B. 1964
C. 1967
D. 1970
E. 1977

F. 1978
G. 1983

1. 914
2. Targa
3. 901
4. 911—6 cyl. and 912—4 cyl.
5. Einspritzung (German for fuel injection)
6. 1974
7. Whale Tail
8. Duck Tail

POPULAR PANELS
1. 1937 Terraplane
2. 1958 Chevrolet
3. 1939 GMC
4. 1961 Ford Falcon
5. 1955-56 International
6. 1937 Autocar

WILD PUT-ON
1. Chevrolet
2. 1972
3. Feathers
   Van Rippler
   Eagle
   Sandman
4. Approx. 4 hours

"HEY, TAXI"
1. 1941 Packard
2. 1960 Studebaker
3. 1953 Checker
4. 1941 Chrysler

YOU LIGHT UP MY LIFE
PICTURE: A
1. It's an auxillary light between high and low beam called Super-Lite.
2. 1970 Dodge Polara
3. 1969
PICTURE: B
1. False—Testing different sealed beam designs.
2. 1953 Chrysler
PICTURE: C
1. True
2. 1984 Lincoln Continental Mark VII
PICTURE: D
1. 1961 Dodge Phoenix
2. Low-cost option

1930 WORD SEARCH #1

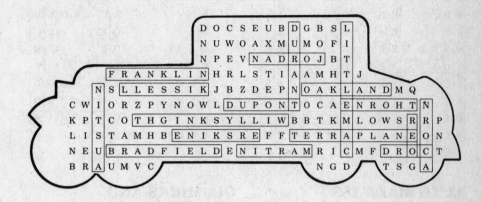

LOOK BUT DON'T TOUCH #1
1. Ford GT-40
2. Its height (40 inches high)
3. 1964
4. 256.3 cu. in.
5. 289 cu. in.
6. 427 cu. in.

THE LOWER FORTIES #1
1. 1941 Cadillac
2. 1966 Mako Shark II
3. 1942 Chrysler Town and Country
4. 1939 Hudson

SPINNERS
1. Dodge
2. Oldsmobile
3. Ford
4. Edsel
5. Plymouth
6. Pontiac
7. Rambler
8. Mercury
9. Dodge
10. Ford
11. Buick
12. Oldsmobile

INDY TWO TIMERS
1. Lou Meyer, 1933 and 1936—Lawson Harris (mech)
2. Gordon Johncock, 1973 and 1982
3. Bill Vukovich, 1953 and 1954

JOY RIDING JEEPS
1. 1941
2. 1946
3. 1959
4. 1960
5. 1963
6. 1963
7. 1971
8. 1975
9. 1976
10. 1976

BLINK BLINK BLINK
1. Thunderbird and Cougar
2. Thunderbird—1965
   Cougar—1967
3. Thunderbird—1971
   Cougar—1973

SMART STICK
1. Turn signals
2. High-low beam
3. Windshield wiper
4. Windshield washer
5. Pulse wiper
6. Cruise control on/off
7. Cruise control resume speed

1940 WORD SEARCH

```
H V D        N A      R B        P L A Y B O Y      Q H S N A M E
A M R C S    T M      N O        I T I S E X S      R E S I A K L
J I     T O  O E      E B        N I R U T I O      A I R H N E I
K D   R N    C R      I B        I L V             R C A N O L B
F R   E A    S I      R I        A A Z             O R     E O M
S A B O N Z  C C      E K        D S S             G O     R M P
I D E L C A R R A     M A        V A A             L S       E R
T E     R O  I N      A R        C L M             Z L Y B O W U
R E     F C  A        A R        O L B             I E C A B L H
U L     C A  A U S T I N        M E Y             G Y A W R I A
K C     A R  D R E K C U T      F R O             P J N D L F O
        T M O Z Y H P
```

AUTO MADNESS
1. '62 Imperial convertible
2. '62 Plymouth wagon
3. '57 Ford
4. VW "Bug"
5. Ford truck

Bonus: '57 Ford with Jimmy Durante

SHOW STOPPERS
1. Freddie Ford
2. 1960 Chevrolet
3. Plymouth (Duster)
4. Chevrolet Corvair

TRIPLETS
1. 1977
2. 1965
3. 1962
4. 1969
5. 1974
6. 1964
7. 1968
8. 1971

THE FACES OF OLDSMOBILE
1. 1948
2. 1953
3. 1951
4. 1954
5. 1955
6. 1957
7. 1958
8. 1950

GIMMICKS AND GADGETS #1
1. Heated rearview mirror
2. Space-saver tire
   1967 Pontiac Firebird
3. Rear deck air spoiler
   1969 Mercury Cyclone Spoiler
4. External hood locks
5. Slide-in license plate holder
   1985 Buick Electra
6. Cornering light
   1965 Cadillac

RADIO HA-HA
1. Ed Wynn
2. Texaco
3. DeSoto

...AND THE NEWS
1. Lowell Thomas
2. Kaiser
3. Walter Winchell
4. Buick

LONG DISTANCE INFORMATION
Bentley
Citroen
Ferrari
Peugeot
Porsche
Triumph
Sunbeam

GAPERS BLOCK
1. 1953-54 Henry J
2. 1951-52 Dodge
3. 1953 Chevrolet
4. 1947 Pontiac

5. 1953 Buick
6. 1949-50 Pontiac
7. 1949-51 Mercury ('51 hubcap)
8. 1951 Ford
9. 1953 Oldsmobile

NAME GAME #1
1. E
2. I
3. A
4. B
5. L
6. C
7. J
8. K
9. D
10. G
11. F
12. H

WHAT A MEMORY
Opel
Buick

MECHANICALLY MINDED #1
Switch
Spark plugs
Resistor
Battery
Ignition coil
Ammeter
Distributor

1. Switch
2. Spark plugs
3. Resistor
4. Battery
5. Ignition coil
6. Ammeter
7. Distributor

TOP DOZEN OF '39
1. Chevrolet
2. Ford
3. Plymouth
4. Buick
5. Dodge
6. Pontiac
7. Oldsmobile
8. Studebaker

9. Mercury
10. Chrysler
11. Hudson
12. Packard

FOUR-FIFTY WAGONS
1. 1959 Mercury
2. 1955 Studebaker
3. 1957 Oldsmobile
4. 1959 Edsel

DIESEL DUZIES
1. 1936 Auburn
2. Clessie
3. Dr. Rudolf Diesel
4. 1977
5. 1982
6. Mack

DAYDREAMS #1
1. '60 Chevy Cerv I
2. '53 Dodge Firearrow
3. '54 Plymouth Belmont
4. '56 Olds Golden Rocket
5. '67 Ford Bordinat Cobra
6. '81 AMC AMX Turbo

MOVIE CAR TRIVIA #2
1. 1974 Dodge Monaco
2. 440 cubic inch
3. 1972 Ford Torino
4. 1969 Dodge Charger
5. The Fall Guy
6. 1971–73 Chevy Vega

FIN FANTASIES
1. 1959 Cadillac Cyclone
2. 1954–55 Ford Mystere
3. 1958 Plymouth Cabana
4. 1956 GM Firebird II
5. 1961 Chrysler TurboFlite
6. 1954 Ford FX-Atmos

PERSONAL PICKUPS
RANCHERO FIGURES

Overall length	208″
Wheelbase	118″
Weight	3840 lbs.

EL CAMINO FIGURES

Overall length	211″
Wheelbase	119″
Weight	3880 lbs.

1. Ranchero
2. Both the same (91″)
3. Ranchero—352 cu. in.
4. El Camino—315 H.P.
5. Grey
6. Chevrolet

SNEAK PREVIEW
Nash (American Motors)

TOP TEN 1942
1. G
2. C
3. I
4. A
5. J
6. H
7. F
8. D
9. E
10. B

COBRA QUICKIES
1. 260
2. 289
3. C
4. A
5. 1966
6. B
7. A
8. B

PUSH/PULL POWER
Jeep Wagoneer

SCHOOL DAZE #1
1. GMC
2. REO
3. Chevrolet
4. White
5. International

FASTER THAN THE FASTEST
1. B
2. C

007
1. For Your Eyes Only
   Lotus Esprit
2. Goldfinger
   Aston Martin
3. Dr. No
   Chevrolet
4. You Only Live Once
   Toyota 2000-GT

NAME THAT STATE #1
1. Alabama—Chevrolet
2. Montana—Lincoln
3. Maine—Pontiac
4. Kansas—Studebaker

BITE THE...
1. Bullitt
2. 1968 Dodge Charger
3. 1968 Ford Mustang
4. Steve McQueen

IMPORT INVASION
1. Volkswagen
2. Renault
3. Ford
4. Fiat
5. Hillman
6. Vauxhall
7. Simca
8. MG
9. Triumph
10. Opel

THE DODGE DILEMMA
1. 1961 Dart
2. 1969 Daytona
3. 1968 Charger
4. 1962 Lancer
5. 1960 Dart
6. 1966 Coronet

SIDE SWIPE
1. 1972 Dodge Charger
2. 1956 Packard 400
3. 1955 Mercury Monterey
4. 1958 Pontiac Bonneville
5. 1956 Plymouth Belvedere
6. 1952 Oldsmobile 98

CARE-FREE CARS
Ford

REAR ENGINES
BMW Isetta
Porsche

SPECIAL DELIVERY
1. REO (Speed Wagon)
2. Dodge
3. Dodge
4. International
5. Chevrolet
6. GMC

REVOLUTIONARY
1. Mercedes-Benz
2. C-111
3. High-powered rotary piston engine
4. Mid-ship
5. 330
6. 162
7. 44.3" tall
8. 1969

KEY BOBBERS #1
1. Volvo
2. Hudson
3. Lancia

KOOL-AID
1. Radiator cap
2. Water pump
3. Upper radiator hose
4. Thermostat housing
5. Cylinder head
6. Freeze plug
7. Heater core
8. Heater hose
9. Heater blower motor
10. Engine block drain
11. Heater hose "return"
12. Water jacket
13. Lower radiator hose
14. Radiator drain petcock
15. Automatic transmission coolant line
16. Drive belt
17. Radiator
18. Fan
19. Radiator expansion tank

LICENSE LAWS
1. 15
2. Alabama, Arkansas, Idaho, Iowa, Kansas, Michigan, North Dakota, Oregon, South Dakota, Tennessee
3. Colorado
4. 18
5. 17
6. 18

CHEVELLE CHALLENGE
1. 1964
2. 1967
3. 1968
4. 1965
5. 1969
6. 1966

TOOTHY BUICKS
1. 1942
2. 1951
3. 1953
4. 1948
5. 1946
6. 1958
7. 1957
8. 1954

UP, UP, AND AWAY
PICTURE A: 1
PICTURE B: 2
PICTURE C: 3

INDIAN SIGNS
1. Six cylinder
2. Eight cylinder

AUTO ART
1. 1967 Plymouth Satellite
2. 1967 Chrysler 300
3. 1967 Plymouth Belvedere GTX
4. 1967 Chrysler Newport

KNOW YOUR NOVAS
1. 1963
2. 1962
3. 1966
4. 1967
5. 1968
6. 1965

BOSS OF THE BONNEVILLE
1. B
2. A
3. C
4. C

MERGING MOTORS
1. 1934
2. 1948
3. 1949
4. 1950
5. 1950
6. 1951
7. 1951
8. 1957
9. 1965
10. 1971
11. 1970
12. 1975

4 OF A KIND
1. 1970
2. 1967
3. 1969
4. 1968

FRAMED #1
"K—Y" Frame
1934 Pontiac

"TRANS"-PLANT
1. Kokomo, Indiana
2. Chrysler Corporation
3. Over 7500 units a day

DASTARDLY DASHES
1. 1949 Ford
2. 1970 Dodge Challenger
3. 1978 Pontiac Grand Prix
4. 1970 Chevy Monte Carlo
5. 1957 Imperial
6. 1957 Chevrolet
7. 1973 AMC Gremlin
8. 1955 Nash

PARKING GARAGE OF TIME #1
1. 1952 Willys
2. 1939 Chrysler
3. 1960 Ford

"A CLEAN SWEEP, BUT A SQUEAKY FINISH"
1. All-American Soap Box Derby
2. Chevrolet
3. 1937
4. Akron, Ohio
5. Derby Downs

DEALERS CHOICE (U.S.A.)
1. F
2. H
3. D
4. A
5. J
6. C
7. B
8. I
9. G
10. E

DUO-DOOR
1. Ford and Mercury
2. 1966
3. "Magic Doorgate"
4. Still in production (1985)

OPEN SESAME
1. 1972 Chrysler
2. 1939 Hudson
3. 1959 Chevrolet
4. 1963 Plymouth
5. 1953 Kaiser Traveler
6. 1958 Dodge

FASTEST THING ON WHEELS
1. "Railton Red Lion"—John Cobb
2. "Macmillan's Ring-Free Streamliner"
3. "Blue Bird II"—Sir Malcolm Campbell

PLEASIN' PICKUPS
1. 1940 Willys
2. 1960 Falcon Ranchero
3. 1971 Dodge Adventurer
4. 1938 GMC
5. 1938 Plymouth
6. 1957 Chevrolet

BIG IS BETTER
Bugatti Royale, Type 41
Wheelbase: 180 in.
Height: 72 in.
Total weight: 5600 lbs.
Engine size: 898.6 cu. in.
Cost: $30,000

TV AUTO TRIVIA
1. Peugeot 404
2. Fords
3. 1969 Dodge Charger
4. Continental convertible
5. 1969 Ford Country Squire
6. 1957 Ford
7. Pontiac Bonneville
8. 1957 Thunderbird

TRUCKIN' ENGINES
1. D
2. F
3. A
4. B
5. E
6. C

SINGING SLOGANS
Chevrolet

TO PROTECT AND SERVE
1. 1962 Pontiac
2. 1935 Plymouth
3. 1966 Dodge
4. 1972 AMC Matador

JUNKERS
1. 1958 Ford
2. 1958 Ford
3. 1961 Chevrolet
4. 1955 Buick
5. 1954 Pontiac
6. 1958 Pontiac
7. 1959 Rambler

VISUAL SLOGANS
1. Chevrolet
2. Oldsmobile
3. Buick Special
4. Plymouth
5. Ford
6. Ford
7. Chrysler
8. Pontiac Tempest

CLUB PAGE—AUBURN-CORD-DUESENBERG
1. It was the date of the go ahead to build the car, August 10, 1935
2. J-101
3. Connersville, Indiana—Dishwasher manufacturing
4. Alex Tremulis—The outside exhaust pipes on the supercharged Cords
5. The 810 Cord
6. Auburn, Indiana—Automotive museum
7. Seven on standard—Eight on custom Beverly
8. The front drive L-29 Cord
9. Three
10. The 810 Cord

RIDE 'EM COWBOY
1. Wyoming
2. B
3. C

EMBLEM QUICKIE
1961 Chevrolet Super Sport Impala 348 cu. in. engine

BOATTAIL RIVS
1. 1973
2. 1972
3. 1971

SIXTIES SLOGANS
1. '64 Olds
2. '65 Plymouth
3. '67 Tempest OHC
4. '63 Ford Galaxie
5. '69 Plymouth
6. '64 Comet
7. '61 Amphicar
8. '69 Dodge
9. '67 Camaro
10. '65 Pontiac
11. '60 T-Bird
12. '60 Imperial

300'S
1. 1958 "D"
2. 1961 "G"
3. 1963 Non-letter model
4. 1965 Non-letter model
5. 1962 Non-letter model
6. 1959 "E"
7. 1955 Non-letter model
8. 1960 "F"

GLITTER AND GLAMOUR
1. 1950 Lincoln
2. 1958 Chrysler
3. 1957 Nash
4. 1958 Studebaker
5. 1951 Buick XP-300
6. 1960 Valiant

VETTE QUICKIE #1
1. 1964
2. 1958
3. 1962
4. 1963

QUEENS FOR A DAY #1
1957 Corvette Super Sport

X MARKS THE SPOT
1. 1970
2. 360 cu. in.
3. 390 cu. in.
4. 325 H.P.
5. 140 MPH
6. Yes

FIRST CLASS DELIVERY
1. GMC
2. Chevrolet
3. GMC
4. Dodge
5. Dodge
6. Autocar

ASSEMBLY LINES #1
1. 1966 Cadillacs
2. 1960 Comets
3. 1940-41 Hupmobile Skylarks
4. 1981 Mercury Lynx
5. 1966 Ramblers
6. 1939 Dodge

DAYDREAMS #2
1. '69 Ford Super Cobra
2. '83 Buick Questor
3. '58 Chevrolet Sebring SS
4. '77 AMC Concept AM/Van
5. '55 Pontiac Strato Star
6. '64 Studebaker "Cruiser" Lark

AMERICAN AUTO GRAFFITI
1. 1958 Chevrolet Impala
2. 1955 Chevrolet
3. 1957 Thunderbird
4. 1960 Cadillac
5. 1961 Ford
6. Mercury
7. Corsair—Blue and white

WHICH WAY IS UP?
Pike's Peak

PANEL PROPHECY
1. GMC L'Universelle
2. 1955
3. 288 cubic inch
4. 180 H.P.
5. Behind and beneath the driver
6. Corvair's Greenbrier Station Wagon
   Corvair's Rampside Pickup

FUN-IN-THE-SUN
1. 1954 Buick (Skylark)
2. 1931 Franklin
3. 1937 Oldsmobile
4. 1963 Pontiac
5. 1959 Ford (Retractable)
6. 1939 Plymouth

DASH DETOUR
1. 1963 Studebaker Avanti
2. 1955 Oldsmobile
3. 1960 DeSoto
4. 1938 Nash
5. 1966 Ford Fairlane
6. 1942 DeSoto

THE PRICE IS RIGHT!

	ETHYL REGULAR
CHI	19.2—17.2
LA	20.0—18.0
NY	21.6—19.6
	PREMIUM REGULAR
CHI	35.9—31.9
LA	37.9—33.9
NY	42.9—36.9
	PREMIUM REGULAR
CHI	37.9—33.9
LA	40.9—38.9
NY	50.9—47.9

PONTIAC POWER
1. 455 cu. in.—1970
2. 287 cu. in.—1955
3. 389 cu. in.—1959
4. 301 cu. in.—1977

PICKUP PASSION
1. 1933 Dodge
2. 1958 Ford Ranchero
3. 1947 Chevrolet
4. 1940 Plymouth
5. 1930 Ford
6. 1955 Dodge

DESOTO DISCOVERIES
1. B 6. A
2. A 7. B
3. B 8. C
4. C 9. B
5. A 10. A

DOUBLE NICKELS
January, 1975

BILLBOARD #1
1935
Chrysler
Airflow on the left and Airstream on the right

BY SHEER DRIVE...
John Hertz
Rent-A-Car, Fleet-Leasing Concept

MUSCLE CAR WORD SEARCH

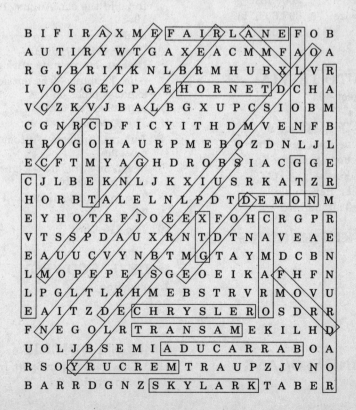

CUT-AWAY CALL-OUTS
1977–79 Cadillac Seville
1. Muffler
2. Taillight
3. Tailpipe
4. Disc brake
5. Leaf spring
6. Differential
7. Universal joint
8. Resonator
9. Catalytic converter
10. Transmission
11. Disc brake caliper
12. Shock absorber
13. Tie rod end
14. Stabilizer
15. Frame member
16. Alternator
17. Power steering pump
18. Alternator drive belt
19. Fan
20. Headlight
21. Air conditioning compressor
22. Fuel line filter
23. Carburetor
24. Spark plug
25. Air filter housing
26. Distributor
27. Master cylinder
28. Vacuum or power brake unit
29. Steering column

BEFORE AND AFTER
1. A-100
2. Deora
3. Golden
4. 1½ feet longer
5. 1½ feet lower
6. Alexander Brothers
7. Through the front by way of a center-hinged door and swing away steering wheel.

BLINKIN' BOBBIES
1966

'55 HORSES
1. 236
2. 270
3. 180
4. 250
5. 200
6. 198
7. 208
8. 225
9. 260
10. 177

SILHOUETTES #1
1. '68 Ford Mustang Shelby
2. '67 Pontiac 2 + 2
3. '60 Chrysler Imperial Limo

4. '68 Ford Ranchero
5. '65 Plymouth Barracuda

TWO SIDES TO EVERYTHING
1. Dodge
2. Sheriff of Scat City
3. "Ya'll drive careful now, heah..."

MADE BY...
Chrysler

MYSTERY CAR #1
1. 1959 Skoda
2. Czechoslovakia
3. 1686.00
4. C
5. B
6. A

DAYDREAMS #3
1. '53 Plymouth Firearrow
2. '54 Olds F-88
3. '70 AMX/3
4. '67 Chevy Astro I
5. '66 Studebaker Sceptre
6. '56 Pontiac Club de Mer

1960's and 70's
1. B
2. A
3. D
4. B
5. C
6. A
7. D
8. A
9. C
10. D
11. B
12. D
13. D
14. B
15. C

CANNIBALIZED CUSTOMS #1
1. Windshield—1951 Kaiser
2. Door Post—1955-56 Ford Crown Victoria
3. Lower Roof, Rear Window—1956 Chrysler
4. Hood Scoop—1970 Plymouth
5. Hood Ornament—1957 Pontiac
6. Right Headlamp Assembly—1967 Pontiac
7. Left Headlamp Assembly—1965 Ambassador
8. Right Front Bumper—1961 Dodge
9. Left Grille—1953 Chevrolet
10. Front Hubcap—1956 Oldsmobile

11. Front Fender, Door Trim—1960 Lincoln Continental
12. Lower Rear Fin—1961-62 Cadillac
13. Rear Front Bumper—1955-56 Imperial
14. Rear Taillight—1959-60 Studebaker Lark
15. Upper Rear Fin—1958 Mercury

HELLO, MA?
Ann Sothern
DeSoto Airflow

DEALER DISPLAYS #1
1. 1938 Terraplane
2. 1935 Chrysler Airflow
3. 1935 Auburn
4. 1933 Nash

TV AUTO TRIVIA #2
1. 1975-77 Dodge Royal Monaco
2. 1970 Mustang
3. 1966 Chevrolet
4. 1974 Buick Century
5. 1956 Chrysler (station wagon)
6. Pontiac Firebird Esprit
7. 1964 Imperial—"Black Beauty"
8. 1960-62 Plymouth

DOWNSIZED DUESY???
1938
American Bantam "60"

EASY PICKUPS #1
1. D
2. F
3. A
4. C
5. B
6. E

KNOCK ON WOOD
1. 1984 Chrysler
2. 1968 Mercury
3. 1946-48 Chrysler
4. 1946-48 Ford
5. 1946 Mercury
6. 1976 Mercury (Bobcat)

SMALL PACKAGE
1. King Midget
2. Rear
3. 1 cylinder
4. '57—23 cu. in.
   '67—29.1 cu. in.
5. Air-cooled
6. '55—one-speed automatic (no reverse)
   '65—two-speed automatic
7. 50 mph
8. 60 mpg

PROUD PARENT
1. F
2. C
3. G
4. A
5. B
6. D
7. E

ICE CAPADE
Pirelli

DETROIT HOODS #1
1. 1969 AMC Javelin
2. 1972 Dodge Challenger
3. 1980 Mercury Capri
4. 1983 Hurst/Olds
5. 1969 Plymouth Road Runner
6. 1970 Pontiac Firebird

WALTER P'S LEGACY
1. 1956
2. 1949
3. 1959
4. 1956
5. 1934
6. 1939
7. 1931
8. 1951
9. 1956
10. 1942
11. 1953
12. 1968

LET'S MAKE A DEAL
1. Plymouth Satellite
2. 3
3. Third

CONVOY UNSCRAMBLE
1. Diamond
2. Chevrolet
3. Mack
4. Autocar
5. Terraplane
6. White
7. Oshkosh
8. Peterbilt
9. Federal
10. Kenworth

SIXES FROM THE SIXTIES
1. E
2. H
3. F

4. B
5. G
6. A
7. D
8. J
9. I
10. C

SON OF COBRA
1. 1966
2. 289 cu. in.
3. 306 H.P.
4. Single four-barrel
5. B

BULLET NOSE
1. 1954
2. 1951
3. 1949
4. 1952
5. 1953
6. 1950

DOOR FIN
1. 1957 Lincoln
2. Landau
3. Futura
4. 368 cu. in.
5. 300 H.P.
6. 1 (1957)

WINDOW STICKER PRICE—1959
1. $2,330
2. $10,418
3. $4,667
4. $1,353
5. $13,250
6. $2,175

BEEP BEEP MY . . . !
Wile E. Coyote

MUNCHIN' MOTORIST
1. 1957 Oldsmobile
2. 1960 Plymouth
3. 1960-61 Chevrolet Corvair
4. 1958-60 Ford Thunderbird
5. 1954-55 Chevrolet Corvette
6. 1960 Pontiac
7. 1960-61 Ford Falcon
8. 1961 Buick

THE BIG BOYS
1. E
2. J

3. G
4. C
5. A
6. I
7. D
8. F
9. H
10. B

TV REPAIR
Brad Sears
The Last Chance Garage
1982

CAR OF PRESIDENTS
1. 1939
   160"
   258"
   72"
   Sunshine Special
2. 1950
   145"
   240"
   65"
   Bubble Top
3. 1961
   156"
   253.7"
   57"
4. 1969
   160"
   258.3"
   59.3"

RUBBER CORD
1. 1964
2. Royalite (by U.S. Royal)
3. Chevrolet Corvair
4. Front
5. Glenn Pray
6. $4000
7. 1966
8. Approx. 90

WELCOME ABOARD
1. 1952 Chrysler C-200 (dream car)
2. 1930 Ford Model A
3. 1949 Nash
4. 1960 Chevrolet Corvair
5. 1954 Chrysler Imperial
6. 1937 Lincoln Zephyr

DETROIT HOODS #2
1. 1970 Dodge Dart
2. 1973 Ford Mustang
3. 1978 AMC / AMX
4. 1969 Mercury
5. 1971 Plymouth Barracuda
6. 1964 Pontiac GTO

TRAVELING TRUNKS
Both are Packards.
A 1953 is on the left, a 1938 on the right.

LIFE-LIKE LOGOS #1
Mack Trucks

STORMIN' STOCKERS
1. 1974 Chevrolet
   427
   A. J. Foyt
2. 1961 Ford
   390
   Fred Lorenzen
3. 1977 Oldsmobile
   358
   Richard Petty
4. 1963 Plymouth
   426 wedge
   A. J. Foyt
5. 1952 Hudson
   308
   Marshall Teague
6. 1955 Chrysler
   331
   Frank "Rebel" Mundy

MUSTANG DIMENSIONS
1965—
2567 lbs.
108"
181.6"
51.1"
1973—
3233 lbs.
109"
193.8"
50.7"
1974—
2743 lbs.
96.2"
175"
49.9"

PUSH BUTTON TRANS.
1. "Teletouch" electric pushbutton transmission
2. 1964
3. 1956
4. "Keyboard" control transmission
5. Chrysler—8 years
6. "Magic Touch" PowerFlite transmission

FARAWAY PLACES #1
1. Seville
2. Sun Valley
3. Mexico
4. Barcelona
5. Manhattan
6. Monte Carlo
7. Torino
8. Saratoga
9. Ventura
10. Bermuda
11. Aspen
12. Calais

MEMORIES #1
Studebaker
Conoco

WOODY WAGONS #2
1. 1938 Plymouth
2. 1972 Chrysler
3. 1954 Ford
4. 1942 Oldsmobile
5. 1947–48 Mercury
6. 1969 Buick

Real wood—#'s 1, 4, and 5
Plus outside trim on #3

CAR PETS
1. Super Bee—Dodge
2. Cobra—Ford
3. Barracuda—Plymouth
4. Dr. Olds—Oldsmobile
5. Hawk—Studebaker
6. Marlin—Rambler/American Motors

HORSIN' AROUND
1. Spark Plug Cleaning Service
2. "Cleenie"
3. AC Spark Plugs

CLUB PAGE—CROSLEY QUICKIE
1. May 1949
2. COpper BRAzed
3. 23,489
4. Hot Shot
5. 1946

WINNERS #1
1. George Robson—1946
2. Rich Mears—1979
3. Rodger Ward—1962
4. Sam Hanks—1957
5. Bill Cummings—1934
   (Earl Unversaw mechanic)
6. Jim Clark—1965

YOU AUTO BE IN PICTURES
Custom built movie camera car
1950 Chrysler Imperial

BIRDS OF PREY #1
1. Ford Falcon
2. Griffith
3. Bentley
4. Pontiac Firebird

BIRDS-EYE-VIEW #2
1. Mercury Comet
2. 1971
3. 302 cubic inch V-8
4. 181.7 inches
5. $2220
6. 1977

GROOVY IDEA
Goodyear experimented with brightly colored neothane tires that lit up at night.
1961 Dodge

STAR WHEELS
1. Judy Garland
   1940 Studebaker
2. Jimmy Stewart and Wendy Berrie
   1936 DeSoto Airstream

GIMMICKS AND GADGETS #2
1. Swing-away steering wheel
   Ford Thunderbird
2. Automatic headlamp beam control
   Chevrolet
3. Adjustable mirrored instrument panel
   Buick
4. Tilt and telescope steering wheel
   Cadillac
5. Portable in-car radio
   Oldsmobile
6. Electronic warning indicator
   Ford Mustang and Mercury Capri

BACK OF THE BARN #1
1. 1939 Plymouth
2. 1930 Duesenberg

MUSCLE CUBES
1. D
2. G
3. E
4. J
5. I
6. C
7. H
8. B
9. F
10. A

DECAL DISGUISE #1
Spirit of America
1974

SOFT TOP QUICKIES #1
1. Lincoln Continental
2. 1940
3. Challenger
4. Cadillac and Oldsmobile

LONG, LUXURIOUS LIMOS
1. 1966 Ford
2. 1937 Chrysler Custom
3. 1936 Packard
4. 1965 Mercury
5. 1960 Imperial
6. 1929–30 Pierce-Arrow

TV AUTO TRIVIA #3
1. Chevrolet Corvette and Ford Thunderbird
2. Sunbeam Tiger
3. VW Karmann-Ghia
4. 1957 Chevrolet and 1982 Camaro
5. Chevrolet
6. *Burke's Law*
7. Volvo 1800
8. Chevrolet Nova

WHAT IS IT #1
Dual Bed
Catalytic Converter

WINNERS #2
1. Wilbur Shaw—1937 Jigger Johnson (mech.)
2. Mark Donohue—1972
3. Graham Hill—1966
4. Kelly Petillo—1935 Jimmy Dunham (mech.)
5. Johnnie Parsons—1950
6. Parnelli Jones—1963

SUMMER CAMP
1. 1965 GMC
2. 1969 Dodge
3. 1973 International
4. 1965 Chevrolet
5. 1967 Ford
6. 1975 Toyota

SUPER HIGHWAY STOMPER STUMPER
1. 1964
2. C
3. B

ROAD WORK
1. Cloverleaf
2. A
3. 1930
4. C

TURBINE TEAMMATES
1. A
2. C
3. One fifth
4. 1963
5. Elwood P. Engel, who designed the car in picture B, also designed the Thunderbird while at Ford.
6. 50
7. 1962 Dodge Dart
8. B
9. C
10. 1977
11. 1956 Plymouth Belvedere

CANNIBALIZED CUSTOMS #2
1. Top—1964-66 Plymouth Barracuda
2. Hood Scoop—1969 Ford Mustang
3. Right Grille—1966 Pontiac
4. Left Grille—1969 Dodge Charger
5. Front Wheel—Dodge/Plymouth
6. Front Fender—1968 Oldsmobile 442
7. Door, Side Scoop—1967 Ford Mustang
8. Rear Wheel—Chevrolet
9. Rear End—1974 Chevrolet Camaro

SLANT SIX
1. 1960
2. 170.9 cu. in.
   225.5 cu. in.

3. 30°
4. 1960-63

BREATHE DEEP
1. B
2. A
3. B
4. A
5. California
6. 1965
7. 1961
8. 1963
9. C

SURFS UP
1973 Dodge Dart "Hang 10"

CAR RAGS #1
1. *Hot Rod*
2. *Speed Age*
3. *Super Stock*
4. *Motor Trend*
5. *Drag Strip*
6. *Mechanix Illustrated*
7. *Popular Mechanics*

JUNKYARD JUMBLE
1. 1959 Oldsmobile
2. 1957 Mercury
3. 1959 Chevrolet
4. 1957 Oldsmobile
5. 1958 Edsel
6. 1959 Ford
7. 1956 Buick
8. 1955 Cadillac
9. 1957 Chevrolet
10. 1960 Chevrolet
11. 1959 Chevrolet
12. 1960 Pontiac
13. 1960 Mercury
14. 1960 Dodge
15. 1953 Mercury
16. 1956 Pontiac
17. 1957 Desoto
18. 1959 Chevrolet

FRONT DOOR SERVICE
1. 1957
2. Germany
3. BMW
4. Isetta
5. 60 MPG
6. Under $1000

WAGONS, WHOA!

1. 1957 Chrysler
2. 1960 Ford
3. 1959 Studebaker
4. 1963 Checker
5. 1955 Rambler
6. 1955 Pontiac (Safari)

HUB HYSTERIA #1

1. Ford
2. Lincoln
3. Jaguar
4. Dodge/Plymouth
5. Buick
6. Ford
7. Mercury
8. Plymouth
9. Isuzu
10. Imperial
11. Pontiac
12. Rambler

BELIEVE IT OR NOT!

Total number of light bulbs: 47
(Four headlights, six taillight bulbs, and 37 others of various sizes.)

INDY 500 PACE CARS 1940-53

1. C
2. E
3. A
4. G
5. H
6. B
7. F
8. E
9. C
10. D

STAR TRUCK?

Name: Nucleon
Year: 1955
Made by: Ford

RACING LEGENDS

1. Dan Gurney
2. Peter Revson
3. Bruce McLaren
4. Mario Andretti
5. Mark Donohue
6. A.J. Foyt Jr.

GENERATION GAP

TOP
1961 Buick Special
Number of cyl.—8
Horsepower—155
Weight—2700 lbs.
Length—188 in.
Height—52.8 in.

BOTTOM
1936 Buick Special
Number of cyl.—8
Horsepower—93
Weight—3660 lbs.
Length—193 in.
Height—67.3 in.

WHAT IS IT? #2

Oil Pan Drain Plug Extractor

AUTO BE FUNNY

1. DeSoto
2. "You Bet Your Life"
3. It's Delovely

PARKING GARAGE OF TIME #2

1. 1958 Rambler
2. 1930 Auburn
3. 1967 Oldsmobile 442

"NICE TO MEET YA!" #1

1. '61 Buick Special
2. '62 Chevy II
3. '63 Corvette Stingray
4. '65 Ford Mustang
5. '67 Chevrolet Camaro
6. '68 AMC Javelin
7. '70 Ford Maverick
8. '75 Chrysler Cordoba
9. '77 Lincoln Versailles
10. '80 AMC Eagle

ELECTRIC HAND

Hudson and Terraplane

PAPAL LIMOUSINE
1. Continental
2. 1965
3. 20 feet long
4. 12 inches

SHOW CAR SHOWDOWN
1. 1965 Mercury Comet Sportster
2. 1970 Dodge Challenger Yellow Jacket
3. 1969 Thunderbird Saturn II
4. 1964 Dodge Charger
5. 1968 Ford Super Cobra
6. 1969 Plymouth Duster I or Beep-Beep X-I

KEY BOBBERS #2
1. Kaiser
2. Lamborghini
3. Alfa Romeo

FIRST IMPRESSIONS
1955 Chevrolet

LAST OF THE MOHEGANS #1
1. 1937 Pierce-Arrow
2. 1940 Cadillac LaSalle
3. 1941 Graham
4. 1951 Frazer
5. 1954 Henry J
6. 1957 Hudson
7. 1958 Packard
8. 1960 Edsel
9. 1961 DeSoto
10. 1962 Nash Metropolitian
11. 1966 Studebaker
12. 1967 AMC Marlin
13. 1969 Chevy Corvair
14. 1971 Dodge Coronet R/T
15. 1974 Plymouth Barracuda

A SLICE OF LIFE
1. 1960 Pontiac
2. 1960 Chevrolet
3. 1959 Oldsmobile
4. 1957 Chevrolet
5. 1959 Ford

HEAVY-DUTY TRUCKIN'
WHITE
Turnpike Cruiser
Payload Special
Road Xpeditor
Road Boss

GMC
Brigadier
Astro
General

CHEVROLET
Pappa Bear Bruin
Kodiak
Titan 90

SCHOOL DAZE #2
1. Dodge
2. Dodge
3. White
4. GMC

BIRDS OF PREY #2
1. Imperial
2. Duesenberg
3. Thunderbird
4. Morgan

WILD HORSES
1. E
2. A
3. H
4. B
5. I
6. C
7. F
8. J
9. G
10. D

EUROPEAN TITLES
1. H—GB
2. K—France
3. F—Germany
4. A—France
5. I—GB
6. B—GB
7. J—Italy
8. C—Germany
9. L—Italy
10. D—Germany
11. E—France
12. G—GB

RARE RUMBLERS
1. 1934 Oldsmobile
2. 1935 Graham
3. 1930 Hudson
4. 1932 Ford
5. 1936 Oldsmobile
6. 1933 Dodge

SLICK SYMBOLS #3
1. D A
2. AMALIE
3. Ring-Free
4. Quaker State

QUEENS FOR A DAY #2
1957 Dual Ghia

T.L.C.
1. October
2. B
3. B
4. C

HOME SWEET FACTORY #1
1. Hartford, WI—Kissel
2. South Bend, IN—Rockne
3. Indianapolis, IN—Duesenberg
4. Willow Run, MI—Kaiser
5. Cleveland, OH—Jordan
6. Toledo, OH—Willys-Knight
7. Syracuse, NY—Franklin

WONDER WILLYS
1. 1940
2. 1932
3. 1939
4. 1955
5. 1953

CONFUSING CONNIES
1. 1968
2. 1963
3. 1966
4. 1964
5. 1962
6. 1967

PREPMOBILES
ACCEPTABLE
2
3
5
6
8
10
UNACCEPTABLE
1
4
7
9

SLICK SYMBOLS #4
1. Kendall
2. OILZUM
3. HYVIS
4. Veedol

CORPORATE GIANTS #1
1. Charles F. Kettering
   Past head of GM research
2. George Romney
   Past president of American Motors
3. H.S. Vance
   Past president of Studebaker
4. William C. Durant
   Founder and past president of General Motors

TRULY THE TRIVIEST #1
1. 1957 and 1959
2. Springfield, MA
3. "Race"
4. 30 hours
5. American Motors
6. 1977
7. 23 years (eight months and 15 days)
8. Honda
9. Studebaker
10. Denise McCluggage
11. Buick
12. Switzerland
13. Scotland
14. Pacer and Citation
15. "Green Monster"
16. Willys
17. Nate Altman
18. Mustang
19. Don Garlits
20. 1950
21. John Dillinger
22. Studebaker
23. 1953
24. W. Edwards Deming

LOOK BUT DON'T TOUCH #2
1958 Buick

TIRE LESS TRAVEL
1. Ford
2. A
3. 1959

DODGE DESIGNED
1. 1956
2. 1967
3. 1957
4. 1978
5. 1958

MYSTERY CAR #2
Dodge Colt

TILT FOR TWO
1. 1940 Hudson
2. 1985 Buick Electra

"LEAVE THE DRIVING TO US"
1. 1954
2. Scenicruiser
3. Raymond Loewy
4. Approx. 11 feet
5. 40 feet long
6. A

FLAT TIRE
Pirelli

MERCURY MUG SHOTS #2
1. 1960
2. 1965
3. 1966
4. 1964
5. 1962
6. 1969

HUB HYSTERIA #2
1. Datsun 240-Z
2. Ford Mustang
3. Jeep
4. Oldsmobile
5. Plymouth Barracuda
6. Dodge

SLICK CHARACTER
1. "Baldy the Slick"
2. Seiberling Rubber Co.

SKY QUEEN
1. Amelia Earhart
2. 1933 Terraplane
3. Six cylinders
4. 193 cu. in.
5. 70 H.P.
6. 106-inch wheelbase

SIGN LANGUAGE #1
1. Environmental Study Area
2. Tramway
3. Dam
4. Post Office
5. Winter Recreation Area
6. Laundry

SYMBOL SPECIALIST #1
1. Opel
2. Kaiser/Willys
3. Packard Clipper
4. Cadillac LaSalle

HOOD VENTS
1. 1936 DeSoto Airstream
2. 1934 LaSalle
3. 1935 Plymouth
4. 1940 Pontiac
5. 1937 Graham
6. 1938 Hudson

BILLBOARD #2
1937
DeSoto

MOTOR TREND CAR OF THE YEAR 1959-68
'59—B
'60—D
'61—E
'62—C
'63—A
'64—G
'65—H
'66—I
'67—F
'68—H

WHAT'S IT MEAN?
"HR" means Hill Retarder
Turboglide transmission
1957 Chevrolet

VETTE VENTS
1. 1956-57
2. 1968
3. 1971
4. 1966
5. 1961
6. 1958
7. 1964
8. 1967

MILLIONTH MODEL

1968
1. 1934
2. 1950
3. 1947
4. 1966
5. 1950
6. 1935

"TRANS"-LATION #1

1. Buick
2. DeSoto
3. Packard
4. Mercury (or Lincoln)
5. Chevrolet
6. Chrysler
7. Studebaker
8. Dodge/Chrysler

BILLBOARD #3

1939
Studebaker

LAGER LORRIES

1. Diamond T
2. White
3. Federal
4. Dodge
5. International
6. Hendrickson

STAR MECHANICS

1. Ricardo Montalban and a 1949 Ford
2. Paul Newman
3. Mickey Rooney and a 1940 Lincoln Zephyr

A ROSE IS A ROSE #1

1. Edsel, Chevrolet
2. Dodge, Pontiac
3. DeSoto, Cadillac
4. Willys, AMC, Chevrolet
5. Dodge, Buick, Studebaker
6. Oldsmobile, Chevrolet
7. Willys, Studebaker
8. Plymouth, DeSoto, Nash, Chevrolet
9. Hudson, AMC

FAIRY TALE

1. Nash-Healey
2. 1951
3. B
4. A
5. C
6. A

HOME AWAY FROM HOME

1. Sleepy
2. TraveLodge

FINE FEATHERED FRIENDS

1. Skylark
2. Firebird
3. Thunderbird
4. Eagle
5. Road Runner
6. Phoenix

1940s AND 1950s

1. D
2. B
3. C
4. D
5. C
6. A
7. B
8. C
9. D
   *Correct name was Kiekhaefer Aeromarine Motors, Inc.
10. B
11. A
12. C
13. D
14. D
15. B
16. D

REBELLIOUS RACER

James Dean
Porsche 356 Speedster

SPYDER WEB

1. C
2. B
3. A
4. A
5. 1964

ROLLING RECORDS #1

Side A—The Rip Chords
Side B—Herb Alpert and the Tijuana Brass

RHINO RIDDLE

Armstrong Rubber Co.

TO PATROL AND PURSUE

1. 1958 Dodge

2. 1964 Ford
3. 1937 DeSoto
4. 1959 Plymouth

HARDTOP HERITAGE

1. F—1950
2. A—1954
3. E—1949
4. B—1951
5. C—1955
6. D—1952

JOHN Z.

1. 1966
2. 1982
3. A. Overhead-cam 6
   B. 1966
4. Tempest

BUSTLE BUTTS #1

1. 1936 Pierce-Arrow
2. 1938 Nash LaFayette
3. 1935 Packard
4. 1935 Hudson
5. 1935 Chevrolet

BROTHERHOOD

Pictures: A. J. Frank and Charles Duryea
         B. John and Horace Dodge
1. D
2. H
3. F
4. B
5. G
6. A
7. E
8. C

SYMBOL SPECIALIST #2

1. Nash
2. International (Trucks)
3. Amphicar
4. Auto Union—DKW

FOR LAW AND ORDER

1. 1946 Ford
2. 1963 Studebaker
3. 1959 Dodge
4. 1939 Plymouth

MECHANICALLY MINDED #2

1. Insulator top
2. Center electrode
3. Shell
4. Lower internal gasket
5. Side electrode
6. Insulator tip
7. Upper internal gasket
8. Center seal
9. Terminal

INDY 500 PACE CARS 1930-39

1. D
2. H
3. G
4. A
5. C
6. B
7. I
8. C
9. F
10. E

STARS IN CARS #1

Clark Gable
1936 Jensen-Ford (English)

COUNT THE MONTE CARLOS

1. 1971
2. 1979
3. 1975
4. 1976
5. 1972
6. 1970

MOVIE SCENES #1

1. The Car
2. Car Wash

MORE WOODY WONDERS

1. 1941 Packard
2. 1937 Terraplane
3. 1940 Willys
4. 1942 Ford

PHOTO FINISH

Car #15: Parnelli Jones
Car #16: Rodger Ward
1963 Mercurys

SUPER LOGO

Mallory

PROBLEM SOLVERS

1. Tire Changer
2. Brake Bleeder
3. Strut Compressor
4. Computer Wheel Balancer

UNCLE T

1. Tom McCahill
2. *Mechanix Illustrated*
3. A

CHROME MOLARS

1. 13
2. 6
3. 11
4. 5
5. 9
6. 3
7. 7
*Toughie—160

FAR AWAY PLACES #2

1. Laguna
2. LeMans
3. Daytona
4. Riviera
5. Southampton
6. Montreal
7. Hollywood
8. Panama
9. Windsor
10. Monterey
11. Granada
12. Monza

THE CADILLAC SIXTEEN

1. 500 cu. in.
2. 1970
3. Heron
4. V-16
5. 1950
6. 1948
7. V-12
8. 1965
9. 1976
10. 1953
11. 1939
12. 1937
13. 1959
14. 1952
15. 1957
16. 1940

MUSCLE MEDALLIONS #1

1. '62 Ford
2. '64 Studebaker
3. '63 Pontiac
4. '67 Plymouth

5. '63 Oldsmobile

"DIP-DIP-DIP BOOM"

1. 1958 Buick
2. 1956 Ford
3. 1958-60 Ford Taunus
4. 1956 Rambler
5. 1955 Oldsmobile
6. 1956 Studebaker
7. 1956 Ambassador
8. 1959 Edsel
9. 1957 Ford
10. 1959 Ford
11. 1953 Packard
12. 1956 Pontiac

BACK OF THE BARN #2

1. 1935 Pontiac
2. 1948 Tucker
3. 1935 LaSalle

IT'S A GAS

1. E
2. I
3. G
4. A
5. C
6. H
7. B
8. D
9. J
10. F

...MORE MOTELS!

1. 1952
2. Memphis, TN
3. 1954
4. Savannah, GA

STRETCHED STEEL

189-inch wheelbase
269.75-inch overall length
64.37-inch height

1. Aerobus
2. 12
3. B
4. 36 inches
5. Kalamazoo, MI

CHRYSLER HINDSIGHT

1. 1970 Plymouth
2. 1964 Dodge
3. 1958 DeSoto
4. 1965 Chrysler
5. 1964 Dodge

"NICE TO MEET YA!" #2
1. '58 Rambler American
2. '61 Pontiac Tempest
3. '67 Front-drive Eldorado
4. '70 Dodge Challenger
5. '74 Mustang II
6. '75 Mercury Bobcat
7. '78 Dodge Omni/Plymouth Horizon
8. '79 Dodge 024/Plymouth TC3
9. '80 Chevrolet Citation
10. '82 Ford EXP/Mercury LN7

SABOTAGED
1. Trouble Shooting Contest
2. Plymouth
3. 1949
4. The most skillful teenage auto mechanic students from schools around the country.
5. Solve 12 major mechanical problems on deliberately sabotaged cars.

DREAMS COME TRUE #1
1. 1955 Chevrolet Biscayne
2. 1953 Pontiac Parisienne
3. 1954 Chevrolet Corvair
4. 1957 Dodge Dart

KNOCK KNOCK
1960 DeSoto

XNR
1. Virgil M. Exner
2. Chrysler Corporation
3. Pontiac
4. Studebaker

VINTAGE MGs
1. M
2. J2
3. PB
4. TA/TB/TC
5. TD
6. TF
7. MGA
8. MGB

INTERNATIONAL INTRIGUE #1
1. Cunningham—England
2. Jaguar—England
3. MG—England
4. Volvo—Sweden
5. Mercedes Benz—Germany

JACKRABBIT
1. 1955 Nash Rambler 90 H.P.
2. 1953 Pontiac 115-122 H.P.
3. 1951 Ford 95-100 H.P.
4. 1950 Buick 115-152 H.P.
5. 1952 Ford 101-110 H.P.

NAME GAME #2
1. Italia
2. Saratoga
3. Concours
4. DPL
5. Terraplane
6. Capri
7. Series 52 Special
8. Powermaster
9. Sebring
10. Streamliner
11. Executive
12. Traveler

CUSTOM LITE
1959 Cadillac

PARTING SHOTS
1. 1973 Chevrolet Monte Carlo
2. 1955 Dodge Coronet
3. 1957 Cadillac Eldorado Biarritz
4. 1955 Chrysler New Yorker
5. 1968 Shelby Mustang
6. 1967 Pontiac Firebird
7. 1967 Mercury Cougar
8. 1959 Continental Mark IV

DEALER DISPLAYS #2
1. 1931 Chrysler
2. 1935 Pontiac
3. 1939 Hudson
4. 1935 Auburn

SECRET COMPARTMENT
1. Ford
2. 1952
3. A. Under left taillight chrome top
   B. Under left gunsight taillight
   C. Behind left flip down taillight
   D. Behind left backup light
   E. Under emblem

BIG BLOCKS
1. C
2. F
3. A
4. D
5. B
6. I

7. E
8. G
9. H

KEY BOBBERS #3
1. Frazer
2. Jaguar
3. Maserati

DIESEL
1. Injection Pump
2. Injection Pump Adapter
3. Injection Pump Drive Gears
4. Timing Chain
5. Prechamber
6. Glow Plug
7. Nozzle
8. Fuel Return System
9. Fuel Filter
10. Vacuum Pump

CHEVY FRONTS
1. 1949
2. 1953
3. 1950
4. 1952
5. 1951
6. 1954

OUTDOOR ADS #2
1. 1975 Datsun 280-Z
2. 1959 Studebaker Lark
3. 1955 Oldsmobile

AMERICAN RULING CLASS #1
1. E
2. D
3. G
4. H
5. B
6. A
7. C
8. F

LIFE LIKE LOGOS #2
Detroit Racing Equipment

KIDDY CARS
1. 1956 Pontiac
2. 1958 Corvette

3. 1976-77 Dodge Aspen
4. 1964 Monza (Chevy show car)

JOHNNIES COME LATELY
1. 1978 Dodge Aspen R/T
2. 1979 Oldsmobile Cutlass 442
3. 1978 AMC AMX
4. 1977 Plymouth Volare Road Runner
5. 1974 Pontiac Ventura GTO

EASY PICKUPS #2
1. F
2. A
3. H
4. G
5. C
6. B
7. D
8. E

TAILOR-MADE
A. Throttle and service break lever
B. Starter control lever
C. Gear Shift control lever
D. Directional Signal lever
E. Clutch pedal extension bar
F. Clutch control switch
G. Headlight dimmer control selector switch
H. Hand headlight dimmer switch
I. Steering wheel—hand or hook grip

MUSCLE MEDALLIONS #2
1. Ford
2. Chevrolet
3. Mercury
4. Studebaker
5. Dodge
6. Pontiac

STOP LIGHT
1. 1950 Chevrolet
2. 1950 Buick
3. 1951 Oldsmobile
4. 1950 Plymouth
5. 1950 Chevrolet
6. 1950-52 Rambler
7. 1949 Chrysler
8. 1949 Cadillac

9. 1951-52 Buick
10. 1952 DeSoto
11. 1950 Pontiac
12. 1952 Studebaker
Bonus: GMC

CANNIBALIZED CUSTOMS #3
1. Top—1966 AMC Marlin
2. Windshield—1956 Chrysler
3. Spoiler—1970 Charger Daytona
4. Rear Fender—1955 Chevrolet Bel Air
5. Door—1958 Thunderbird
6. Right Fender—1974 Chevrolet Monte Carlo
7. Hood Scoop—1954 Mercury
8. Hood—1953 Studebaker
9. Left Grille—1954 Studebaker
10. Right Grille—1953 Studebaker
11. Left Fender—1957 Nash
12. Bumper—1968 Corvette
13. Left Lower Grille—1970 Corvette
14. Right Lower Grille—1968 Corvette
15. Front Hubcap—1953 Studebaker
16. Rear Hubcap—1957 Ford

WOOD'NT RUST
1957 Chevrolet

WHAT IS IT? #2
A $14.95 accelerator holder (a cheap cruise-control)

FIREBIRD FRONTS #2
1. 1977
2. 1975
3. 1976
4. 1978
5. 1979
6. 1974

GREENHOUSE #1
1. 1956 Lincoln
2. 1956-57 Rambler
3. 1960-64 Corvair
4. 1959 Ford
5. 1978 AMX
6. 1957-59 Imperial

MOTOR TREND CAR OF THE YEAR 1949-58

'49—B	'53—D	'57—A
'50—D	'54—D	'58—C
'51—A	'55—D	
'52—B	'56—E	

SO SENSITIVE
It was a micro-moisture switch that would automatically raise the convertible top and windows at the first drop of rain.

AUTO PARTS #1
1. Air Lift Company
2. Edelbrook Company
3. Holley Hi-Performance Products
4. Rotunda (products of FoMoCo)

DEALERS CHOICE (TRUCKS)

1. D	5. B	9. E
2. H	6. J	10. G
3. A	7. C	
4. F	8. I	

FIRST OF ITS KIND
1949 Holden; Australia

DECAL DISGUISE #2
Sprint Decor
1972

SLOGANS OF THE FIFTIES
1. Chevrolet
2. Dodge
3. Kaiser
4. Chrysler 300/C
5. Ford
6. Chrysler
7. Buick
8. Corvette
9. Mercury
10. Plymouth

THOSE MISCHIEVOUS GREMLINS

1. 1973	4. 1972
2. 1977	5. 1976
3. 1970	6. 1975

THE HORNETS NEST

1. 1972	5. 1981
2. 1978	6. 1970
3. 1973	7. 1975-77
4. 1980	8. 1979

CARS FROM CROPS?
1. Henry Ford
2. 1941
3. Plastic
4. Soybean derivative

MISSION-"INITIALS"
1. Road & Track
2. Rally Sport
3. Four-barrel, four-speed, dual exhaust (400 cid, four-barrel, dual exhausts after 1964)
4. Hertz (Rent-A-Car)
5. Gran Sport
6. Two Seat—Mid-engine—Four cyl.
7. Gran Turismo Omologato
8. American Motors Experimental
9. Super Sport
10. King of the Road

'84 LITERS
1. D
2. I
3. E
4. A
5. G
6. C
7. B
8. J
9. F
10. H

DEVIOUS DODGES
1. 1954
2. 1956
3. 1950
4. 1952
5. 1953
6. 1957
7. 1949
8. 1955

DON'T LET IT "BUG" YOU!
1. 1951-1963
2. 1958
3. 1950
4. 1977
5. 1952
6. 1976
7. 1955
8. 1978
9. 1962
10. 1871
11. 1964
12. 1970

13. 1953
14. 1966
15. 1968
16. 1956
17. 1966

FIVE MILLIONTH HARDTOPS
1. 1949
2. Roadmaster
3. 1970
4. LeSabre

ROLLING RECORDS #2
Side A—Wilson Pickett
Side B—Jan and Dean

TOP TEN 1957
1. H
2. F
3. D
4. J
5. I
6. G
7. C
8. A
9. B
10. E
Bonus: DeSoto

CHARGER CHOICES
1. 1971
2. 1977
3. 1975
4. 1972
5. 1970
6. 1976

PICKUPS TO PONDER
1. 1960 Ford
2. 1930 Willys
3. 1933 Terraplane
4. 1979 Chevrolet (El Camino)
5. 1961 Dodge Dart
6. 1940 Chevrolet

MEMORIES #2
Japan—Toyota
Pure

SYMBOL SPECIALIST #3
1. Reo-Royale
2. Simca
3. Subaru
4. DeSoto Adventure

CALL ME BY MY FIRST NAME
1. L
2. H
3. F
4. A
5. I
6. B
7. K
8. C
9. E
10. D
11. G
12. J

NAME GAME #3
1. H
2. E
3. J
4. A
5. L
6. B
7. I
8. D
9. K
10. C
11. G
12. F

SEE NO EVIL—HEAR NO EVIL
Side view mirror and radio aerial

SPEED WEEK
1. 1957 Mercury Monterey
2. Driving stability
3. A
4. C

PARKING GARAGE OF TIME #3
1. 1957 Lincoln
2. 1938 Graham Paige
3. 1982 Ferrari Mondial

MOVIE SCENES #2
1. *Grease 2*
   1951 Studebaker
2. *Grand Prix*
   Formula 1
   James Garner

PIERCE-ARROW CLUB PAGE
1. Stamped into the base of the archer ornament

2. 1932 (112.9 mph); 1933 (117.8 mph); 1934 (127.2 mph)
3. Red—Stoplight
4. The Studebaker Corporation
5. Norman
6. Club Sedan
7. Pierce-Arrow's fender-mounted headlights
8. Ice boxes, bird and squirrel cages, wire goods, household tinware.
9. The Shah of Persia
10. False (The Model A was the largest)
11. True
12. Seagrave, to power its fire engines.

RAIL-CAR
1936 Chrysler Imperial Airflow

BIG IMPRESSIONS
1. A
2. C
3. B
4. Giant earth-moving equipment

POSTWAR OUTPUT
1. Chevrolet
2. Ford
3. Plymouth
4. Buick
5. Dodge
6. Pontiac
7. Oldsmobile
8. Kaiser-Frazer
9. Mercury
10. Studebaker

"A PAT ON THE BACK"
1926–1951

PASSION PITS
1. 1956 Pontiac
2. 1955 Ford
3. 1959 Pontiac
4. 1959 Ford
5. 1958 Ford
6. 1957 Chevrolet
7. 1958 Pontiac
8. 1961 Rambler
9. 1955 Pontiac
10. 1956 Cadillac
11. 1957 Plymouth
12. 1955 Ford

MAN & MACHINES
1. C
2. E
3. H
4. J
5. A
6. I
7. B
8. D
9. G
10. F

PLAYMATE CARS
1. 1969 Shelby GT 500—Connie Kreski
2. 1972 DeTomaso Pantera—Liv Lindeland
3. 1966 Dodge Charger—Allison Parks
4. 1968 AMX—Angela Dorian
5. 1967 Barracuda—Lisa Baker
6. 1965 Sunbeam Tiger—Jo Collins

NAME THAT STATE #2
1. Oklahoma—Chrysler
2. Colorado—Mercury
3. Georgia—Oldsmobile
4. Michigan—Packard

BATTERY BAFFLERS
1. Vent Cap
2. Terminal post
3. Negative plate
4. Separator
5. Positive plate
6. Sediment space
7. Cell partition
8. Plate feet
9. Element rests
10. Post strap
11. Case
12. Cover

FORD DREAMING
1. 1956 Mercury XM-800 or Turnpike Cruiser
2. 1963 T-Bird Cougar
3. 1961 Ford Gyron
4. 1977 Ford Megastar
5. 1967 Seattle-ite
6. 1952 Continental Nineteen Fifty-X

OPERA WINDOWS
1. 1976 Ford Elite
2. 1974 Olds Toronado
3. 1978 Ford Thunderbird
4. 1974 Dodge Charger
5. 1981 Continental Mark VI
6. 1956–57 Ford Thunderbird

LONG AND SHORT OF IT!
1. C
2. E
3. G
4. B
5. I
6. J
7. H
8. A
9. D
10. F

SLICK SYMBOLS #5
Texaco

FIND THE DIFFERENCES
1. Traffic signal changed
2. Model year changed from 6 to 8
3. Hood ornament missing
4. One port hole on fender is gone
5. The car occupants clothing is missing
6. Hubcap center missing
7. Gas filler door flap is gone
8. Rear bumper guards missing
9. Tie on pedestrian changed
10. Sidewalk curb missing

AMERICAN RULING CLASS #2
1. G
2. A
3. B
4. F
5. H
6. C
7. E
8. D

SLICK SYMBOLS #6
Gulf

DASH DANG-IT
1. 1961 Imperial
2. 1955 Thunderbird
3. 1956 Pontiac
4. 1966 Mercedes-Benz 250 SE
5. 1964 Dodge Custom 880
6. 1964 Ford Falcon

QUIZ DELIVERY VAN

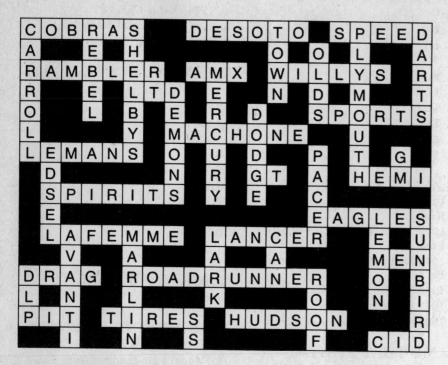

NAME THAT STATE #3
1. Iowa—Rambler
2. Arkansas—Buick
3. Louisiana—Plymouth
4. Minnesota—Cadillac

CORVAIR CLUB PAGE
1. October 2, 1959 to the Ypsilanti (Mich) Press, at 12:01 am, only one minute after its introduction.
2. Forward-control vans (Greenbrairs, Corvans)
3. 1961
4. 1960–61 and 1966–69
5. 1961
6. 1965
7. Four-door hardtop
8. 1965
9. Lucy Baines Johnson—1963 Spyder convertible
10. Two-door hardtop

CANNIBALIZED CUSTOMS #4
1. Hood Trim—1946 Pontiac
2. Center Grille Bar—1952 Ford
3. Inboard Headlight—1956–57 Rambler
4. Left Headlights/Fender—1957 Lincoln
5. Left Bumper/Lower Grille—1958 Edsel
6. Right Bumper/Lower Grille—1960 Dodge
7. Right Upper Grille—1959 Checker
8. Right Headlight/Fender—1959 Oldsmobile
9. Right Windshield—1935 Hupmobile

NAME GAME #4
'65 Pontiac 2 + 2
'70 Buick GSX
'63 Studebaker Hawk
'65 Corvair Corsa
'70 Olds Rally 350
'69 Plymouth GTX
'67 Rambler Rogue
'73 Challenger Rallye
'67 Cougar Eliminator
'67 Dart GTS

FASTBACK FOOLERS
1. '78–'84 Mazda RX-7
2. '84 Dodge Shelby Charger
3. '69 Mercury Cyclone
4. '70 AMX
5. '80 Pontiac Firebird
6. '65 Chevrolet Corvette
7. '69 Plymouth Barracuda
8. '76 Alfa Romeo Alfetta-GT

CAR RAGS #2
1. *Popular Science*
2. *Car Life*
3. *Motor Trend*
4. *Speed Age*
5. *Car Life*
6. *Popular Hot Rod*
7. *Hot Rod*

ONCE UPON A TIME...
LeSabre—Invicta—Electra
1959 Buick

"NICE TO MEET YA!" #3
1. '56 Continental Mark II
2. '58 Packard Hawk
3. '63 Buick Riviera
4. '64 Chevelle
5. '66 Toronado
6. '66 Charger
7. '68 AMX
8. '70 Monte Carlo
9. '73 Oldsmobile Omega
10. '75 Cadillac Seville

INTERNATIONAL INTRIGUE #2
1. Goliath
2. Renault
3. Nash-Healey
4. Ferrari
5. Borgward
6. DeLorean
Bonus: 1. Tiger
       2. Sammy Davis Jr.

NAME GAME #5
1. 600
2. State Star liner
3. Dragon
4. Jet Liner
5. Medalist
6. Jetfire
7. Commando
8. Cricket
9. Sizzler
10. MPG

MUSCULAR MASSAGE
1. Hastings Manufacturing Co.
2. "Tough Guy"
3. piston rings
4. Tough on oil-pumping Gentle on cylinder walls

MYSTERY CAR #3
1. Arnolt-Bristol
2. 1954
3. S. H. Arnolt, Inc., Chicago, IL, U.S.A.
   Bristol Cars of England
   Carrozzeria Bertone of Italy
4. 2.0 litres
5. Six-cylinder
6. 130 H.P.

BIRD COLORS
Blue—Red—Yellow

MOVIE SCENES #3
1. Corvette Summer
1. The Love Bug
2. Herbie

EXPOSED
1. 1959 Pontiac
2. 1935 DeSoto Airflow
3. 1968 Checker Superior
4. 1964 Dodge D-100
5. 1955 Nash
6. 1965 Dodge Monaco
7. 1978 Datsun 280-ZX

THE HOLE TRUTH
1. 1949
2. 1978
3. 1953
4. 1961
5. 1954
6. 1957
7. 1950
8. 1962
9. 1952

NAME GAME #6
1. Astre
2. Big Boy
3. Fireflite
4. Virginian
5. Caliente
6. Concord
7. Invicta
8. Royal
9. Super
10. LaFayette
11. Meadowbrook
12. Futuramic 76

GRANDPA DUKE
1939 Studebaker Champion

PLYMOUTH PICTURE PUZZLER
1. 1968
2. 1961
3. 1960
4. 1963
5. 1960
6. 1968
7. 1966
8. 1962

SKY LIGHT
1. Buick and Oldsmobile
2. Skylark SportWagon and Vista Cruiser
3. 1964
4. four inches
5. 1970

DRIVE-IN QUICKIES
1. A
2. B
3. A
4. C

AUTO LANGUAGE #1
1. Bezel—E
2. Diode—C
3. Coil—F
4. Pinion—F
5. Linkage—G
6. Spark—A
7. Bearing—B
8. Flywheel—D

STOCK STARS
1. 1966 Chevrolet Chevelle
   427 cu. in.
   Curtis Turner
2. 1970 Javelin
   304 cu. in.
   Jim Paschal
3. 1951 Chrysler
   331 cu. in.
   Aaron Woodard
4. 1969 Ford Talladega
   429 cu. in.
   David Pearson
5. 1957 Ford
   312 cu. in.
   Joe Weatherly
6. 1970 Chevrolet Monte Carlo
   427 cu. in.
   Bobby Allison

MOTOR PSYCHO
1. 1956 Ford

2. Arizona, ANL-709
3. 1959 Ford
4. 1957 Ford

ORIGINAL ROUGH RIDERS
1. Roosevelt
2. Marmon
3. 1929
4. B
5. 1931

AUTO LANGUAGE #2
1. Bore—D
2. Cowl—F
3. Injector—H
4. Torque—B
5. Valve—G
6. Pushrod—A
7. Idle—C
8. Dash—E

MOPAR FINS
1. 1959 Plymouth
2. 1956 Dodge
3. 1961 Imperial
4. 1958 Chrysler
5. 1960 Dodge
6. 1959 DeSoto

PISTON POPPERS
1. 1977 Olds Cutlass
   358 cu. in.
   Cale Yarborough
2. 1965 Dodge Coronet
   426 Hemi
   James Hylton
3. 1976 Chevrolet Malibu
   358 cu. in.
   Benny Parsons
4. 1962 Ford Galaxie
   406 cu. in.
   Fred Lorenzen
5. 1969 Plymouth Road Runner
   426 Hemi
   Roger McCluskey
6. 1970 Ford Torino
   429 cu. in.
   Donnie Allison

SECRET AGENT
Bardahl
1. B— Dirty Sludge
2. A—Blackie Carbon
3. D—Gummy Rings
4. C—Sticky Valves

NICK NAMES
1. E
2. D
3. F
4. G
5. A
6. C
7. B

ENGINE ABBREVIATIONS
1. IL—In-line engine with "L" Head
2. VO—V-engine with Overhead Valves
3. VHV—V-engine, Horizontal Valve Arrangement
4. IO—In-line engine with Overhead Valves
5. VL—V-engine with "L" Head

CAR TUNES #1
1. Fun Fun Fun
2. Johnny Bond
3. Cadillac
4. The Cadillacs

HALF-DOZEN INDYS...
1. Bobby Unser—1968, 1975, 1981
2. Al Unser—1970, 1971, 1978

LOVE THOSE 8'S
1. Ferrari
2. Nash Ambassador
3. La Salle
4. Ford/Mercury
5. Plymouth/Dodge
6. Porsche

T-BIRD TEASER
1. 1960
2. 1963
3. 1958
4. 1962
5. 1959
6. 1961

ENGINE SPECS
1. B
2. A
3. C
4. C
5. B
6. A
7. B
8. B

ASSEMBLY LINES #2
1. 1937 Plymouth
2. 1946 Packard
3. 1955 Hudson
4. 1963 Dodge
5. 1960 Buick
6. 1958 Chevrolet

GRAND PRIX GAME
1 & 6 1973
2 & 3 1978
4 & 7 1972
5 & 8 1977

HOME SWEET FACTORY #2
1. Indianapolis, IN—Marmon
2. Lansing, MI—Viking
3. Detroit, MI—Essex
4. Elkhart, IN—Elcar
5. Cincinnati, OH—Crosley
6. Cleveland, OH—Peerless
7. Buffalo, NY—Pierce-Arrow
8. Elizabeth, NJ—Durant

PAST REFLECTIONS
1. 1953 Hudson
2. 1946 Pontiac
3. 1961 DeSoto

AMX CLUB PAGE
1. A
2. 1968-69
3. False—They were standard
4. 1970
5. 1969
6. False
7. AMX/3—6 units
8. Senator Barry Goldwater of Arizona
9. Australia
10. B
11. False
12. 1971-74 Javelin AMX
1977 Hornet AMX
1978 Concord AMX
1979-80 Spirit AMX

DO-IT-YOURSELF KEY
1971 Ford Pinto
1. Ignition point and spark plug gauge for .030" gap
2. Regular screwdriver

3. Phillips screwdriver
4. 1½—inch ruler
5. Spark plug setter tool
6. Distributor point and spark plug gauge for .025" gap

NAME SAKES
1. Ransom Eli Olds
2. James Ward Packard
3. Joseph W. Frazer
4. Louis Chevrolet
5. Frederick Samuel Duesenberg
6. Walter Percy Chrysler
7. Howard C. Marmon
8. Henry Ford
9. Charles W. Nash

BUSTLE BUTTS #2
1. 1935 Dodge
2. 1935 Pontiac
3. 1940 Continental
4. 1935 Auburn
5. 1936 Nash Ambassador
6. 1936 Hupmobile

MORE EL CAMINO/RANCHERO
1. 1960
2. 1964
3. 1967
4. 1979

SLICK SYMBOLS #7
Humble Oil

"TRANS"-LATION #2
1. Chrysler
2. Studebaker
3. Ford
4. Buick
5. Hudson
6. Cadillac
7. Chevrolet
8. All Chrysler Corp. makes

OPEN SEASON
1. 1957 Pontiac Star Chief
2. 1968 Oldsmobile 98
3. 1960 Ford Sunliner
4. 1950 Nash Rambler
5. 1964 Lincoln Continental
6. 1957 Dodge Custom Royal

MOVIN' MASCOT
1. "Tiger Paws" by Uniroyal
2. "Power Brute" by Borg-Warner

RAINY DAY RAGTOPS
1. 1942 Plymouth
2. 1942 Oldsmobile
3. 1949 Lincoln Cosmopolitan
4. 1955 Chrysler Windsor
5. 1956 Ford Sunliner
6. 1937 Pontiac

THIS MUST BE "Z" CAR
1. Fairlady Z
2. 1970
3. 2.4 liters/146 cu. in.
4. False (all steel)
5. *Car and Driver*
6. B
7. 1974
8. A
9. 1975
10. 1979
Bonus: 2000 GT

SPORTS CAR SILHOUETTES
1. Austin-Healey
2. MGA
3. Jaguar
4. Saab
5. Triumph TR-3
6. Porsche

UNDERWATER DREAMS
1956 Norseman by Chrysler on the Andrea Doria

CHEVY BLOCKS
1. 1931
2. 1934
3. 1955
4. 1957
5. 1962
6. 1969
7. 1960

SYMBOL SPECIALIST #4
1. Plymouth
2. Bricklin
3. Citroen
4. Packard

PICKUPS OF THE PAST
1. 1951 Dodge
2. 1961 Willys Jeep
3. 1955 GMC
4. 1939 Federal
5. 1938 Willys
6. 1957 Ford

WAR YEARS
1. Hudson
2. February
3. A
4. Chrysler
5. A
6. B
7. Ducks
8. 1941
9. American Bantam and Ford
10. 1945

LAST OF THE MOHEGANS #2
1. 1931 Ford Model A
2. 1934 Franklin
3. 1937 Terraplane
4. 1941 Hupmobile
5. 1952 Crosley
6. 1955 Willys
7. 1956 Nash Statesman
8. 1957 Hudson
9. 1961 Chrysler Windsor
10. 1963 Buick Invicta
11. 1965 Dodge Custom 880
12. 1970 Ford Falcon
13. 1971 Plymouth GTX
14. 1974 Pontiac GTO
15. 1978 AMC Gremlin

MYSTERY EMBLEM
1. Vauxhall
2. England
3. Pontiac

PARKING GARAGE OF TIME #4
1. 1956-57 Continental Mark II
2. 1935 Terraplane
3. 1960 Mercury Comet

PASS WITH CARE
1. 1966 Plymouth Barracuda
2. 1949 Crosley

NAME GAME #7
1. Cosmopolitan
2. Hollywood
3. VIP
4. 1000
5. Skyway Champion
6. Pacemaker
7. Royale
8. Mirada
9. Superba
10. Fleetline

11. Vista Cruiser
12. Corsair

WILD HORSES #2
1. E
2. A
3. H
4. B
5. I
6. C
7. F
8. J
9. G
10. D

TAIL END OF TRIVIA
1. 1959 Edsel
2. 1955 Imperial
3. 1958 Plymouth
4. 1966 Pontiac Tempest
5. 1970 Chevrolet Monte Carlo
6. 1969 Mercury
7. 1959 Mercury
8. 1967 Dodge

LENGTHY LIMOS
1. 1984 Chrysler
2. 1938 Packard
3. 1930 LaSalle
4. 1966 Ford
5. 1964 Imperial
6. 1967 Lincoln Continental

WILD HORSES 1958
1. D
2. F
3. A
4. H
5. G
6. B
7. E
8. C

FLYING CAR FACTS
Aircraft wingspan: 34'6"
Make of aircraft engine: Lycoming
Horsepower rating: 190
Horsepower rating: 26½
Make of car engine: Crosley

SLICK SYMBOLS #8
Mobil

FIN FUN
1. 1959
2. 1948
3. 1956
4. 1961
5. 1960
6. 1964
7. 1957
8. 1957 (Eldorado Biarritz)

BODY BUILDERS
From left to right: Alfred J., Lawrence P., Charles T., Fred J., William A., Howard A., and Edward F. Fisher

FOMOCO FIRST
1. 1939
2. 1951
3. 1954
4. 1946
5. 1960
6. 1971
7. 1932
8. 1962
9. 1951
10. 1962½
11. 1939
12. 1957

FLATTERY
1. 1942 Chrysler New Yorker
2. 1970 Lincoln Continental
3. 1940 Graham
4. 1982 Dodge Mirada

LIL' HUSTLER
Datsun

EXOTIC GT SPORTS
1. Urraco
2. Mulsanne
3. Khamsin
4. Lagonda
5. Interceptor
6. Zagato
7. Spider
8. Mondial
9. Alpine
10. Eclat

ZEALOUS PATRIOT
1934 Dodge

DREAMS COME TRUE #2
1. 1962 Ford Mustang I
2. 1955 Chrysler Falcon
3. 1953 DeSoto Adventurer I
4. 1968 Ford Mustang Mach I

BADGE BRAINBUSTERS
1. Mercury Comet
2. Plymouth Duster
3. Ford Maverick
4. Buick Centurion
5. AMC Gremlin

REAR VIEW
1. 1962 Plymouth Sport Fury
2. 1969 Ford Torino Cobra
3. 1971-72 Chevrolet Chevelle SS
4. 1966-67 Dodge Charger
5. 1963 Pontiac Grand Prix
6. 1965 Rambler Marlin

"SHIFTY" HURST
1. 1961 Pontiac
2. 1968
3. 1975
4. AMC Gremlin-X
5. 1970
6. Linda Vaughn
7. 1970
8. Twin Olds Engines
9. Jack Watson
10. 1965

BILLBOARD #4
1937

Lincoln Zephyr

V-12

1966-70 TORONADO FRONT ENDS
1. 1967
2. 1968
3. 1970
4. 1966
5. 1969

TV..."AND NOW A WORD FROM OUR SPONSORS!"
1. F
2. G
3. A
4. H
5. B
6. E
7. D
8. C

TREE-MENDOUS
Chrysler

SILHOUETTES #2
1. '62-'64 Studebaker Gran Turismo
2. '61 Plymouth Fury
3. '70 Buick Riviera
4. '66-'67 Dodge Charger
5. '63 Mercury Comet
6. '68-'69 American Motors AMX

STAR SHIP COMMANDER
Ronald Reagan

1954 Cadillac La Espada

GRILLE GREATS #1
1. '70 Rebel "Machine"
2. '62 Pontiac Tempest
3. '59 Plymouth Fury
4. '66 Comet Cyclone GT
5. '64 Studebaker Hawk
6. '69 Ford Torino Cobra

SUPER BIRD
1. One
2. Charger Daytona
3. Yes
4. 440 Six Pack
5. Petty Blue

Overall length: 221"

Nose cone length: 19"

Rear wing height: 25"

HIS & HERS
1. Hurst
2. Dual Gate
3. Normal automatic shifting
4. Manually shift the transmission
5. Pontiac Grand Prix
   Oldsmobile Starfire
   Chrysler

SHOW GIRLS
1. 1960 Mercury
2. 1951 Packard
3. 1958 Rambler
4. 1953 Hudson
5. 1957 Packard
6. 1951 Crosley

LICENSE TO QUIZ #2
1. Florida
2. 1955
3. Montana
4. Washington, Jefferson, Lincoln, Roosevelt
5. There is none
6. Canal Zone

TORONADO FRONTS
1. 1971
2. 1973
3. 1974
4. 1978
5. 1977
6. 1972

VETTE QUICKIE #2
1. 1956
2. 1970
3. 1974
4. 1967

OFFICIAL RESULTS
1. 18.7
2. 17.8
3. 19.2
4. 20.8
5. 20.5
6. 18.0

FIVE GENERATIONS
1. 1955-63
   190 SL
2. 1963-71
   230/250/280 SL
3. 1971 to present
   350/450/380 SL
4. 1957-63
   300 SL Roadster
5. 1954-57
   300 SL (Gullwing) Coupe

MYSTERY HUBCAPS
Pontiac
1. 1969
2. 1962
3. 1957
4. 1960
5. 1963
6. 1967

WHAT IS IT? #4
Automatic pressure-lubricating for car chassis fittings.

HEAVY TRAFFIC MPG
1. B
2. D
3. E
4. F
5. A
6. C

GIMMICKS AND GADGETS #3
1. Back window louvers
   1970 Dodge Challenger
2. Rear wheel "liquid tire chain"
   1969 Chevrolet Camaro
3. Sun roof
   1940 Cadillac
4. Headlamp washer
   1971 Dodge Charger
5. Mobile radio-telephone equipment
   1950 Ford
6. Louvered rear vent for passenger area ventilation system
   1966 Studebaker

SIGN LANGUAGE #2
1. Tunnel
2. Showers
3. Interpretive Auto Road
4. Spelunking
5. Information
6. Grocery Store

TIRELESS TYCOONS
1. John Boyd Dunlop
   (Inventor of pneumatic tire)
2. Harvey S. Firestone Sr.
   (Founder of Firestone Tire Co.)

AS THE WORLD TURNS
1. 1971
2. 3 (1974)
3. 1976
4. 1978

RUBBER MAN
1. Michelin
2. Bibendum
3. Bib
4. A

PROTOTYPE
Desoto

KNUDSEN KAR
1. 1957 Bonneville
2. A
3. B
4. B
5. C
6. C
7. C
8. There was none

GAS WAR
Mobilgas—.21 9/10
Mobilgas Special—.23 9/10

LIL' RAMBLERS
1. 1961
2. 1966
3. 1959
4. 1968
5. 1963
6. 1960
7. 1962
8. 1967

BIRTH ANNOUNCEMENT
5½ seconds

KEY BOBBERS #4
1. Rover
2. Excalibur
3. Fiat

STAR ENDORSEMENT
1. C
2. B
3. E
4. F
5. D
6. A

CAN'T DODGE 'EM
1. 1933
2. 1946
3. 1953
4. 1963
Bonus: Custom 880

STARS IN CARS #2
Elton John
Jaguar

CODE 7
1940 Plymouth
1. Rear view mirror missing
2. Steering wheel missing
3. Mustache on policeman shaved off
4. Badge on other cop missing
5. Door handle missing
6. The number 22 missing
7. One chrome strip at the front of hood missing
8. The word "Police" missing from the front emergency light

BEACH PARTY BAFFLE
1936 Terraplane

A RARE SIGHT
1942 DeSoto

SOUNDS GOOD
1. 1930
2. Motorola
3. Paul V. Galvin

SPEEDWAYS
1. Bridgehampton
2. Elkhart Lake
3. Indianapolis
4. Laguna Seca
5. Langhorne
6. Marlboro
7. Mexican Grand Prix
8. Phoenix

TOP THESE #2
1. 1954 Buick Skylark
2. 1930 Jordan
3. 1931-32 MG Midget
4. 1957-61 Metropolitian 1500
5. 1940 Hudson
6. 1931 Ford Model A

INDY TRILOGIES
1. Wilbur Shaw
   1937, 1939, 1940
2. Johnny Rutherford
   1974, 1976, 1980
3. A.J. Foyt
   1961, 1964, 1977
4. Mauri Rose
   1941 (co-driver), 1947, 1948

ROLLING RECORDS #3
Side A—The Rip Chords
Side B—The Beach Boys

HORSE RACING 1954
1. G
2. C
3. E
4. F
5. A
6. H
7. B
8. D

BEWILDERING BUMPERS #1
1. 1958 DeSoto
2. 1967 Pontiac GTO
3. 1941 Continental
4. 1977 Chevrolet
5. 1972 Pontiac Grand Prix
6. 1958 Imperial
7. 1958 Ford
8. 1984 Dodge Daytona

FIRST PRIZE
1931

HEY, SPORT FANS!
1. 64,000
2. 163,000
3. 145,000
4. 85,000
5. 116,000

DAGMARS
1. 1950
2. 1954
3. 1953
4. 1957
5. 1942–45
6. 1951

GALLANT MEN?
1. Elephant Engine
2. Shifty
3. Wind Tunnel
4. Esses
5. SPY

HUB HYSTERIA #3
1. Imperial
2. Pontiac
3. Chevrolet Corvette
4. Ferrari

5. Buick
6. Oldsmobile
7. Chevrolet
8. Ford Mustang

MECHANICALLY MINDED #3
1. Axle
2. Differential Case
3. Pinion Shaft
4. Pinion Gear
5. Ring Gear
6. Side Gear
7. Spider Gear
8. Spider Shaft
9. Universal Joint

DREAM STAR
1. Lincoln Futura
2. 1955
3. 330 H.P.
4. *It Started with a Kiss* (1959)
5. A. Radio Aerial
   B. "Audio approach" microphone that amplified the sound of any car approaching from the rear.
6. Pushbutton control, located in the pedestal between the two seats.
7. 18' 11" long and 52.8" high
8. The Batmobile

PONTIAC PICKERS
1. D
2. C
3. B
4. A

DREAMS COME TRUE #3
1. 1954 Pontiac Bonneville
2. 1954 Chevrolet Nomad
3. 1962 Pontiac Monte Carlo
4. 1954 Olds Cutlass

SIX CYLINDER QUICKIES
1. C
2. B
3. A
4. B
5. A
6. B

SMILEAGE
B. F. Goodrich

STARS IN CARS #3
Leo Carrillo (Poncho on *The Cisco Kid* TV series)
1947 Chrysler Town and Country

FARAWAY PLACES #3
1. Cordoba
2. Caribbean
3. Biarritz
4. Concord
5. Capri
6. Newport
7. Park Avenue
8. Versailles
9. Bonneville
10. Malibu
11. Monaco
12. Catalina

CAR TUNES #2
1. 1965
2. The Medallions
3. Mercedes-Benz
4. Nash Rambler and a Cadillac

PASSING DREAMS #2
1. '55 Chrysler Flightsweep I
2. '73 Chevy Astro III
3. '40 Chrysler Thunderbolt
4. '83 Chevy Aero 2002
5. '51 Chrysler K-310
6. '56 Plymouth Plainsman

TAIL WATCHING
1. 1960 Mercury Montclair
2. 1954 Plymouth Belvedere
3. 1970 Firebird Trans Am
4. 1957 Hudson Hornet
5. 1958 Ford Fairlane 500 Skyliner
6. 1968 Oldsmobile Cutlass
7. 1946 Continental
8. 1970 Plymouth 'Cuda

ENGINE WEIGHT
1. D
2. E
3. F
4. B
5. A
6. C

CB LINGO
1. Well-marked police car
2. Passenger car pulling a tractor
3. Volkswagen Beetle
4. Police listening on CB
5. Cars made by AMC
6. Good, clear transmission signal
7. Talk to you on the radio on a return trip
8. Accelerator
9. Traffic court that fines everybody
10. Dollars
11. To get the police out of hiding
12. Motorcycle
13. Exterior car color
14. A police radar unit
15. Occupants driving in cars
16. Last vehicle in a convoy
17. Highway truck weigh station
18. Drive safely

LOOK BUT DON'T TOUCH #3
1. 1965
2. Mercer-Cobra
3. Ford
4. 289 cu. in.
5. Copper Development Association, Inc.

RAINDROPS KEEP FALLING
1. 1933 Ford phaeton
2. 1957 Oldsmobile 98
3. 1936 Jaguar
4. 1937 DeSoto
5. 1958 Ford Skyliner (retractable)
6. 1940 Cadillac LaSalle

SUSPENSION QUICKIE
1. Moog
2. A. Ford
   B. 1965
   C. Twin I-Beam
3. Corvette

HERE TODAY, GONE TOMORROW #1
1. 1964
2. 1958
3. 1969
4. 1969

5. 1958
6. 1969
7. 1970
8. 1962

HOW MUCH?
$9.95

DASHING DESIGNS
1. 1959 Rambler
2. 1968 Triumph TR-250
3. 1940 Pontiac
4. 1941 Oldsmobile
5. 1984 Chevrolet Corvette
6. 1939 Chrysler

DUAL PERSONALITIES
A. Ransom E. Olds
   1. Oldsmobile 2. REO
B. Harry C. Stutz
   1. Stutz 2. H.C.S.
C. Henry J. Kaiser
   1. Kaiser 2. Henry J

STEER CLEAR
Citroen

TV CAR #2
1. *Knight Rider*
2. K.I.T.T.
3. Knight Industry Two Thousand

HOOD WINKED
1. 1957 Dodge
2. 1956 Rambler
3. 1956 Buick
4. 1954 Mercury

HIGH OCTANE
1. C
2. D
3. E
4. A
5. B

FALCON FRONTS
1. 1962
2. 1969
3. 1966
4. 1960
5. 1964
6. 1963

SAFE STEERING
1967
Collapsible, energy-absorbing

CHRYSLER—300 WORD QUIZ

1. Fifty-five
2. Three hundred horsepower
3. G, sixty-one
4. Fifty-seven
5. Sixty-two
6. B, fifty-six, J, sixty-three
7. Fifty-six, sixty-four
8. Seventy-one
9. E, fifty-nine
10. Sixty-five, L
11. Father
12. Seventy-nine

GRILLE GREATS #2

1. '68 AMC Rebel SST
2. '68 Plymouth Barracuda
3. '67 Oldsmobile 4-4-2
4. '66 Studebaker Daytona
5. '68 Chevy Camaro SS
6. '63 Ford Falcon Futura

LEAPIN' LOGOS

1. Stud
2. High performance oil treatment
3. Union Carbide

CORPORATE GIANTS #2

1. William S. Knudsen
   Past GM president
2. Henry M. LeLand
   Founder and past president of
   Cadillac Motor Car Co. and
   Lincoln Motor Car Co.
3. K. T. Keller
   Past president of Chrysler
4. George W. Mason
   Past president of
   Nash-Kelvinator Corp.

INDY 500 PACE CARS
1954-64

1. F
2. H
3. K
4. J
5. B
6. I
7. E
8. C
9. D
10. A
11. G

PANEL PLEASERS

1. 1954 Ford Courier
2. 1935 Terraplane
3. 1937 Dodge
4. 1941 International
5. 1941 Plymouth
6. 1941 Chevrolet

BIRD'S-EYE VIEW #3

1. Chevrolet
2. 1962
3. 283
   327
   409
4. 409 H.P.

SMILIN' SYMBOL

1. Humble Oil (also Oklahoma,
   Carter, or Pate brands)
2. Motoring

SLICK SYMBOLS #9

Richfield

ALL WHEEL DRIVE

1. International Scout Comanche
2. Jeep Commando
3. Land-Rover

A ROSE IS A ROSE #2

1. Dodge, AMC
2. Packard, Pontiac
3. Hupp, Buick
4. Henry J, Edsel
5. Crosley, Chevrolet
6. Studebaker, Dodge
7. Ferrari, Pontiac
8. Plymouth, AMC
9. Willys, Ford
10. Packard, Chevrolet, Graham

MEMORIES #3

1. A; Flying "A" Service
2. GMC
3. C

INDY 500 PACE CARS
1965-75

1. E
2. G
3. H
4. B
5. H

6. A
7. I
8. D
9. F
10. D
11. C

HUBBA BUBBA

1974

HUB HYSTERIA #4

1. Oldsmobile
2. Plymouth
3. Pontiac
4. Jaguar
5. Ford
6. Dodge
7. Rambler
8. Oldsmobile
9. Mercury
10. Ford/Mercury
11. Ford
12. Pontiac

TRIVIAL TWENTY

1. 1953 and 1976
2. Chevrolet
3. April 1969
4. It was welded shut
5. DeSoto
6. Three (54-56)
7. Sun Valley
8. 1970
9. Cadillac Eldorado coupe
10. Lincoln-Zephyr Continental
11. Graham
12. 1932
13. 1958-60
14. 1962
15. Nine years (1949-57)
16. Suburban
17. Challenger
18. 1968
19. Jet
20. Argentina

AMERICAN RULING
CLASS #3

1. F
2. D
3. G and H
4. C
5. A
6. H
7. E
8. B

SLICK SYMBOLS #10
Standard Oil

THE LOWER FORTIES #2
1. 1937 Chrysler Royal
2. 1957 Rambler Rebel
3. 1951 Frazer
4. 1937 Hudson victoria
5. 1954–58 Bristol 405
6. 1946–48 Lincoln Continental

GUILT TRIP
1979 Dodge Aspen

WHAT'S UP DOC?
Doctor of Motors
Perfect Circle (Piston rings)

MYSTERY CAR #4
1. Davis
2. 162 cu. in.
3. 58 H.P.
4. Wheelbase: 109½"
   Height: 60"
   Weight: 2148 lbs.

CLUB PAGE—KAISER-FRAZER-WILLYS
1. Howard A. "Dutch" Darrin
2. The hood scoop
3. Clyde Paton
4. 1953-54
5. B.
6. Woody Woodill, a Willys dealer from Downey, California
7. Carleton Spencer
8. 1951-54
9. None
10. Allstate
11. Kaiser-Darrin DKF-161
12. 1952-54
13. Brazil
14. Renault Dauphine—Willys Gordini
    Renault Alpine—Willys Interlagos
    Alfa Romeo 1900—Kaiser Bergantine.
15. Brooks Stevens
16. Front-wheel drive
17. Dragon
18. Dinosaur vinyl
19. 1952-55
20. True

SO SURREY
PICTURE 1
A. 1961

B. Pink, green, or blue candy stripes
C. Low-cost rentals for guests at resort hotels and vacation centers
PICTURE 2
A. Fiat
B. Jolly
PICTURE 3
A. 1978-79 Plymouth Volare
B. Fantasy Island

TRULY THE TRIVIEST #2
1. 1964
2. 1960
3. Seven lbs.
4. Oklahoma City, Oklahoma
5. 1935
6. Borg-Warner Award
7. John Z. DeLorean
8. 1955
9. Garden Grove, California
10. Dick Smothers
11. Acceleratti Rapidus Maximus
12. Volkswagen Fastback
13. 1965
14. 1967
15. Society of Automotive Engineers
16. 1958 Chrysler
17. 1970
18. 1957
19. Oldsmobile Toronado
20. American Express Company
21. 1965 Ford Mustang
22. BradField
23. Studebaker-Packard
24. 14,000

INTERNATIONAL INTRIGUE #3
1. Mercedes-Benz 540 K—Germany
2. Saab Sonett III—Sweden
3. Fiat 500—Italy
4. Porsche 356 Speedster—Germany
5. Alfa-Romeo 2300 berlinetta—Italy
6. Sunbeam Tiger—Great Britain

RUSH HOUR
1. 1955 Plymouth
2. 1953 Mercury
3. 1956 Buick
4. 1956 Chevrolet
5. 1955 Pontiac
6. 1950 Chevrolet
7. 1955 Plymouth

8. 1957 Studebaker
9. 1957 Ford
10. 1956 Ford
11. 1955 Ford
12. 1951 Oldsmobile

FOUR EYES
'57—DeSoto, Lincoln, Imperial, Nash, Mercury
'58—Packard, Cadillac, Rambler, Buick, Continental

EASY RIDER
1939 Oldsmobile

DAYDREAMS #4
1. 1964 Ford GT-40
2. 1938 Buick Y-Job
3. 1964 GM Runabout
4. 1965 Chevy Mako Shark II
5. 1971 Ford Mach 2 (mid-engine)
6. 1977 AMC Concept II

FRAMED
Tucker

NAME GAME #8
1. C
2. G
3. A
4. J
5. L
6. B
7. D
8. K
9. F
10. H
11. I
12. E

COMMERCIAL CUTIE
1. Plymouth
2. Mean Mary Jean
3. Judy Strangis

TOP TEN '66
1. Chevrolet
2. Ford
3. Pontiac
4. Plymouth
5. Oldsmobile
6. Buick
7. Dodge
8. Mercury
9. Rambler
10. Chrysler

CALL ME A CAB
1. 1946 Packard Clipper
2. 1961 Dodge Lancer
3. 1963 Studebaker
4. 1935 Terraplane

ROOF RELICS #1
1. '64 Olds/Buick
2. '55 Chrysler
3. '57 Mercury
4. '60 Ford/Edsel
5. '56 Ambassador
6. '55 Dodge
7. '54 Cadillac
8. '58 Ford (retractable)

OPEN FOR BUSINESS!
1. 1956 Pontiac
2. 1977 AMC Pacer
3. 1982 Mercury Cougar
4. 1954 Chevrolet
5. 1955 Plymouth
6. 1963 Studebaker

SHOW TIME
1. 1958 Packard
2. 1951 Henry J
3. 1952 Nash Rambler
4. 1957 Hudson
5. 1951 Muntz Jet
6. 1950 Packard

HAPPY ANNIVERSARY
1939 and 1979 Mercury

MULTI-CARBS
1. B
2. C
3. A
4. B
5. B
6. C
7. A
8. C

THE MAN BEHIND
A. Charles S. Schwab

LIFE LIKE LOGOS #3
1. Bear Mfg. Co.
2. Detroit Racing Equipment
3. Mack Trucks

PERPLEXING PONTIAC PICTURES
1. 1957
2. 1955
3. 1956
4. 1959
5. 1954
6. 1958

ROOF RELICS #2
1. '58 Mercury
2. '64 Dodge
3. '58 Pontiac
4. '56 Rambler
5. '61 Oldsmobile
6. 1956–62 Corvette
7. '79 AMC Pacer
8. '55 Chrysler Corp.

GREEN HOUSE #2
1. Ford Anglia
2. Olds Toronado XS
3. Mercury Turnpike Cruiser
4. Chevy Nomad
5. Maserati Merak
6. Nash Rambler Country Club

ROLLING RECORDS #4
Side A—Jan and Dean
Side B—The Routers

RISING SUN
1. E
2. D
3. A
4. H
5. J
6. C
7. B
8. F
9. G
10. I

TOPLESS MODELS
1. 1963 Oldsmobile
2. 1933 Pontiac
3. 1954-55 Kaiser-Darrin
4. 1942 Mercury
5. 1969 Plymouth
6. 1960 Edsel

COLOR ME WILD
1. Orbit Orange
2. Big Bad Blue
   Big Bad Green
   Big Bad Orange
3. Anti-Establish Mint
   Hulla Blue
   Freudian Gilt
   Thanks Vermillion
   Original Cinnamon
4. Citron Yella
   Plum Crazy
   Green Go
5. Vitamin C
   Lime Light
   Lemon Twist
   Tor Red

TOP SECRET INITIALS
Kaufman Thuma Keller

F.O.B. FACTORY
Packard #6
Terraplane #3
Plymouth #1
Chrysler Airflow #8
Pierce-Arrow #9
Studebaker #4
Chevrolet #2
Cadillac #7
Buick #5
Bonus—Free on Board

WOODY WONDERS
1. 1957 Rambler
2. 1940 Oldsmobile
3. 1939 Chevrolet
4. 1941 Hudson

KEY BOBBERS #5
1. Datsun
2. Abarth
3. Triumph TR3

BUG BUS
1. 1950
2. Type 2
3. "Bully" after its bulldog appearance
4. Four
5. A
6. B
7. C
8. A
9. 1968
10. 1980

1930 WORD SEARCH #2

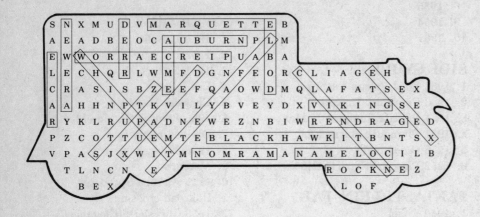

CUDA-DRAGIN'
1. 1970
2. Martin
3. 1966
4. Hurst/Hemi
5. 1969
6. 1964-65

NAME GAME #9
1. Mayfair
2. Carolina
3. Fiesta
4. Roundup
5. Pioneer
6. Challenger
7. Talladega
8. Scamp
9. Stallion
10. Can Am

UP IN SMOKE
1. Vacuum-operated ash tray disposal
2. Mercury

MOVIE SCENES #4
1. *Magnum Force*
   1970 Cadillac
2. *Grease*

MORE MUNCHIN' MOTORISTS
1. 1955
2. Des Plaines, IL
3. "Speedee"
4. 1954
5. 1953
6. Howard Johnson's
7. 1940
8. Pennsylvania Turnpike

CLASSIC CONTINENTALS
1. 1955-57 Mark II
2. 1941 Mark I
3. 1958 Mark III
4. 1970 Mark III
5. 1942 Mark II
6. 1972 Mark IV

MOVIE SCENES #5
1. *Hud*
   1958 Cadillac
2. *Christine*
   1958 Plymouth Fury

FAMILY RESEMBLANCE

1936 Chevrolet (older car)	
109 in.	Wheelbase
182.4 in.	Overall length
67.4 in.	Height
70.3 in.	Width
2775 lbs.	Weight

1960 Corvair (dotted line car)	
108 in.	Wheelbase
180 in.	Overall length
51.3 in.	Height
66.4 in.	Width
2340 lbs.	Weight

ROLLING RECORDS #5
Side A—Beach Boys
Side B—The Playmates

SECRET SYMBOL/SLOGAN
Saab
Sturdy—Stylish—Swedish

TOURIST INFO
1. Lancia—Italy
   Panhard—France
   Ford Anglia—Great Britain
2. Panhard
3. Ford Anglia
4. Lancia
5. American Oil

HUB HYSTERIA #5
1. AMC Javelin
2. Ford
3. Jeep
4. Ford Mustang II
5. Mercury
6. Oldsmobile
7. Cadillac
8. Edsel

INDEPENDENT QUICKIE
1. Powell Crosley Jr., and we'll never know
2. 1940 Crosley

CAR PHONES
Mustang
Packard
LaSalle
Crosley
Riviera
Rambler
Corvair
Pontiac

GRAND PRIX GRILLES
1. 1964
2. 1962
3. 1967
4. 1966
5. 1963
6. 1965

SYMBOL SPECIALIST #5
1. Stutz
2. Hudson Hornet
3. Dodge Demon
4. Peugeot

HERE TODAY, GONE TOMORROW #2
1. 1970
2. 1977
3. 1970
4. 1977
5. 1963
6. 1959
7. 1961
8. 1969

"HONEST INGINES"
1. Ford, 8 cyl., 1930's
2. Chevy, 8 cyl. (fuel injection), 1950's
3. Chevrolet Corvette, 6 cyl., 1950's
4. Porsche, 6 cyl. (fuel injection), 1960's and 1970's
5. Nash, 6 cyl., 1950's
6. Chrysler, No cyl. (turbine), 1970's

"HOME, JAMES"
1. 1939
2. 1932
3. 1938
4. 1936
5. 1937
6. 1933

PREHISTORIC POWER
1. Sinclair
2. Dino
3. 1970
4. Arco (Atlantic Richfield)

TEN LITTLE INDIANS
1. 1957
2. 1964
3. 1967
4. 1969
5. 1962
6. 1964
7. 1969
8. 1955
9. 1954
10. 1961

SIDE SWIPE #2
1. 1962 Ford Falcon Futura
2. 1958 Chevrolet Impala
3. 1961 Pontiac Tempest LeMans
4. 1971 Plymouth Barracuda
5. 1958 Oldsmobile
6. 1952 Packard Patrician 400

FANTASTIC FIN–FAD
1. 1960 Edsel
2. 1959 Chevrolet
3. 1957 Hudson
4. 1959 Imperial
5. 1959 Studebaker
6. 1956 Chrysler

ENGLISH EAGLE
1. Sir Malcolm Campbell
2. Bluebird
3. 1936 Hudson

SPARK ART
1. Autolite
2. AC

NOSTALGIC UNSCRAMBLER
1. Crosley
2. Frazer
3. Graham
4. Hudson
5. Tucker
6. Willys
7. Hupmobile
8. Packard
9. Studebaker
10. Nash

COVER QUIZ
1. 1938 LaSalle
2. Frazer
3. 1951 Nash
4. Lee Iacocca
5. Chrysler Hemi-V8
6. 1956 Pontiac Club de Mer
7. Divided highway
8. 1938-39 Graham
9. Mercury
10. 1929 Auburn Speedster
11. Railroad crossing
12. 1953 Chrysler d'Elegance
13. William Crapo Durant
14. Cadillac
15. 1971 Barracuda show car

MOTOR TREND CAR OF THE YEAR 1969-78
'69—B
'70—E
'71—A
'72—F
'73—C
'74—I
'75—J
'76—D
'77—H
'78—G

BACK IN THE USSR
ZIS

SEEING-EYE SYMBOL
1. Moon
2. "Mooneyes"
3. Dean Moon